THE FIRST AND THE LAST OF THE

SHEFFIELD

CITY

BATTALION

JOHN CORNWELL

Pen & Sword
MILITARY

AN IMPRINT OF PEN & SWORD BOOKS LTD.
YORKSHIRE – PHILADELPHIA

First published in Great Britain in 2019 by
PEN & SWORD MILITARY
an imprint of
Pen & Sword Books Ltd
Yorkshire - Philadelphia

Hardback ISBN 978 1 52676 224 5
Paperback ISBN 978 1 52676 736 3

A CIP catalogue record for this book is available from the British Library.

Typeset in 10/12.5 & Times New Roman
by Aura Technology and Software Services, India

Printed and bound in England by TJ International Ltd, Padstow, Cornwall

Pen & Sword Books Ltd incorporates the Imprints of Pen & Sword Books Archaeology,
Atlas, Aviation, Battleground, Discovery, Family History, History, Maritime, Military,
Naval, Politics, Railways, Select, Transport, True Crime, Fiction, Frontline Books,
Leo Cooper, Praetorian Press, Seaforth Publishing, Wharncliffe and White Owl.

For a complete list of Pen & Sword titles please contact

PEN & SWORD BOOKS LIMITED
47 Church Street, Barnsley, South Yorkshire, S70 2AS, England
E-mail: enquiries@pen-and-sword.co.uk
Website: www.pen-and-sword.co.uk

Or

PEN AND SWORD BOOKS
1950 Lawrence Rd, Havertown, PA 19083, USA
E-mail: uspen-and-sword@casematepublishers.com
Website: www.penandswordbooks.com

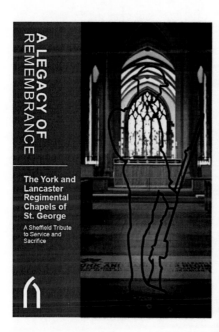

A LEGACY OF REMEMBRANCE

The York and Lancaster Regimental Chapels of St. George

A Sheffield Tribute to Service and Sacrifice

The book will be on sale
in the Cathedral Gift Shop following the
launch, priced £4.

SHEFFIELD CATHEDRAL
A PLACE FOR ALL PEOPLE

Contents

Foreword

Colonel I. Geoffrey Norton TD DL
York and Lancaster Regiment

On 6 May 2014, I received an email from Hannah Brignell, Curator of Social History at Sheffield Museums telling me that she been contacted by an auction house in Bristol about archival material coming up for sale on 5 June about the first man to join the Sheffield City Battalion who also played for Sheffield Wednesday. As it was an archive, it couldn't really go into the Sheffield Museum collection, but she felt that it needed to come to Sheffield and wondered if I might be able to spread the word.

In a subsequent telephone conversation I established that she had not been in touch with the Regimental Museum of the York and Lancaster Regiment in Rotherham, so in a further telephone conversation with Karl Noble in Rotherham, it became evident that they would be interested in purchasing the collection but would have to raise the money first and that would take some months.

On 22 June, my friend Helen Ullathorne from Sheffield University and I went to Clevedon Salerooms to view the items that made up the collection of Captain Vivian Simpson, which included his Military Cross and of even more interest, two leather bound volumes of letters that he had sent home to his brother George before he was killed on 13 April 1918. It rapidly became obvious to us that these volumes contained an invaluable historical background to life in Kitchener's Army, and I arranged to make a telephone bid after we had spent most of the day copying out salient points from the letters in case our bid was not successful.

It was. A bid up to £8,000 was agreed but was successful at £5,300. The total sum paid was £6,944 including costs and VAT. After the auction, Toby Pinn from Clevedon Salerooms put me in touch with the vendor, Patrick Simpson – Vivian's grandson – and I was able to tell him the future of our purchase which Toby handed over to me on 3 July.

Before the Museum could apply for grants, an independent valuation had to take place and this was held on 13 August to which I was accompanied by my colleague Peter Bayliss who subsequently copied out all the letters in the two volumes and many of the photographs. The full purchase price was upheld at the valuation.

The Museum was eventually able to purchase the collection with aid of grants from ACE/V&A Purchase Fund, Western Front Association, Rotherham Military Community Veterans Association, the Friends of Clifton Park Museum and Rotherham Archives and the York and Lancaster Regiment. I presented the collection on 20 October 2015, with agreement from Rotherham Metropolitan Borough Council that the contents could be used for a possible book.

On 22 February 1993, I had had the privilege of sitting opposite Captain Reg Glenn on the occasion of the lunch given to him by the York and Lancaster Regiment to celebrate his 100th birthday, and next to his son Don. I had known Reg for many years because of my interest in the Sheffield City Battalion in which my father's cousin, James Norton, had been one of the first recruits and with whom I worked for many years. Sadly I was unable to attend Reg's funeral but kept up the connection with Don and subsequently Reg's granddaughter and grandson, Diane and Michael. They accompanied us to Serre on the Somme in 2007 where their grandfather had been in action on 1 July 1916.

Through Diane, I have got to know a great deal about her grandfather's life and it became obvious to me when considering the possibility of a book about Vivian Simpson that the contrast in his and Reg's lives would make interesting reading. I had the conceited idea that I could write such a book but, through meeting John Cornwell and reading the books he had written concerning the service of Old Boys of King Edward VII School in Sheffield in two World Wars, I realized that it would be better written by an experienced author rather than me, an amateur.

I am grateful to John for his efforts in producing a fascinating historical record of the service of two soldiers from the Sheffield City Battalion of the York and Lancaster Regiment.

Colonel I. Geoffrey Norton TD DL

Acknowledgements

I was privileged to work with a small group of people who are either intimately connected to the story of Reg Glenn and Vivian Simpson or became so during the writing of this book in 2017-18. Firstly, my thanks to Colonel Geoffrey Norton, Chairman of the Trustees of the York and Lancaster Regiment, who conceived the idea of a book based on a juxtaposition of the military careers of Vivian Simpson and Reg Glenn and their differing, but changing, social backgrounds. He has been a constant supporter and guide to me during the writing of the book and his knowledge of the history of his regiment, the York and Lancaster Regiment, has been invaluable. Similarly, I have benefitted enormously from the knowledge, recordings and family photographs that Diane Glenn, Reg Glenn's granddaughter, has made available to me. Along with four other people she has carefully read the proofs and ensured that the spirit and character of her grandfather has been faithfully recorded.

Mark Goodwill has been a massive help to me throughout the writing of the book. He has an encyclopaedic knowledge of the individual men of the 12th Battalion and of the actions they fought in the Great War and has generously made that information available to me at all times. In the latter stages of preparing the book for the publishers he has taken responsibility for the reproduction of the photographs, something that was quite beyond my level of competence.

Peter Bayliss also played a critical role in the project transcribing all the Simpson letters from two magnificent leather-bound albums and also identifying all the photos and artefacts that were part of the Simpson collection. He also proof read every chapter as did Patrick Simpson, the grandson of Vivian Simpson, who also gave permission for the use of the photographs of Simpson family used in the book.

My thanks also to the late Ralph Gibson and Paul Oldfield for permission to use the information in their 1988 book *The Sheffield City Battalion*. This excellent account of the life of the battalion was a most useful guide to understanding Vivian Simpson and Reg Glenn's journey through the years from 1914 to 1918.

My thanks also to the Rotherham Museum at Clifton Park, where the York and Lancaster Regimental Museum is housed, for permission to use items from the Simpson collection.

I am also appreciative of the help given by Alan Hampshire, the Secretary of the Wortley Golf Club; Richard Ibbotson, the Chair of the Sheffield Collegiate Cricket Club; Richard Tims and Alan Dixon, respectively Chair and Historian of Sheffield F.C., the oldest football club in the world; and Linda Gooden, Headteacher at King Edward VII School in Broomhill. There was considerable help from Matt Naughton, a Volunteer Research Worker at the Staffordshire Regiment's Museum at Lichfield.

My thanks also to the Editor of Sheffield Newspapers for permission to use a number of photos in the book that originally appeared in the *Sheffield Daily Telegraph* or the *Sheffield Independent.*

I am also most appreciative of the advice and guidance I received from Heather Williams, the Commissioning Editor at Pen and Sword books in Barnsley, as well as the painstaking editing of Carol Trow, who has corrected all my deficiencies of punctuation and, when it was needed, helped set my syntax straight.

J.C. Cornwell

About the Author

John Cornwell was born in Hull in 1939 and read International History at the LSE. He taught in Sheffield for 23 years and also in Jamaica and Canada. He was the Deputy Leader of South Yorkshire County Council, a member of the Arts Council of Great Britain, Chair of Sheffield Theatres (the Crucible and Lyceum Theatres), Chair of the Rugby League's Youth Commission and Vice Chair of the Yorkshire and Humberside Sports Council. In retirement he became an author and has written nineteen books mainly about aspects of local history. He lives in Sheffield and his interests include military history, writing poetry and rugby league.

Introduction

This is the story of two men of Sheffield coming from different social backgrounds, who both volunteered in early September 1914 and joined the new Pals battalion that became the 12th Battalion York and Lancaster Regiment. This battalion was raised by a joint initiative of the City Council and the University and was blatantly aimed at recruiting just middle-class volunteers. Until July 1915, it was paid and provided for by the City Council and from the first the volunteers were treated as heroes already by the local press and Sheffield public, even if they had to parade and train in their civilian clothes. Later, in December 1914, a camp would be built for them at Redmires on the bleak moors west of the city, but until they left for Cannock Chase in May 1915, they were a very visible presence in the city.

The first man to volunteer was Vivian Simpson, a 31-year-old solicitor who was well known in the city, partly because he was an outstanding sportsman who had played for Sheffield Wednesday and had been an England trialist. He was the first man to enrol for the new battalion and was exactly the sort of volunteer that the City Battalion wanted to recruit. He was not among the first group of subalterns who were selected to command the platoons of the new battalion, but he was commissioned in January 1915 and from the first was marked out as an effective and efficient officer.

The other man was Reg Glenn, a clerk in the Education Offices who served as a signaller throughout his time in the Battalion, serving with them in Egypt and then in France from March 1916 until the summer of 1917. He was in the front line trench during the 12th Battalion's failed assault on Serre on 1 July 1916, when two thirds of those committed to the attack were casualties, including 265 fatalities. Reg came through the battle unscathed but lost so many of his friends and later was in all the action that the 12th Battalion saw on the Somme and Arras fronts until the summer of 1917, when he was selected to become an officer.

Vivian Simpson to his annoyance was kept back in England as a training officer until after the Battalion's disaster on the first day of the Somme in 1916. However, once in France, he soon proved himself to be a most energetic and courageous officer winning the Military Cross in 1917 for his planning and leadership of a raid on the Cadorna Trench at Gavrelle. He was the only officer in the 12th Battalion to win an MC. Although he railed at his slow promotion, he was invariably in charge of a company until he was injured patrolling east of Vimy ridge in September 1917. Invalided back to England, he was offered a training position that would have meant his survival, but he opted to go back to France and was killed during the German offensive on the Lys in April 1918.

Reg Glenn also went back to France in the spring of 1918 as a subaltern in the North Staffordshires and was wounded on the Aisne in his first day of combat as an officer. He was never fit enough to go back to the trenches and became a training officer in Northumberland with his new regiment and later with the Cameronians at Invergordon.

He therefore survived the war and lived to be 101 years old and was by some margin the last survivor of the 12th Battalion.

It has been a privilege to write the story of these two brave men and gain some understanding of their character and their life before the war, when they lived in very different circumstances from each other. Reg Glenn still had most of his life to live when he was demobbed in 1919 and the book details some of the public service and voluntary work that he undertook, becoming a well-known and respected local, even national, figure.

Chapter 1

Born in the City of Steel

This is the story of two men, James Reginald Glenn and Vivian Sumner Simpson, born in the city of Sheffield in the latter part of Queen Victoria's reign, whose fortunes came together when they volunteered for military service in the first week of September 1914. They answered the call of the City Council to join a special infantry battalion that the Council was preparing to equip and finance until such time as the Regular Army was ready to take it over and allow it to join the other battalions of the 'New Armies'. These battalions would then be formed into new brigades and divisions, created from the 500,000 volunteers that Field Marshal Kitchener's recruitment campaign had raised to meet the challenge of the German invasion of Belgium and Northern France.

Before Reg Glenn and Vivian Simpson joined this brand new 'City of Sheffield' Battalion, one of the early 'Pals' battalions that harnessed local enthusiasm for the war among men who wished to serve alongside their mates, work colleagues and neighbours, they had never met each other. Vivian was ten years older than Reg, 31 when the war broke out, and had already been a partner in his family's firm of solicitors for eight years, while 21-year-old Reg (always known as Reg, not James or Reginald) was a junior clerk in the Council's Education Department, more an office boy he would say in later years, who had already had a couple of short-term jobs since he had left school in 1907.

However, Reg would know of Vivian Simpson because as a fan of Wednesday FC (the club only changed its name to Sheffield Wednesday in 1929) he would most probably have seen Vivian playing for them, when, as an amateur, he guested for the club in 38 matches between 1902 and 1907. In his nineties, Reg would recall that as a boy he would manage to get into Wednesday's ground – then called Owlerton – for the last ten minutes of a match when the exit gates had already been opened, so that lads with no money could sneak in and watch the end of a game free of charge.

The city where these two men had been born and raised had seen massive changes during the nineteenth century, as it grew exponentially from a small town famous for its cutlery trade, to become one of the great industrial cities, not just of Britain, but throughout the world. Sheffield was the Industrial Revolution city par excellence and its reputation for steel and engineering was famous on every continent. By the end of the century, this importance was recognised when the city was created a County Borough in 1893. It now had a Lord Mayor as its first citizen, and for the first two years the post was held by the Duke of Norfolk, further underlining the awareness of its new prestige and importance. In the next decade, the City Council, dominated by professional men including many lawyers in both the Conservative and Liberal Parties, would create the buildings and institutions commensurate with the city's new status. Thus, the palatial Town Hall, a mix of renaissance styles designed by E.W. Mountford, would be built at the top of Fargate, and in 1905, the new University, based in a defiantly red brick building on Western Bank, would be opened by Edward VII. Queen Victoria had opened the new Town Hall in 1897 and although she did it from her carriage and never set foot in the building, her very presence in the city added to the immense pride Sheffield people felt for their home town, a city that by 1914 had a population that was close to half a million people.

As Sheffield had grown from almost 46,000 inhabitants in 1801, large areas of countryside had been built on to create the terraced homes of factory workers in the east of the city, as well as suburbs for artisans and the burgeoning middle class on areas adjacent to the town centre. While further out at Ranmoor, steelmasters like John Brown and Mark Firth, the new aristocracy of the industrial revolution, built majestic mansions such as Endcliffe Hall (later the headquarters of the York and Lancaster Regiment's Hallamshire Battalion) and Oakbrook, now part of Notre Dame High School's campus.

Reg Glenn was born in February 1893 in one of those new suburbs, high up on Burngreave cliff on one of Sheffield's many hills. His father, Richard, a rate collector for the Water Board, rented what was then a modern terraced house, No.107 Nottingham Street, a house with a narrow front garden, its own backyard, a private outside toilet and enough bedrooms for his young family that included Reg and his two sisters Edith and Ada. Nottingham Street was a bit of a cut above the side streets that ran into it and as you went further north along the street the houses became more substantial, some of them double fronted with bay windows, carved portals and larger front gardens.

Richard Glenn and his wife Elizabeth would have considered themselves as new members of the lower middle class. Apart from their superior terraced house, Richard had a white collar job, where he wore a suit and probably a bowler hat to work and had a certain status as a representative of management. The family would still find it difficult to manage on his weekly wage and there would be few treats for his wife and the children, but as a good church-going family, they would be considered respectable by their neighbours, and the children would be well brought up in a strict but loving home.

Their church was down steep Spital Hill, through the Wicker Arches – more like the triumphal gateway to the city than the functional railway bridge that was

Reg with his mother and two sisters, Edith (r) and Ada, at the rear of their house in Nottingham Street, Burngreave.

its reality – and then round the corner to Holy Trinity Church on Nursery Street, where Reg was baptized in March 1893. At the age of five, Reg went to school for the first time when he enrolled at Pye Bank School, a building that he would have been aware of all his young life because it was just across the road from his home. The school had been built in 1875 and was one of the earliest of the Sheffield Education Board's outstanding elementary school buildings. Designed in a confident Gothic Revival style, it looked out over the valley of the River Don to the city centre on the hill opposite and from some angles it looked more like a Victorian church than a school. Pye Bank School, when it had been completed, was clearly a statement that education was important for the children of all classes and vital for the continued progress of the British economy, the nation state and its armed forces.

When Reg was eight and presumably because his father had been re-assigned to work in the north-west district of Sheffield, the family moved to new rented accommodation at 60 Holme Lane, above a handsome parade of shops named Hillsborough Market. Their new house was entered from a generous back yard that served several houses in the block, and one can easily imagine the football-mad Reg kicking a ball about with his pals in that yard that was their playground, serving alternatively as a football pitch or a cricket wicket depending on the season

Morley Street School, now called Rivelin Primary School, was only completed and opened in 1901. Reg and his two sisters were the first three pupils to be enrolled at the new school.

of the year. However, for eight year old Reg the most exciting thing about the new house was that it was next door to a huge tram shed with its high red brick double gateway, where in the back of the yard there were stables where horses had once been rested after they had pulled the horse-drawn trams from the city centre up to Hillsborough, before the trams were electrified after 1898.

The move to Hillsborough also meant a change of school. So in the autumn term of 1901, Reg and his two sisters started at the brand new Morley Street School, half a mile from their home, where they were the first three names to be entered in the enrolment register. The school was designed for over 800 pupils and it would be some time before it reached its full capacity, but these Sheffield Board Schools were supremely functional, as well as being aesthetically pleasing and the school is still in use today, although it has been renamed the Rivelin Primary School. Reg loved his new school and excelled at his studies, always coming top of the class, despite the fact that he was always scrapping with other boys and often playing truant, a fairly regular occurrence at Board Schools in turn of the century Sheffield. Perhaps the teachers would not miss a few truants because the classes were huge by modern standards with 60 pupils to a class, whilst two classes often shared the main hall where the atmosphere was always noisy. Reg remembered many decades later how the Headmaster was very strict, as were all the male teachers, who all carried a cane and most probably believed that in teaching the 'little urchins' from the back streets that an unrelenting ferocious discipline came first and learning second. It was a style of teaching that has bedevilled British education since, where all classrooms, even at the most prestigious schools, are potential battlegrounds if the teachers cannot keep immaculate order.

On the other hand, Reg found the women teachers much more friendly. All unmarried, they had to resign when they married to stay 'respectable', so most of them were quite young and they could often interest and engage with their pupils better than their male colleagues. Clearly Reg was a bit of a scamp at school and probably at home as well, a bit of a lad who was growing in confidence, who could look after himself in the scrapes and predicaments of those pre-teenage years but continued to show academic promise, so much so that his school put him forward for admission to the Central Secondary School in Leopold Street in the seemingly awesome world of the centre of town – the hub of Sheffield politics, its posh shops, and important looking offices.

He was selected for the Central Boys School in 1905 when he was almost twelve and this move to what was in effect a new grammar school – albeit a school with a most significant history over the previous quarter of a century – was a game changer for Reg. It set him on an upward trajectory that would lead to a middle-class job and eventually a commission in the army during the First World War, something he could never have imagined when growing up in Hillsborough, or even when he first joined the army in 1914.

Vivian Simpson's early life could not have been more different from Reg Glenn's. Vivian was born in Beech Hill House, a building that was a mixture of the neo-classical and Victorian Gothic styles, ideally situated at the top of Beech Hill Road in Broomhill, close by St Mark's Church. Today, it is a pre-school nursery but at that time it housed the whole Simpson clan of eight children and three servants in an exclusive enclave off the Glossop Road. Everything about the house shouted success and wealth, emphasizing that the Simpson family were people of stature and significance in Sheffield and had all the right connections to the people who made the city tick.

In the mid-Eighties, the Simpson family moved to the centre of fashionable Nether Edge when they purchased 13 Moncrieffe Road, another massive solid Victorian villa, secluded behind its handsome stone walls and thick holly hedge. Why George Simpson Snr felt the need to move house every decade is a bit of a puzzle, but by the mid-Nineties they had moved again, to Warleigh House, returning to the exclusive Victorian suburb of Broomhill. Their new home at 19 Southbourne Road was situated in a very attractive area of leafy, gently sloping avenues and substantial detached stone houses, an address much favoured by the successful members of the new expanding professional class. Warleigh House (since renamed Broombank) is a very imposing double fronted villa, close by the attractive Botanical Gardens, although by the turn of the century most of the Simpson children had left home and only Vivian and an older sister and brother still lived at the house after their father had died suddenly in May 1900.

George Joseph Simpson, born in 1837, the year that Queen Victoria ascended the throne, and his wife Gertrude, some seven years his junior, had eight children neatly balanced by gender with four sons and four daughters. Such large families were the norm for the Victorian age but in a wealthy family like the Simpsons, they all survived childhood and into adult life, unlike the sad children of poorer families in the city's slums, where almost always a number of children died as babies or when very young. Vivian, born in February 1883, was the family's last child and eighteen years separated him from his oldest sibling, his brother Francis. Francis, and his sister Ethel (born 1867), would seem awe-inspiring to the young Vivian as he grew up and indeed, they were already adults, although in the Eighties all the Simpson children were still living at home. Two of his older brothers, including George, to whom he would later write a hundred letters from the trenches, were already articled to his father's legal firm, whose office was in the Independent Building at 21 Fargate, where Vivian would be articled in turn, when he left school in 1899.

Vivian always seemed closer to his three youngest sisters, Frances (born 1872), Julia (born 1874) and Margaret (born 1877), but even Margaret was born almost six years before him. Whether Vivian was spoilt by his older sisters, or whether he was the butt of their ragging and teasing is not known, but the chances are that as the youngest by quite a margin in a high-achieving family, the young Vivian would have to prove himself from a very early age and it most probably made him very independent and self-reliant.

Not that he had to do everything for himself, because the Simpsons had the status and the wealth to employ servants. Three young girls aged between 16 and 20 lived in at Warleigh House and did all the domestic chores and prepared the meals, so that living with servants in the home would render normal to Vivian the social divisions of Victorian society and emphasize the sense of the superiority of families like his own.

The Simpsons were part of the social elite of the Sheffield. Not the very highest rank – that was reserved for the families of the steelmasters out at Ranmoor – but the next highest level of Sheffield society. There is a report in the local newspaper of 1891 of a fancy-dress party organised by the Cutlers' Company at the Cutlers' Hall for almost 400 children of the City's most notable families and Vivian and his sister Julia were not only invited but they both performed in a small play to amuse the other children at the party.

So perhaps it is surprising that Vivian was sent at the age of nine to Wesley College and not to one of the more famous public schools that had revolutionized British boarding school education in the nineteenth century, whereas in 1915 Vivian's

Warleigh House, now called Broombank, was the third home that Vivian Simpson had known in his young life. The family lived at Warleigh House during the 1890s and Vivian spent his teenage years there until the family moved out in the early twentieth century after the death of his father.

nephew, Gordon, went to Winchester, an indication of the social aspirations and ambitions of the Simpson family a couple of decades later.

However, Wesley College, founded in 1837, was the most prestigious school in Sheffield, especially after the Collegiate School, founded by Anglicans in 1836 on Ecclesall Road, had folded because of a shortage of fee-paying pupils and consequent financial difficulties. Wesley College was the Methodists' reply to the Collegiate School and it opened its doors in 1838 on a hillside site between

Glossop Road and Clarkehouse Road, part of the new prestigious suburb of Broomhill. Wesley College's style and curriculum was modelled on the successful new modernising public schools like Rugby and Uppingham and among other aspects of the school's ethos it placed great importance on games as part of a 'manly' education. The school had great ambitions academically and in 1844 it became an outlying college of London University and ran courses for older students leading to London external degrees.

Established as a boarding school for the sons of wealthy Methodist laymen, it took students from all over England and even some from abroad. However, by the late 1890s it was also in financial difficulties because it could not achieve its optimum numbers of around 350 pupils and it was increasingly relying on day boys and not necessarily Methodists either.

So in 1892, at the age of nine, Vivian joined twenty other new boys in the First Form of Wesley College and spent the rest of decade at the school leaving

Wesley College in Broomhill where Vivian received his education in the late Nineties. It became King Edward VII School in 1905 and the exterior of the main building looks exactly the same today as it did when Vivian was a pupil there. This is a photograph of the whole school in 1897 and Vivian Simpson is somewhere among the number.

in the summer of 1899. The school, only a quarter of mile away from his home in Southbourne Road, could boast a main building as grand as any school in Yorkshire with its great Palladian frontage of sixteen Corinthian pillars. 'A palace for the children of the King of Kings' was the hyperbole used to describe it at the official opening, when it was considered a triumph of design by the young, ambitious architect, William Flockton, the first of a family of architects who would leave their mark on their city and whose buildings are still very much admired today.

Never among the academic high flyers, Vivian Simpson found the College had one great advantage for him. Success at games could ensure popular recognition and a high status in the school and from an early age Vivian was clearly a very accomplished all-round sportsman. The school also placed great emphasis on gymnastics, usually under the instruction of a former army drill sergeant who also served the College in the combined role of school porter and NCO instructor to the cadet corps. Unusual for its time, the school had an open air swimming pool and insisted on all its pupils learning to swim, whilst on the Close in front of the main building, the school played its home football and cricket matches. It is clear from newspaper reports that in his last year or two at the school, Vivian Simpson was already making a name for himself in Sheffield sporting circles as a footballer and as a cricketer. The school history records that Wesley College was rarely beaten at either game and they had a prestigious fixture list that included Manchester Grammar School, Nottingham High School and Queen Elizabeth Grammar School, Wakefield, although for courtesy's sake they did play the local Sheffield Royal Grammar School and in one year in the Nineties, before Vivian played for the First XI, Wesley College won 29-0 (although in the SRGS magazine it was claimed it was only 27-0).

One other experience at Wesley College that would be of some use in later life was his membership of the College Cadet Corps. Membership of the Corps was not compulsory, but it numbered around 35 boys and was attached to the 1st West York Royal Engineers (Volunteers) at their Glossop Road barracks, half a mile down the hill towards the city centre. Vivian would later write that when doing initial training in 1914 with other volunteers in the new City Battalion, it was all rather familiar to him from his time as a cadet at school.

With no interest in going to university and performing very ordinarily in his final exams – mainly second-class grades in a lower standard exam run by the South Kensington Examination Board – Vivian Simpson left Wesley College at sixteen in 1899 and he became an articled clerk at his father's legal firm as he always knew he would. His future career and prosperity now seemed secure and he appeared set up for life as a person of substance in the civic and social life of his home city.

Reg Glenn entered the Central Secondary School in Orchard Lane in the centre of town, at a pivotal time in the school's history. Founded in 1880 as the Sheffield Higher Grade School, part of an extraordinary complex of educational buildings in an area that had previously been depressing slums, it was a national trailblazer for

Vivian Simpson is the sixth from the left on the back row in this photo of the College Cadet Corps taken in camp at Lydgate in 1897. The Corps wore scarlet uniforms and blue trousers and a pill box hat that was then common headgear but is now only worn by the Gurkhas.

secondary education for the children of working and lower middle-class families. Bright pupils, both boys and girls, at the city's Board Schools could be sent to the Higher Grade School in the city centre and given a free secondary education that could compare with the education on offer at the fee-paying Sheffield Royal Grammar School on Collegiate Crescent. Sheffield School Board had no legal power to run a Higher Grade School on the rates but for almost twenty years no one challenged them and the school grew in importance and standards.

In 1905, under the provisions of the new Education Act of 1902, the school became two schools, a Central Boys Secondary School and a Central Girls Secondary School, now in separate buildings but still on the Leopold Street campus. The boys' school, now essentially a grammar school in all but name, stayed in the original building in Orchard Lane and it was here that the young Reg arrived for the Spring term of 1905 aged eleven. He found that it was not so easy to be top of the class now when there were so many able pupils in his year group. Still he rose to the challenge of the school's curriculum where he studied seemingly esoteric subjects such as geometry, trigonometry and science for the first time. His favourite subjects were French and German where the teachers were both Swiss nationals, one was from the western, French-speaking cantons and the other one from the eastern, German speaking area.

This was the original building of the Central Higher Grade School founded in 1880 and designed by Thomas Flockton, son of William Flockton, who was the architect of Wesley College. In 1933, the school moved to High Storrs into a purpose-built palatial Art Deco building and in 1940 the school changed its name to High Storrs Grammar School.

Reg got on well with his German teacher, who also ran the school's gymnastics teams. Gymnastics was taken very seriously by educationalists at the beginning of the twentieth century and schools put on extravagant displays of their skills to admiring parents and visitors. Reg was in one of these teams, which usually ended their performance forming a tall pyramid of students where Reg, the smallest in the group, would scale the pyramid and lodge two flags on the summit. He recalled in later years how, in a competition at the Albert Hall in Barker's Pool (the site is now the John Lewis store), he reached the top of the pyramid but as he was about to fix the flags he was dazzled by the lights just above his head and fell off, crashing down on the table where all the prizes and trophies were displayed. With characteristic humour he would later recall, 'That was the only time I ever got near a prize for gymnastics.'

The German teacher also caused a small 'international' incident at the school when he took it upon himself to teach the boys the words of 'Deutschland Uber Alles'. He asked them to sing it softly, but the boys soon got into the swing of the tune and belted it out so that the Headmaster heard them. Enraged, he burst into the classroom making it quite clear that he was not having any German national anthem sung in his school. At the time, Reg could not understand this hostility, but it was a small example of how the tide of British public opinion was swinging against Germany in the Edwardian era, even if young Reg was at that time unaware of the build up of tensions on the continent that would lead to 'his' war.

The Central School, now it was a grammar school, needed proper games facilities. Prior to 1904, the boys and girls had had to use the school yard where many footballs, hockey and cricket balls went through windows over the years and clearly you could not play home fixtures against other schools without your own fields. In 1899, the City Council, who now ran the Central Schools, had bought land at High Storrs intending to build houses on an extensive site that had been farm land. Local opposition killed the idea, so when playing fields were needed for the new school, the High Storrs site was the obvious solution. Not that it was at all convenient for students whose school was in the centre of town, and whose homes were unlikely to be anywhere near these new grounds in the hills of the far south-west of the city.

So Reg, like other pupils at Central School, had to take a tram to the Ecclesall Road terminus and then undertake a steep hike up country paths to High Storrs. For the first year, he helped dig up, level and seed the fields so it wasn't until 1906 that he could play football there during games periods and when he represented the school in the Under14 team. The site was ideal for cross country running and Reg enjoyed ten-mile steeplechases up and down the Mayfield valley and onto the moors beyond Ringinglow, demonstrating a fortitude that would serve him well in facing the rigours and tribulations of the trenches less than a decade later.

In 1907, Reg was faced with a major decision: should he stay on at school or go out into the adult world and find a job? At 14 years of age, education at Central School was no longer free, but there were two hundred scholarships for able pupils who might progress to the new Sixth Form and possibly on to university. Reg sat the required examination but did not gain a scholarship and so therefore like many bright pupils in the early twentieth century, he decided to leave school, perhaps encouraged by his family who would have to find the fees to keep him on at school and subsidize his keep at the family home.

He did not feel he was ruining his life chances. His mates in Hillsborough and at Wadsley Church had already left elementary school at thirteen and he believed that those who stayed on at Central School were all planning to be teachers, something Reg did not fancy as a life time career. As for going on to university, that would not have been an option, as only a very small percentage of the population went to university and very few of them were from a background like his.

So, as with Vivian Simpson, his education was foreshortened, as he opted for the world of work. There was no teenage culture in those times and boys left school wanting to prove themselves capable of a man's job at the first opportunity. Reg appreciated getting a weekly wage, contributing to the family budget, yet saving a few shillings to spend on himself. He would trust to the future that it would bring advancement, a wife and family one day and a reasonable level of security and prosperity.

Chapter 2

Edwardian Days

Somewhat ironically, Reg Glenn's first foray into the world of work in 1907 was as an office boy in a solicitor's office in the centre of town. He might even have made contact with the newly qualified Vivian Simpson at the offices of Simpson and Sons on Fargate, although, if he did so, he never commented on it later. It was not an exciting introduction to the adult world, mainly fetching and carrying large ledgers and searching in the vaults for wills, deeds and other legal documents and, although he was keen to obtain an office job, this one very quickly appeared a dead end as far as Reg was concerned. He moved on when he was sixteen and got another office boy's job at Thomas Ashton's, who were engineers. He found that job more interesting, largely because he had to regularly pass through the engineering works where the tumult of monstrous machinery clattering away left him more than a little awestruck. The tough-looking workforce tending those colossal machines seemed more like the real world of work than a dusty solicitor's office, where a permanent torpor appeared to lie across every room of the building and most of the staff.

To balance the disappointment of his day job, Reg became even more active in his leisure activities, most of which centred around the parish church at Wadsley where the family worshipped. Always a participant rather than a shy observer, Reg joined the local company of the Church Lads' Brigade, founded by the Anglican Church in 1891, whose motto was 'Fight the Good Fight'. The Brigade based its organisation on military routines and discipline, intending to give some purpose and structure to the lives of children from deprived backgrounds

Reg at 14 when he started his first job at a solicitor's office in Sheffield.

who might otherwise be running around wild and be up to no good. Still very much a young boy in years, Reg had joined the Church Lads' Brigade (CLB) partly because he rather liked the uniform, modelled closely on the regular army's new pattern khaki dress but in navy blue, with a pill box cap and leather belt. He found that the emphasis in the Brigade was on marching and drilling, although there was instruction in map reading that got him out into the countryside and the fresh air. Continuing the deliberate military theme, the Brigade used army ranks and chevrons, but there is no evidence that Reg made it to Lance Corporal or higher. The officers saw the advantages of using the nearby spectacular countryside for training, with the result that Reg's unit undertook regular route marches along Pennine roads that tested the boys' stamina. Reg would find this useful experience when he joined the City Battalion in 1914, because they too had a penchant for long route marches, important training for troops who would expect to march from billet to battlefield and back to their billets.

Apart from the more overtly military activities, Reg's Company went camping and played sports as did all youth organisations of whatever national, religious or political colour that flourished in the late nineteen and early twentieth centuries. There was also emphasis in the Brigade on Christian teaching, church attendance and church parades and a general support for the values of the time, honouring the King, the British nation and the Empire. Nor did it need to be stated that should war come, the CLB boys would play their part in the ranks of the army. In fact, the 16th Battalion of the King's Royal Rifle Corps, a London 'Pals' battalion, was

The local Wadsley company of the Church Lad's Brigade in 1908 with Reg third from right back row.

entirely recruited from the Church Lads' Brigade and twenty-two former members of the Brigade were winners of the Victoria Cross in the First World War, the highest number of awards of any civilian organisation.

Shortly after the Boy Scouts were formed in 1910, Reg jumped ship from the Church Lads' Brigade and enlisted in a new scout troop that was attached to Wadsley Church. The troop had been started by a teacher at Morley Street School and he offered Reg, now nearly twenty, the opportunity to be a scoutmaster in the new troop. Soon after the troop was formed, they were visited by General Robert Baden-Powell himself, who congratulated them on their progress, although Reg's abiding memory of the inspection was that he could clearly see that Baden-Powell was remarkably bowlegged, as he was wearing the regulation Scouts' shorts.

The Scouts captured Reg's imagination and enthusiasm as they have continued to do for teenagers all over the world in the decades since their foundation. He loved leading their activities and performing their small rituals, but most of all he appreciated the sense of freedom, enjoying life in the open air, camping at weekends, cooking meals and practising woodcraft in the familiar beautiful countryside along the Rivelin and Loxley valleys. There were occasionally longer periods of camping away from Sheffield and Reg would later recall a week's camp in North Wales where the troop had to stay up all night to sit on the marquee to prevent it from blowing away after it had collapsed in the face of a fierce gale coming in from the Irish Sea.

Among the skills that Reg acquired in the scouts and the CLB were signalling with flags and the ability to blow a bugle. Both of these skills would be in demand later when he joined the City Battalion and he was even forced to make a choice in 1914 between joining the battalion signallers or becoming a bandsman, because he was equally proficient at both skills.

In 1910, Reg changed jobs again and this time it would lead to a lifetime's

Reg in his Assistant Scoutmaster's uniform shortly before the outbreak of the Great War, after he had left the Church Lad's Brigade and joined the new Scout movement founded by Baden-Powell.

public service with the City Council working in the Education Department – the Sheffield LEA. His old Headmaster, the legendary J.W. Iliffe, who was the Head of Central School for twenty-four years, knew that the Education Department was looking to recruit new clerks and encouraged Reg to apply, whilst no doubt putting in a good word for him with those who counted.

When Reg asked the manager at Thomas Ashton's for permission to go for an interview at the Education Offices on Leopold Street, he got a dusty reply. 'Whether you get the job or not, you are finished here!' the unsympathetic manager grunted, but undaunted, Reg went for the interview and his bright, confident attitude ensured his success. So, with some satisfaction he gave a week's notice to Ashton's and left.

This was in essence more than just a promotion for Reg, because the Education Department, that had taken over from the Sheffield School Board after the 1902 Education Act, was living through an exciting period of development. This was a golden decade for education in the city, with so many important institutions created, driven by strong support from councillors and leading citizens who regarded education as the Council's most important function, one that always commanded the largest revenue item in city's annual budget. The City Council was not only repositioning the Central School as a Boys' Grammar School and a Girls' Grammar School in their own separate buildings, but they had launched a teacher training college on Ecclesall Road in the enlarged buildings that had originally been the Collegiate School. In 1905, the Council had also finessed the amalgamation of Wesley College and the Royal Grammar School to create a high performing boys' school to which the king granted permission to call King Edward VII School. On top of that, the City Council, in the same year, was the driving force in establishing the new university on Western Bank that initially they envisaged as largely serving able pupils from Sheffield and the adjacent area, as few students went away to university in those days unless they got a scholarship.

Working for the Education Department was a matter of some prestige and Reg would have been told repeatedly that he had made a good decision, now had a job for life and opportunities for advancement. The reality was somewhat different when he first took up his post at Leopold Street. He might have the title junior clerk and arrive at work in a suit, stiff collar and a tie but much of the work was routine. His immediate boss was almost eighty, who hung on in the job unable to retire because there was no pension available for him. All Reg ever saw him do was sit in the same chair all day with a rug over his knees using an official rubber stamp to authorise letters to and from the department. The atmosphere was still Victorian, with clerks perched on high stools at high desks checking formidable, heavy ledgers. One of Reg's tasks was to collect a monthly record from each school and write it up in those ledgers, while another was to produce a bulletin every day indicating which teachers were teaching where the following day. As there were only two telephones in the entire building, Reg had to send the

The Sheffield LEA Education Offices in Leopold Street close by the Town Hall. It was part of the same complex of education buildings as the Central School where Reg was educated. It was completed in 1880 and was also designed by Thomas Flockton. In recent years, it became an upmarket hotel.

information out by post before 10am so that it would get to the schools by the 4pm post in the afternoon. Seventy years later, he would still be able to recite by heart all the sixty schools in alphabetical order that he had to contact every day in those years before the war.

They were long hours but punctuated by a generous dinner time. Reg started work at 8.30, having got there by tram from Hillsborough or by cycle. When he was a young lad, he had often sneaked a free ride on the tram by jumping on the rear open platform when the conductor was otherwise engaged, hanging on until summarily forced to jump off. Now as a respectable member of the Council's staff, he would have to pay his fare, so he usually travelled in to work by cycle, a matter of three miles from Hillsborough but fortunately almost all of the journey was along the flat valley of the River Don. Officially, the work day ended at 6pm, but if work still needed to be done, Reg could be in the office till past 9pm with no suggestion of overtime payments. He did have an hour and a half off for lunch and invariably he cycled home to Hillsborough for a lunch prepared by his mother. For all this effort, he got the meagre sum of five shillings a week, equivalent to a wage of around £94 today. He gave most of this to his mother to help with the housekeeping, and with two sisters working as well, the family finances became more comfortable, so much so that they could afford a family holiday at the sea-side.

Usually this meant a week in Cleethorpes, in those days Sheffield's place of choice by the sea, presumably because it was the nearest resort offering the

The Glenn family with his father, Richard, and his mother, Elizabeth, and two sisters Edith and Ada (left) in a formal portrait circa 1901.

traditional British holiday. For a shilling a night, they could get a room and have their cooking done for them by the landlady, provided they bought the food for the landlady to cook. Their treats were also remarkably cheap and you could buy an ice–cream for a halfpenny and try out the amusements along the front for a similar amount. More likely, you would just enjoy an afternoon or evening stroll along the promenade, gazing at the North Sea seemingly miles away across the vast expanse of Lincolnshire sands.

In August 1914, they tried the considerably more exciting North Riding coast instead, and took the train and stayed in Whitby. It was while they were away that they read that Britain had declared war on Germany over the issue of Belgian neutrality. Like many holiday makers that summer, caught out by Asquith's government's declaration of war, they did the very British thing and just continued with their holiday, rather optimistically thinking that it would all blow over. They were, no doubt, further comforted by the belief that the British Empire was invincible and that the Royal Navy guaranteed the nation's ultimate safety, whatever happened on the continent.

For Vivian Simpson, the opening of the twentieth century was marked by great sadness, as his father died of a sudden heart attack in May 1900 at the relatively young age of 63. Vivian had just left school the previous summer and was expecting to be tutored by his father when he became articled to the family firm. Instead he would be a pupil of his elder brother George, who was thirteen years older than Vivian and who would become his guide and confidante over the next few years. For a few years after Warleigh House was sold, Vivian moved into George's home in Meadowbank Avenue, Nether Edge, before seeking out his own bachelor rooms in Broomhall. George Harold Simpson was now the senior partner in the firm that had already been renamed in the Nineties, George J. Simpson and Son, and when Vivian qualified, he would become a partner as well and the title would be changed again to George J. Simpson and Sons.

Seventeen when his father died, Vivian was of an age when his natural resilience would allow him to quickly come to terms with his father's death and get on with his own new life in the adult world. His connections to the professional, social and political world of Sheffield marked him out as a young man on the rise in the early Edwardian period, a cheerful man about town for whom money was no problem, who would dine at the Grand Hotel in Barker's Pool and for entertainment take a box, or a front row dress circle seat, at the Lyceum, Sheffield's most fashionable theatre.

However, it was his sporting ability, already noticed by Sheffield football and cricket clubs when he was playing for Wesley College, that made him famous as a young man in his native city. In December 1899, Vivian made his choice of football clubs and his decision was to join Sheffield FC, the gentlemen's club formed in 1857 by Nathaniel Creswick and William Prest, along with other former students of the Collegiate School. Sheffield FC were not just the oldest and most prestigious amateur club in Sheffield, but they are recognised today by FIFA, no less, as the oldest football club in the world and are still playing as a leading amateur side at their Dronfield ground on the outskirts of the city.

At the end of 1900, Vivian also signed amateur forms for the Wednesday FC, who had just moved to their new ground on the north west fringe of the city that they called Owlerton Stadium (it was renamed Hillsborough Stadium in 1914). The Wednesday had turned professional in 1887, a controversial move among many of their well-heeled supporters, who had a Corinthian view of sport, that football was a noble exercise for gentlemen who played for the pure enjoyment of the game and not for any tawdry financial reward.

This was very much Vivian Simpson's attitude as well and it was an attitude that persisted in British sport well into the twentieth century. England, even Yorkshire County Cricket Club, still had amateur cricket captains in the 1950s, whilst in Rugby, the clash of clubs containing mainly ex-public schoolboys and those in Yorkshire, Cumbria and Lancashire that relied on the skills of working-class players led to a split in the game in 1895, with Rugby Union holding out officially against professionalism until the 1990s.

Vivian solved this problem by playing most of his games for Sheffield FC but guesting in crucial matches for Wednesday, in a side where he was the only amateur in a team of professionals. The other players in his team invariably came from a social background more akin to Reg Glenn's or even from the Victorian slums of Scottish and northern towns and Vivian's accent and clothes would have marked him out as a chap more like the club's directors than the players and coaches. Nevertheless, he was popular amongst his team mates who called him 'Vivvy' and appreciated his sportsmanship and his skill on the ball. Most of all they were impressed with his courage, as he was only 5ft 6in tall and weighed about 9 stones. Several former players in later years testified to their amazement how he would take on tall, tough defenders with reputations for ferocious, even illegal, tackling and unconcernedly and deftly slip past them, although he did take some punishment and missed the 1907 FA Cup Final because of a serious ankle injury.

In another English city, Vivian might well have played Rugby Union, but Sheffield could justly claim to be the premier home of Association Football where the influential Sheffield Rules of the Game had been written in 1858. It was also the home to Sheffield FC and Hallam FC, the world's two oldest clubs. There were two professional clubs, which in the first decade of the century were among the game's giants, United winning the FA Cup in 1902 and Wednesday winning the League twice between 1902 and 1904 and the FA Cup in 1907.

At the Sheffield Club, Vivian was called 'Simmy' and here he was playing alongside his social peers. His first game for FC in December 1899, two days after Christmas, was against Attercliffe in the Wharncliffe Cup, but he had to wait until the following season for his first goal in September 1900. He usually played inside forward or centre forward for Sheffield FC, the positions he had played at Wesley College, and if he had to wait for his first goal for the club, plenty of other followed. In 229 games for Sheffield FC between 1899 and 1909, when he played his last game against Northern Nomads, he scored 169 goals. Not bad for a little chap in a crowded penalty box where burly defenders would attempt to block his progress and not necessarily in a very gentlemanly way.

There were to be days of disappointment as well. The bitterest was when he missed the 1904 FA Amateur Cup Final against Ealing at Valley Parade, Bradford. Vivian had been crucial to the club's progress in the earlier rounds and a hat trick against a Darlington side had seen the club through to the semi-finals, but then he had been injured playing for Wednesday in an FA Cup tie against Spurs. However, in recognition of his part in the club's 3-1 triumph, he received a compensatory medal and when the team returned home they went straight round to Vivian's house to show him the cup that he had helped to win.

During Vivian's time with the club, Sheffield FC played their matches at the Niagara ground at Wadsley Bridge (now South Yorkshire Police sports ground) and Vivian's talent was recognised by selection for England in an amateur international match against Ireland in 1907. More significantly, in January 1907 he took part in a trial match for the full England side, although he was still an amateur. This was organised on a North v South Select XI basis and Vivian made a good impression in the trial, despite the presence of so many of the star players who were available to England in that decade. Finally, the selectors decided he was too slight for international football and he never won a full cap.

Vivian's first game for Wednesday was on 28 March 1902, when he was just nineteen years old. The club had been performing badly and the directors feared they would be relegated, so they insisted that some of the younger players were brought into the team and that is how Vivian got his break. His first game was against Manchester City at Maine Road, then as now one of the leading clubs in

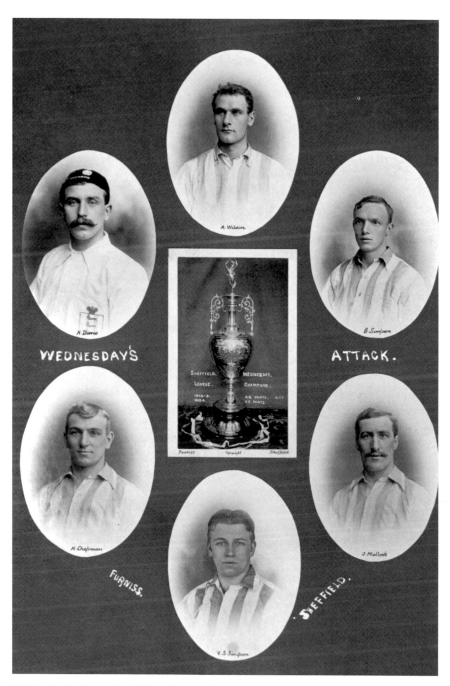

Vivian (at the bottom) and the other members of The Wednesday's formidable forward line in the season they won the FA League Trophy in 1904.

the Football League and the infusion of youthful talent did the trick, as Wednesday won 3-nil. Moreover, they avoided relegation and the following season they topped the League with Vivian turning out for them on an occasional basis during the next five seasons, usually playing on the wing where his size did not matter so much but his pace did.

Wednesday seemed to have accepted that Vivian's first loyalty was to Sheffield FC and they called on his services when they had a key match against top sides or FA Cup matches. If the Sheffield public still did not know much about Simmy, they did after 20 February 1904, when Wednesday drubbed Manchester United by six goals to nil, with Vivian scoring a hat -trick. Because he played on the wing for Wednesday, he only scored eleven goals in his seasons with the club, but he made thirty-eight appearances and was clearly in demand when there was a crucial match. Again, Vivian was to suffer a great disappointment in 1907, when, having starred in the earlier rounds, he was injured against Liverpool and was unfit to play in the FA Cup Final when Wednesday beat Everton at Crystal Palace by two goals to one, although he did receive a medal for his part in the Cup run but it would have been of limited consolation.

That third-round tie against Liverpool in March 1907 proved to be his last game for Wednesday. Although Vivian recovered from the injury, he never played for them again, although he was asked to play for the Wednesday in January 1908 in an FA Cup tie that fell on the same day as Sheffield Club had a key Amateur Cup replay against Blackburn. So Vivian faced a clash of loyalties, but he chose his first love, the amateur club (they lost 1-0), and perhaps because of that, rather than his recurrent ankle injury, he never pulled on the blue and white striped shirt again.

Vivian played two more seasons for Sheffield FC and, rather surprisingly, he played as an amateur for one game for Norwich City in November 1907, when they were still in the Southern League. The local press was excited that such a talented and well known player should turn out for their team, but he only played that one game for the 'Canaries' and why he agreed to play for them at all is a bit of a mystery. Vivian's last game for the Sheffield Football Club was in April 1909 against the powerful amateur side Northern Nomads (SFC lost 4-0), and at the age of twenty-six he hung up his boots and took up golf instead.

It was in the Edwardian era that sport finally achieved a dominant position in British society, the subject of earnest discussions and intense loyalties of millions of men and boys, and the platform for the exploits of popular heroes whose fame was as great as the politicians, generals and royalty, who had been the most famous celebrities of the late nineteenth century. True, W.G. Grace had been a cricket super hero for over three decades but he was the exception. Now there were many popular heroes and many of them were amateur gentlemen like the cricketers C.B Fry and Gilbert Jessop, or Adrian Stoop of the Harlequins. Britain had hosted the all-amateur Olympic Games in 1908 and won 147 medals (including 59 Golds, more than twice the USA's haul), and a Yorkshire amateur, the Hon. F.S. Jackson, later Sir Stanley, an MP and Governor of Bengal, had captained the England side in a winning Ashes series in 1905, whilst all counties had several leading players who were amateurs from public school backgrounds.

Vivian Simpson's sporting success would not therefore seem as unusual as it might in a modern sporting context. He would be well known in the city several years after he stopped playing football and certainly a celebrity among his own social set. As early as 1903, his old school, Wesley College, had invited him to their Sports Day to present prizes, a recognition already of his local sporting fame. At Wesley College, Vivian had also starred for the cricket team as an all-rounder but principally as a batsman, then the true gentleman's calling. Cricket was clearly regarded as the nation's premier game, possibly because it was still the preserve of the aristocracy and the upper middle class who ran the world game through their private club, the MCC at Lords. In the summer, Vivian played for the Collegiate Club that had also been founded by Old Boys of the Collegiate School in 1881, initially playing their games at the school on Ecclesall Road. It was among the leading amateur clubs in the region, certainly the most exclusive, and Vivian would naturally gravitate to joining that club rather than another. When Vivian played for Collegiate, they had acquired a ground at Tinsley and their First XI played in the Sheffield and Hallamshire League, however, the club does not have any individual records that would indicate how Vivian performed. Nevertheless, his obituary in the *Star* in 1918 referred to him scoring centuries for the club and he obviously had very good hand-eye co-ordination, as was soon to be demonstrated by his success at golf.

Towards the end of Vivian Simpson's football career, he appears to have fallen in love with golf. Here was a game you could play without suffering leg and ankle injuries, one you could play competitively until your fifties, if not longer. Moreover, you could join a club where you were among people of your own background because golf was an expensive game to take up and private golf clubs in the first half of the twentieth century usually had a rigorous vetting process for aspiring new members. Perhaps because of Queen Victoria's enthusiasm for all things Scottish in her later years, their 'national game' of golf became very popular in England in the last decade of the nineteenth century and really caught on with the English upper middle class after 1900.

Sheffield was a classic example of the development of the game. In England, there were only twelve golf courses in 1880, by 1914 there were over 1,000 and Sheffield had more than its fair share of outstanding courses. Starting with Lindrick in 1891 (just inside the West Riding, but founded in Sheffield), the Hallamshire Club opened in 1897, Dore Golf Club (later renamed Abbeydale) in 1895, Lees Hall and Tankersley clubs in 1907 and Dore and Totley in 1913. The 'Great Triumvirate' of golfers, Harry Vardon, James Baird and J.H. Taylor, were three more of the sporting super-stars of the Edwardian golden age and their exploits helped to popularise the game, although all three were professionals and came from modest backgrounds themselves.

So it was not surprising that Vivian Simpson took up golf in his mid-twenties and very soon proved a very adept player, who had got his handicap down to

Wortley Golf Club around the time of the Great War. Originally it had been the Earl of Wharncliffe's shooting lodge and though now enlarged it still serves as the clubhouse for Wortley Golf Club, which was founded in 1894.

'scratch' by 1914. His course of choice was perhaps surprisingly a nine-hole course nine miles from his home in Sheffield on the Earl of Wharncliffe's estate at Wortley, out in the West Riding countryside. Francis, 2nd Earl of Wharncliffe, had been a Royal Navy Commander before he inherited his title from his uncle and after taking up residence at Wortley Hall he indulged his enthusiasm for golf by creating a nine-hole course in 1894 in beautiful wooded parklands, that had been part of the family's deer park since medieval times.

Vivian Simpson regarded it as an 'oasis of calm' in a busy world and played there regularly. He probably made the choice to play at Wortley, rather than one of the courses within the city boundary, because his brother George was already a member there, as was his future brother-in-law, Freddy Belcher. George, in fact, was so well established at Wortley that he was elected Captain of the Club in 1913. The course became even more attractive to Vivian when the Earl extended it to 18 holes in 1911, and also allowed his old shooting lodge, relatively close to the first tee, to become the clubhouse, a clubhouse with bedrooms, so that players and guests could stay overnight and enjoy a full weekend's golf before driving back to Sheffield.

Vivian would have played with old fashioned hickory irons while his woods would have been made of hardwood, all carried in a stovepipe bag, but there was still a considerable cost in being kitted out as a golfer, and membership fees and green fees would have been prohibitively high for less well-off members of the public. By 1911, the Simpsons had motor cars and getting to Wortley would be easier, with no longer any need to rely on the train and the stiff mile walk from the station. Another attraction for Vivian was that Freddy Belcher's sister, May, also played golf at Wortley and by now Vivian and May, who knew each other from the Broomhill social whirl and St Mark's Church were something of a couple and before the war broke out, they had got engaged.

Romance was also beckoning for Reg Glenn in those last months of peace before the outbreak of war in August 1914. He had formed an attachment to Elsie Gosling who he had known for a few years while she was growing up in a house at the bottom of Stannington Road near Malin Bridge. Still only seventeen in 1914, Elsie had had her share of sadness when her father, Fred Gosling, a former Coldstream Guardsman, and latterly a member of the Sheffield City Police Force, was recalled to the colours in 1899 and sent out to South Africa to join the Coldstreamers' Second Battalion. Soon in action, Fred was killed shortly afterwards at the battle of Modder River in November 1899, after the Boer forces had swept all before them and besieged Kimberley.

Only two years old when her father was killed in South Africa, Elsie would never have known him, whilst her brother Frank was born in 1900 after their father's death. Her mother, Edith, had to bring up two children and leave her home in Heeley after she was offered a position as Matron at West Bar police station looking after the general welfare of a number of unmarried policemen who lived in at the station. There was further sadness years later, when Frank succumbed to TB and died in 1919.

In 1908, Elsie passed the examination to go to the Central Secondary Girls School, now housed in the building at the end of Leopold Street that had once been Firth College. She now embarked on a grammar school education under another famous Head, Florence Cousins, who built up the reputation of her school and its Sixth Form until she retired in 1925. Reg's office in the Education Department was next door on Leopold Street and he would already know Elsie quite well after she had joined the congregation at Wadsley Church. Although Elsie would just be a young lass at that time, she might, however, have been a trifle sweet on the handsome young clerk with whom she may have demurely exchanged glances during church services on Sundays.

By 1914, Reg and Elsie were sweethearts, and Elsie, now seventeen, was a very attractive young lady who was destined for a career in teaching, at least until she got married, although that was a long way off in her thinking at that time. Having made her career choice, Elsie embarked on initial teacher training at the Pupil Teacher Centre adjacent to the Central Girls School. Reg recalled years later that he used to find an excuse to accompany Elsie

An attractive photo portrait of Elsie probably taken in late 1914 or early 1915, because she is wearing a York & Lancaster Regiment cap badge as a brooch.

back home to Hillsborough on the tram and one way and another their relationship moved on until they could be said to be courting. When Reg joined up, Elsie was very proud to be seen walking out with a soldier, especially one who had volunteered for the battalion everyone in Sheffield was talking about. When Reg went off to war, Elsie continued at the Pupil Teacher Centre before travelling right across the country to undertake her advanced teacher training at Truro Diocesan Training College. This college had been established by the Diocese of Truro after the Cornish town became a bishopric, with a new cathedral started in 1880 but only finished a few years before Elsie arrived at her college in Truro in September 1916.

It is not clear why Elsie went to Truro for her two-year course, about as far as you could go in England from Sheffield. It may be nothing more complicated than it was the college that said yes and offered her a place. In normal times, it is more than likely that she would have trained at the Sheffield City Training College on Ecclesall Road, but the buildings were requisitioned in 1914 as a hospital for wounded soldiers and therefore were not available to train teachers during the war. At least in Truro, Elsie was safe from Zeppelins, one of which bombed Sheffield in late September 1916, with everyone in the city expecting more of them to return.

Teaching was vital war work too, because so many male teachers had volunteered for the army in 1914 and 1915 (teachers won more gallantry medals than any other profession) and increasingly the nation turned to young unmarried women to fill the posts in the nation's schools, mainly in its primary schools. This trend had clearly been occurring already in the early twentieth century but became more pronounced during the war. So once qualified, Elsie was a part of an important social development of the new century. Few middle-class professions were open to women in sizeable numbers, but teaching was one job where the ranks of the teaching profession could only be filled if the Local Education Authorities recruited large numbers of qualified women teachers. Young ladies like Elsie were trailblazers for women's emancipation, even if not one them was yet allowed to vote.

By early 1914, Vivian Simpson was engaged and planning to marry during the next year. His fiancée was Marion May Belcher, the younger daughter of a leading figure in the business world of the town. Her father, John

May Belcher standing on the front steps of Rossleigh the family home on Broomfield Road, Broomhill in 1914.

Frederick Belcher, was manager of the Sheffield branch of the London, City and Midland Bank and had been the manager of the Sheffield and Hallamshire Bank whose city centre premises were close by the Cutlers Hall. He had a strong link to civic politics, for he had been the Treasurer of the City Council when that post had been held by an independent figure not employed by the City Council. Born in Ecclesfield, a village to the north of the city, by the early twentieth century the family were all living in Rossleigh, a huge house partly modelled on a French chateau across the road from St. Mark's Church in Broomhill.

So the forthcoming marriage was a dream match between two well-established Broomhill families and Vivian would have considered himself very fortunate to have been accepted by the strikingly appealing May Belcher. Never called Marion among the family – she was always known as May – she was also born in Ecclesfield when the family lived there. Born on New Year's Day in 1889, May was twenty-five years old in 1914 and was a lady of leisure with two servants in the house, young women who did the cooking and the housekeeping. Within her social circles, May Belcher would not have been expected to go out to work but rather help organise social events and support acceptable charities. Vivian, who was six years older, always called her 'Maykins' in his letters, and that was probably their private name of endearment for they seemed to be very much in love. During their engagement they

Vivian leaning on the stone wall with his dog and May (extreme right) enjoying a picnic with a group of friends in Derbyshire just before the Great War started.

organised the purchase of a new house on Hagg Lane at Crosspool that they intended would be ready for them to move into when they got married.

Hagg Lane is a precipitously steep road that would have been a rough surfaced lane in 1914. It led from the heights of Crosspool down the steep incline into the Rivelin Valley with unsurpassed views across the valley to the fields on the hillside below Stannington Village. It was an unbelievably beautiful place to have a house and although it was on the outskirts of Sheffield it was close to the Hallamshire Golf Club where May was a member; Vivian had recently joined as well.

In the meantime, Vivian had found rooms of his own at Travis Place in Broomhall, near Moorfoot, in a house that was different from the rest of the row of smart, but modest, town houses. No.3 Travis Place was at an angle to the street and may well have been a farm house from the previous century when the area was still agricultural land. This address gave Vivian some independence away from the family, and in those years before the war, he would establish himself as a successful lawyer before branching out into other business activities.

The Simpson brothers became directors of the Sheffield Cinematograph Company who owned two cinemas, the Electra (opened 1911) in Fitzalan Square and the Cinema House (opened 1913) in Barker's Pool. Just before Easter in 1914, the *Sheffield Telegraph* reported that Vivian had appeared before the Licensing Magistrates to get approval for his Easter programme at the two cinemas. The Licensing Committee, chaired by Sir William Clegg, the City Council Leader, was very critical of the programme planned by a cinema in Heeley, claiming its content did not show due reverence to the message of Easter, but Vivian's defence of their cinemas' programmes received their full approval. The Heeley cinema was turned down for an Easter licence and the proprietor was told to model his programme on that outlined by Mr. Simpson in future.

Cinemas and the films they showed, were the most exciting and newest aspect of the entertainment industry at that time. It was an industry that was welcomed enthusiastically by working people and the powers-that-be viewed it with some concern and worried about the moral effect of its appeal, especially as the USA had taken a leading role in popular cinema and the British Establishment could be very snooty about Americans and uncertain how to deal with the new phenomenon of American popular culture that had started to appear in Britain. However, Vivian enjoyed going and seeing the films his cinemas showed and clearly the Simpson brothers had the foresight to get in on the ground floor, seeing the potential of this new medium, that would within the next twenty years have a revolutionary effect on the entertainment industry and also on society's attitudes.

Neither Reg Glenn nor Vivian Simpson would have had an inkling before 28 June 1914 of how their lives were about to be transformed, nor is it likely they had ever heard of Sarajevo. And for one of them, their young life would be drastically foreshortened in less than four years' time, at a nondescript crossroads at the end of a nondescript village near a dull, flat stretch of land near the Franco-Belgian border.

Chapter 3

Joining Up
September-December 1914

Vivian Simpson was the first man to enrol in the new City Battalion on the morning of 2 September, in the magnificently appointed reception room on the first floor of the Town Hall. It is most likely, given his connections, that he was already in the building and did not have to wait on the steps of the Town Hall to be let in at 10am when enrolment began. He would claim later that he had been one of the first to have the idea of a rather special City Battalion, because he had had a discussion with his fiancée's father, John Belcher, in late August, suggesting that he would be prepared to join up as a private in the New Armies if he could serve alongside people of his own class. John Belcher was well connected to the key men in the Town Hall, especially Sir George Franklin, a former Lord Mayor and still a leading Conservative Alderman, who became a prime mover in the creation of the City Battalion. Vivian may well have heard that some London stockbrokers had started the idea of the Pals Battalions by forming a battalion from members and staff of the Stock Exchange (a battalion that would eventually become the 10th Bn Royal Fusiliers), and thought why could something similar not happen in his city as well?

The credit for the genesis of the idea to form a special middle-class battalion is usually given to two anonymous undergraduate members of the Sheffield University OTC. They are said to have persuaded the Vice-Chancellor, Herbert (H.A.L.) Fisher, an enthusiastic supporter of Britain's entry into the war, to consider the idea of a Pals Battalion drawn from students from the university. Fisher was most receptive to the idea, but it was soon clear that the university could not produce enough volunteers for a whole battalion and that they needed a wider constituency of volunteers and the financial and organisational strength of the City Council.

No doubt leading figures on the Council had been having similar, if unfocussed, thoughts along the same lines, especially after Lord Derby over in Liverpool had raised four battalions of 'Pals' for the local King's Regiment (they became 17th, 18th, 19th and 20th Bn King's Regiment) in under a week. In Yorkshire, Hull, a city with only half the population of Sheffield, had already raised one Pals Battalion (later the 10th East Yorks) in August and they had looked to limit their recruiting to professional men, white collar staff and men from a middle-class background.

At the very end of August, the men who counted in the city's politics had decided to talk directly to the War Office in London with a view to raising a Pals Battalion in Sheffield. The city's delegation was led by the Duke of Norfolk and Sir George Franklin, who was also a member of the Court of the University, so he could represent the university's interest at the talks as well. The Duke, who owned vast areas of land in Sheffield, was such a senior Member of the Lords that he added great weight to Sheffield's case. They found the War Office was well disposed to their proposals, as well they might be, because the Pals Battalion idea was taking off like wildfire and proving an absolute winner in raising the volunteers to meet Kitchener's target of an army of seventy divisions.

Back in Sheffield on 1 September, a hurriedly convened meeting at the Town Hall, chaired by the Lord Mayor, George Branson VD JP, himself a Lieutenant Colonel, established the new battalion and agreed that the Council would finance, quarter and train it pending repayment by the Government at some future date. This ad hoc committee included everyone who mattered. Apart from the Duke and Sir George, there was Sir William Clegg and Colonel Herbert Hughes, respectively the Leaders of the Liberals and the Conservatives on the Council, and the University Vice-Chancellor H.A.L. Fisher, who would became the Liberal MP for Hallam in 1916. The Labour Party was not involved or invited, although they were a growing force in Sheffield politics and had won the Attercliffe Parliamentary seat in 1909, but they never had more than four councillors on the Council in any year before 1914. In early September, the Labour Party was still uncertain about whether it supported the war or not, although its voters clearly did, but if it had been a power in the Town Hall at that time it would have certainly opposed ratepayers' money being spent on a battalion that was only for 'posh' people and intended to exclude working class men.

By mid-morning, when enrolment started, there was already a line of volunteers outside the Town Hall and all day young men would be queuing up on the grand marble staircase inside the Town Hall that led to the reception room where enrolling was taking place. The committee had acted quickly and posters were out by the morning of 2 September, calling for volunteers to enrol immediately. The committee also decided that for the moment the name should be 'The Sheffield University and City Special Battalion'. The University name came first to ease their sensibilities because they thought of themselves as the initiators of the idea of the battalion; special because this was going to be a battalion for the middle class only. The War Office on 11 September announced that they would be accepted as a battalion of the York and Lancaster Regiment, because this was always going to be an infantry battalion, and the Regiment recruited in Sheffield, Barnsley and Rotherham, an area that sixty years later would become the county of South Yorkshire. So their formal title became for the time being the Sheffield City Battalion of the York and Lancaster Regiment.

The posters also made it clear who this battalion was for. One of them stressed the desire for volunteers who were present or former university students, or old boys of public schools. Another listed those who were welcome to join in declining order of social status. 1. Professional men; 2. Businessmen; 3. Teachers; 4. Clerks; 5. Shop Assistants – essentially anyone who needed to go to work in a suit, a collar and tie and probably a waistcoat as well for good measure. Four-fifths of Sheffield's population in 1914 were intended to be excluded from this Battalion, although the York and Lancaster Regiment was also recruiting for other Service Battalions who would take fit volunteers from any class. Meanwhile, the Territorial Force battalion, the Hallamshires (the 4th Battalion York & Lancaster), was contemplating raising another battalion in October and there were many skilled workmen from the city's engineering firms who joined the Royal Engineers.

On that first day, when enrolment closed at 4pm at the Town Hall, 250 men had signed up, indicating their willingness to serve in the new battalion. The Duke of Norfolk stayed all day in the reception room, his presence adding to the importance and significance of the occasion, telling the volunteers that their city and their country was proud of them and lauded their sense of duty and their spirit of adventure. During the afternoon, the University OTC, dressed in their khaki uniforms with badges and buttons specially bulled up for the occasion, marched down en masse to the Town Hall and enrolled. Apart from the officers and the former Regular and Territorial Force NCOs who joined to help train the battalion, they would be the only ones to have the proper army uniform for some weeks.

A sizeable crowd had hung around the entrance to the Town Hall on Pinstone Street, enjoying the excitement, no doubt aware they were watching Sheffield history in the making and perhaps a few waverers were carried along

---

SHEFFIELD UNIVERSITY
AND
CITY SPECIAL BATTALION

Col. Hughes, C.B., C.M.G., Acting Commandant.
Capt. E. A. Marples, Acting Adjutant.

For Professional Men,
For Business Men,
For Teachers,
For Clerks,
For Shop Assistants,
Etc., Etc.

Enrolment at the Town Hall
TO - DAY,
10 a.m. to 7 p.m.

ENROL NOW.

Newspaper Advertisement of 2 September, describing the volunteer battalion as the Sheffield University and City Special Battalion.

by the crowd's enthusiasm and decided to enrol. This all helped to promote recruitment and the local papers carried photos of young men going in to sign up and that encouraged another 270 to enrol the next day. Some may have been impelled to join up because the news from the France was quite disastrous. The British Expeditionary Force, serving alongside the French Army, was retreating after their first contact on 23 August with the German First Army, just over the Belgian border at Mons. By the 24th, the five British Divisions were back to Le Cateau and by the 29th they were trying to hold the line at St. Quentin but could not stop the German army from reaching the Marne on 31 August, their spearheads now only 10 miles from Paris. If people in Britain thought the war might be over by Christmas, they seemed to have underestimated. It was looking possible that the German army might have the whole thing wrapped up in a couple of months, as they did in 1870, and the BEF might be looking for an escape through Le Havre or Cherbourg, In the same way that British troops were evacuated from Dunkirk 26 years later.

Reg Glenn had been thinking about joining up, but it was not until 4 September that he took the plunge. He said later it had nothing to do with King and Country, or the situation in France, or even the basic appeal to a young man's courage. It was more that he was fed up with office work and the war offered a chance to travel and see other countries, as few Sheffielders would have visited Europe, let alone the Middle East, as Reg would do in the next twenty months. In the end, it was a decision taken at the mid-morning break at the Education Department offices and the initiative was taken by Reg's friend and colleague, Edward (Ned) Muxlow, who lived with his family over the Wicker Post Office.

'Shall we go and enlist?' asked Ned and Reg replied; 'Yes, let's do it, we can go at dinner time'. But Ned having made up his mind to sign on, countered; 'No let's go now!'

So the two friends slipped out of the building walked the hundred yards up Leopold Street and into the Town Hall and signed up. Like volunteers, reservists and even conscripts in all the armies now involved in the war, they were carried away by the exuberance of the moment and rather proud of their decision. However, that day of civic celebration at the Town Hall would profoundly change their lives, even though both of them would survive the war, unlike many of those who signed up for the City Battalion that week. Ned Muxlow would be severely wounded at Serre on the first day of the Somme, his leg and groin injuries keeping him out of the front line for almost a year. Later, he was twice wounded within a week in April 1918 during the German offensive, this time it was the other leg that was injured and in 1919 when he was demobbed from the army, he was given a disability pension because of the injuries to both his legs.

When Reg and Ned got back to the office, they found they were feted rather than disciplined. Several of the department staff had joined up but Reg's boss seemed supportive of their decision, although Reg suspected he was easy about losing so many staff, because his department was overstaffed and fewer clerks would ease his budget worries.

Back in Hillsborough, where the family were now living in May Road, Reg's parents were not at all pleased that he had signed up, especially as he had made no effort to discuss it with them. Perhaps older people could see that war was not a macho game, not a bit of a lark, but a deadly serious business where people got killed, as had happened to Elsie's dad in the Boer War only fifteen years earlier. They probably thought that all the nonsense about it being over by Christmas was wild press talk, remembering that the last time the British Army had taken on a 'European' enemy in South Africa it had not performed very impressively. Furthermore, tales of the horrific conditions in the Crimean War were still fresh in popular culture and everyone knew Tennyson's 'Charge of the Light Brigade', and how the hubris and apparent glamour of war preparations can quickly turn into ugly carnage on the battlefield.

In the week after the enrolment at the Town Hall, the volunteers got on with their normal jobs and waited for the postcard from the City Battalion Adjutant telling them when and where to report for a medical examination and attestation. The Council used the Corn Exchange building, built by the Duke of Norfolk at the bottom of Commercial Street in 1881, a famous Sheffield landmark in the Tudor palace style that was knocked down in 1964 to make way for Park Square roundabout. The key officers of the new battalion had been selected from men the organising committee members knew personally. They were mainly Territorial Force officers who had a connection, or were still serving, with the 4th (Hallamshire) Battalion of the York and Lancasters. These men, along with volunteer clerks, organised by the local Liberal and Conservative parties, and forty–five doctors who offered their services, made the preparations for the next stage of processing the volunteers. These officers included Captain Edward Marples, who had Boer War experience and who became the Battalion's first adjutant; Captain William Kerr, who agreed to become the temporary medical officer; and Captain T. Carter Clough, who would soon become the Battalion's second in command. The first appointment was Alderman Herbert Hughes, who was chosen by

Colonel Herbert Hughes, a leading member of the City Council and the first commanding officer of the Sheffield City Battalion 2 September to 10 October 1914.

the senior members of the Council's organising committee to be the initial Commanding Officer. He was the obvious choice, one of an inner group who ran Sheffield's civic affairs, well fitted to fill the role having considerable military experience, as well as serving as the Treasurer of the University.

Colonel Hughes CB CMG VD JP at 61 was far too old to lead a battalion in action, but his task was to get the whole concept of a council-run battalion off the ground, until such time as the War Office appointed a regular officer as the Commanding Officer. Born in Oxford in 1853, he had spent his professional life in Sheffield, been Lord Mayor in 1905-06 and was currently the Leader of the Conservative Group on the City Council. The senior partner in the law firm of Younge, Wilson and Co., Colonel Hughes was the Law Clerk to the Cutlers' Company, but more relevant to the present exercise he had served in the Hallamshire Rifles for thirty-one years, a volunteer unit that he went on to command from 1899-1908.

His admirers called him big hearted, honourable and chivalrous. However, Vivian Simpson in one of his letters sent to his brother George in mid-September took a more caustic view:

'What a blustering cad old Hughes is. Talk about a cheap auctioneer– they're not in it. The claptrap he turns out makes one positively mal de mer!'

These remarks were written after the Colonel's opening speech to the recruits at their first parade at Norfolk Barracks on Edmund Road on 14 September, when he had said that his motto was 'Work! Work! Work!' But Vivian would have known Colonel Hughes quite well from the legal world of Sheffield. He might also have been influenced by the fact that he had not been selected to be one of the initial group of junior officers who Colonel Hughes had chosen from the volunteers. Later in the autumn, Vivian Simpson would claim he did not want to be an officer but changed his mind and was eventually commissioned in January 1915.

Those who attended at the Corn Exchange on 10 September would be buoyed up by the recent news from France. After a month of retreat, the BEF and the French Armies had counter-attacked on the Marne on 6 September and the overstretched Germans, following their modified Schlieffen Plan, had to admit their inability to continue their advance on Paris. The original idea had been to capitalise on the slowness of Russian mobility in the East by encircling Paris and knocking out the French quickly. Over the next week, they would pull back on their western front, back across the Aisne and start digging trenches along the line of the Chemin des Dames ridge, where they would stay on the defensive for the next three years until the spring of 1918. The war was not going to be over by Christmas, nor for the following three Christmases and the volunteers of the City Battalion would see plenty of action, becoming involved in unforeseen cataclysmic events, as yet beyond their imagination.

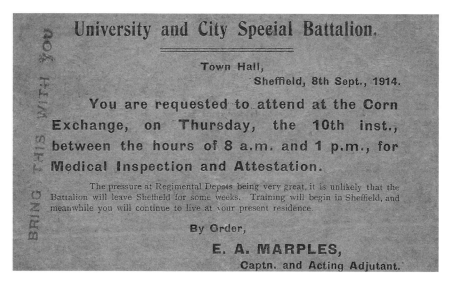

James R. Glenn's card from the adjutant telling him to report to the Corn Exchange to attest and have a medical.

When Reg Glenn arrived at the Corn Exchange, the first thing he noticed was a placard saying 'To Berlin via the Corn Exchange' but once inside he had to first undertake a medical. He was pretty sure that he was fit but his main worry was that he was too short because he believed there was a minimum height requirement of 5ft 6in and he was just under this. He need not have worried because quite a number of men who were shorter than Reg were being attested, although no-one under 5ft 3in, the army's normal height requirement, were being accepted. At separate tables around the Corn Exchange sat Col. Hughes, and Captains Marples and Clough who administered the Oath of Allegiance. Reg was in the queue that was being attested by Captain Clough and when it was his turn, he filled in the answers to the seventeen questions, including agreeing to General Service (that meant service overseas) and serving three years with the colours. There was some even smaller print that he probably did not notice at the time that said he could be retained after three years if his services were needed, but only for an extra six months. If the war did not last three years, the wording promised 'you would be discharged with all convenient speed'.

Reg's answers were officially witnessed by one of the clerks, as Reg recited the Oath and signed his acceptance. It read:

'I, **James Reginald Glenn,** swear by Almighty God that I will be faithful and bear true Allegiance to His Majesty King George the Fifth, His Heirs and Successors, and that I will in duty bound, honestly and faithfully defend

His Majesty, His Heirs and Successors, in Person, Crown and Dignity against all enemies, and will observe and obey all orders of His Majesty, His Heirs and Successors, and of the Generals and Officers set over me. So help me God.'

Captain Clough then signed Reg's attestation form and with that he had taken the final plunge and enlisted in the British Army for the duration. Later, he was given the number 12/928 when the recruits had been sorted out into companies, his high number indicating that he was serving in D Company, not signifying how early he had attested. There was one more ancient military tradition to take place when he moved to another table and was given the king's shilling for enlisting, except for some reason Reg got 1/6d that he quietly accepted, telling Elsie and his family later that it must be because he was so good looking.

The following Monday, 14 September, around 1,000 volunteers who were accepted for the City Battalion mustered at Norfolk Barracks, the home of the 3rd West Riding Brigade, Royal Field Artillery on Edmund Road. There were over 200 who had been turned down mainly on medical grounds, but also a few who failed to meet the Army's height requirement. Never before 1914, in all of British military history, had such a group of men volunteered for the ranks of an infantry regiment. They were a remarkable collection of volunteers, including £500 a year businessmen – a tidy salary when a graduate teacher only received £170 pa – bankers like Aubrey Benniston who lived on Western Bank, architects like George Roberts who had worked for the City Council, civil engineers like Alec Brook, another former Wesley College pupil and university graduate. There were men who helped run their family businesses and would one day take over from their fathers like John Harrison of Chesterfield, educated at Denstone College, or the Gunstone brothers, Frank and William, who lived in Nether Edge and whose family business was a well-known bakery firm in Sheffield. There were many who worked in the Town Hall like Frank Meakin, an architect with the City Surveyor's Department and several accountants and their articled clerks, like John Thorpe who also lived in Nether Edge. Among the volunteers were a large number of teachers, among whom was Edward Curwen MA Oxon. who was a classics master at Rotherham Grammar School. Numbered among the very many Sheffield University representatives in the battalion was Alexander Robertson, who was a lecturer in History and an accomplished and published poet.

A number of journalists joined up, including Richard Sparling of the *Sheffield Daily Telegraph*, who would end up as a sergeant with the Meritorious Service Medal, and who in 1920 published a heartfelt tribute history of the City Battalion. There were a fair number of solicitors and their clerks besides Vivian Simpson. One was an articled clerk, Harry Morris, who would survive the war, qualify as a solicitor and become a City Councillor in 1920, joining the Labour ranks in

Norfolk Barracks on Edmund Road today. In essence, apart from the cars and the road signs, the building will have looked much the same to the volunteers in 1914.

1926 when Labour gained control of the City Council for the first time. In 1945, he would become the Labour MP for Sheffield Central and end up in the House of Lords as Lord Morris of Kenwood. Another with a parliamentary connection was Eric Roberts, the son of Sir Samuel Roberts, the MP for Sheffield Ecclesall, who was a great supporter of the City Battalion. Eric, who lived at Queen's Tower, the family home on Grange Road, was the first to attest on 10 September. Later, his father threw a thank-you supper for the whole battalion a week before they left Norfolk Barracks for the wet and windy uplands at Redmires in early December.

The City Battalion was not unique in having such highly educated middle-class personnel. The 'Public School' battalions raised by the Royal Fusiliers and the Middlesex Regiment appealed to 'Old Boys' of public schools, mainly from their numerous ranks living in London and the Home Counties but also wider afield – a master at King Edward's joined a 'Public School' Battalion in August at Kempton Park racecourse. It was not the most intelligent form of recruitment by the Army. These men, who now joined the ranks, were the calibre of men the War Office would need to recruit as the officers of the New Armies and also fill the decimated ranks of the Regular and Territorial battalions. Similarly, the City Battalion was recruiting men as private soldiers who would have been better suited to be selected as officers at an early stage after some basic training, as happened later in the war. The Americans, when they eventually joined the war in 1917, had to build an officer corps up from virtually nothing and to help them select capable men, they used the new IQ tests to identify potential officers, before fast tracking them into commissions.

Still the 'Pals' battalion concept worked in Sheffield and in many other towns and counties. Serving with your mates caught the imagination of potential recruits as well as the general public. The men were doubly proud to serve in a regiment that was local to their county but also encouraged their visceral pride in their own town or city and no citizens were prouder of their town than Sheffielders, then and now. Visitors might wonder why they had such affection for their soot black city, plagued by continuous smoke from its numerous factories that shrouded the houses on most days. A city where the locals joked about 'ducks flying backwards!' and the 'Mucky Picture in the Golden Frame!', a reference to industrial Sheffield surrounded by moors, verdant hills and valleys, but most of the recruits to the City Battalion lived close enough to the Golden Frame to enjoy living in a different kind of city, one of tree clad suburban hillsides, full of lofty spacious stone houses, in what had been in previous centuries the green foothills of the Pennines.

Eventually, the army would realise that the City Battalion was a fruitful source of recruitment of subalterns with around 300 members of the Battalion being commissioned before the war was over. This number would include Reg Glenn, who would never have conceived in September 1914 that a chap like him could be considered an officer; he was a junior clerk and the social hierarchy above him looked impenetrable. Indeed, the number of subalterns who first saw service as rankers in the City Battalion would have been even higher if so many potential officers had not been slaughtered on the first day of the Somme Offensive.

That day at Norfolk Barracks the volunteers stood in long lines the length of the drill hall and listened to high flown speeches from civic leaders. The Lord Mayor, speaking from a high balcony, batted first. Lieut. Colonel Branson had until recently been the CO of the Hallamshires, now called the 4th (Hallamshire) Bn. of the York and Lancaster Regt. and so his words carried some weight with the young men below him. H.A.L. Fisher got embroiled in some hyperbole telling the men that; 'they would carve for themselves a niche in the temple of history!' One can imagine Vivian Simpson snorting to himself about that phrase, but the Vice-Chancellor was right. The 1,000 men gathered there did make history, both nationally and certainly within their own city, where their story is still very much alive.

Colonel Hughes was more blunt, starting off by calling them 'a CROWD! But a good looking one!' and he too hit the nail on the head. Aged between 18 and 35 (70 per cent were under 25) they looked and were an intelligent, educated, handsome and fit bunch of men. Parading there in suits or tweeds, they look remarkably like people today, a hundred years later. If those volunteers in 1914 had looked back a hundred years to Waterloo and the dress and appearance of the men of Wellington's army, they would have regarded them as people from a totally different world. But the men of 1914 are instantly recognisable as Sheffielders, especially the officers whose uniforms are still essentially the same design as that worn by all ranks of the British Army today. The volunteers were nearly all clean shaven – walrus moustaches were now only worn by middle aged men and full beards had almost disappeared by 1914 except for elderly gentlemen, so that if you met them today in Fargate with their short back and sides haircuts, they would not look at all out of place. Perhaps this is one of the contributing reasons why the British have such a fascination with the First World War even a century later.

Like all the other volunteers, Reg would not be marching off after that first parade to the regimental depot, or a new hutted camp in deepest Yorkshire. The army needed all the existing camps and barracks for their own new recruits and demanded that the Pals Battalions find, or build, their own accommodation. So Reg returned that night to live in his own home in May Road, a neat terraced house in a pleasant cul-de-sac half way up the hill from Hillsborough towards Wadsley. From there, he reported for duty every morning at 9.00am and when his drill and exercises were over for the day, he would be free to live his normal life as if he was just returning from work at his civilian job.

On top of that, there were no uniforms ready to hand out to the volunteers, so apart from the University OTC men, ex-Regulars and Territorials among them who had khaki uniforms and wore them on parade, they trained in civilian clothes until the middle of November when their new, but unusual, uniforms finally arrived. As there were no casual styles of clothing for British men until the late 1930s, they paraded in their suits and tweeds, often with a waistcoat. For hats most of them seem to have adopted the ubiquitous flat cap that had become classless in the North by the twentieth century.

Vivian Simpson returned each night to 3 Travis Place and some evenings he would no doubt spend with May, and occasionally they dined at the Grand and took in a show at the Lyceum or the Hippodrome or visited one of his cinemas. In one of his letters to his brother dated 1 November, he enclosed a 10/- note asking him to get the office boy to go and book four seats for the second house at the Hippodrome for himself, May, George and his wife, after they have dined at the Grand at 7.15.

D Company, to which Reg was assigned, became quite well known for their nights out at the King's Head, in Angel Street, one of Sheffield's best known old coaching inns. Although Reg was a teetotaller, he would have been a leading figure in their revels, joining many other talented performers who had been brought together by war, now forming a closer comradeship over ale, refreshments and communal singing. Reg called his D Company the 'Odds and Sods', because he believed their members were the least posh among the four companies, whereas Vivian Simpson was in A Company, by common agreement the 'Toffs' company. Reg was convinced that 'they' had graded the membership of the four companies by social status, even though there were many professional men, especially teachers, in each company. To fill up the numbers, and have a full complement of soldiers, some working men, usually skilled artisans, had been accepted into the Battalion as well, men like William Micklethwaite, a plumber of Broomspring Lane, (who was commissioned in 1918) and Jack Baun, a mechanic from the bottom end of Abbeydale Road.

This was an odd period for the new soldiers of the City Battalion. They were officially in the Army but still felt like civilians, yet, for the first few weeks they were treated as celebrities in the city. The two main Sheffield daily newspapers, the *Daily Telegraph* and the *Independent*, covered their activities faithfully with many photographs and people were proud to be associated with them, especially their girlfriends who were now keen to be seen out with them. Parents, still worried about the future, were relieved that nothing had happened yet and their son was still at home, while those who had not joined up kept themselves in the shadows, while the new recruits were so clearly a popular presence in the city.

After a time, there were those among them who questioned what was going on. Their mood was not improved by kids who made fun of them as they marched around the city in civilian clothes without rifles and there were adults who hinted that they were really playing at soldiers and were not real troops, unlike those Sheffielders in other Service Battalions of the York and Lancaster Regt. who were training at the Regimental Depot in Pontefract. Also, there were not a few in the Battalion who wondered why they had to do so much drilling, especially after they had proved they could perform drill movements competently. An ex-regular Guards NCO attached to them had said, 'They grasped the essentials in three weeks whereas it would have taken ordinary recruits three months to reach the same standard.' The local press jumped on this to announce that in their opinion the Battalion was ready for action and were needed to stop the Germans in northern France or Belgium, so what was the delay?

Training had started promptly at 9am on the morning following that first parade at Norfolk Barracks. The men had been formed into squads within their new companies and they were marched out to nearby venues to start their military careers with a three hour drill session. Reg's company went to Norfolk Park, no great distance from the Barracks and he enjoyed the drill session as he had done years before in the Church Lads' Brigade. They also got ten minute breaks at intervals and Reg and his pals could nip into the cafe in the park for a quick coffee. On other days, he was drilling at Bramall Lane, the famous Sheffield sports ground home to both Sheffield United and Yorkshire County Cricket Club. The press arrived in numbers and there were many photos taken of the squads forming fours against a backdrop of the cricket pavilion and against the football stands and terraces. At first, the ground management let them use the whole field; like so many local firms and organisations they were keen to be seen helping the volunteers of the new Battalion, but Sheffield United's management soon cried foul, pointing out that there may be a war on but the new season had started and the drilling volunteers were churning up the turf. Keen Wednesday fans in the ranks might not have been too concerned about what happened to Bramall Lane's playing surface, but the Battalion accepted that from now on they could only practice drilling on the cricket outfield, turf that would have six months to recover.

Vivian Simpson's squad was confined at first to what he described as a muck heap behind the Drill Hall:

> 'Some lucky blighters are performing at Bramall Lane but I suppose our lot are being trained for mountaineering! Up to the present we have been taught nothing we didn't learn in the College Cadet Corps, although we have one or two duds who spoil our squad. I think a large proportion of them have done some kind of drilling as they march well, and the University OTC boys are pretty good.'

He was full of praise for his elderly sergeant who put the squad through their paces, saying he did not mind having his leg pulled, while still getting the best out of his volunteers. His sergeant was one of a number of experienced ex-regular NCOs who had volunteered to join the battalion for the present to knock the volunteers into shape. They were led by RSM Miller, a regular Coldstreamer, who

One of the platoons of new City Battalion soldiers drilling in civvies in a local park in September 1914. Vivian Simpson is fourth from left on the front row.

had just retired from the army in June 1914, while one of the Company Sergeant Majors was the legendary Charles Polden, who would take over as RSM in January 1915 and be an indefatigable figure in bringing the battalion up to scratch, before distinguishing himself on the battlefield and winning the Battalion's first Military Cross in 1917.

Vivian may have had a high regard for the NCOs, but he was highly critical of most of the first batch of junior officers whom Colonel Hughes had selected, appointments that the Colonel felt he had to run past the key members of the organising committee for their approval. Vivian wrote:

> 'The commissioned men are a poor lot on the whole and George Beley [a 42 year old surgeon who Vivian probably knew from the Freemasons] is by far the nicest of the crowd. In our company we have three subalterns who were university lecturers and Douglas Allen, who is the son of Sir Charles. None of them strike me as likely gents to lead you into Hell.'

Hughes was faced however with the problem of picking out a few individuals to be officers when he had a battalion full of capable men, many of whom made excellent officers when they were commissioned later in the war, so he went for education and experience to select his platoon commanders. The University was well represented, with William Jarrard and James Kenner among the university lecturers fast-tracked to full lieutenants. Kenner was both PhD and DSc, two rare academic honours in pre-1914 Britain. Other subalterns had University OTC experience where they had been senior NCOs, having gained their Certificates A and B, certificates that were devised to qualify the holder for a commission. One former Sheffield University student, working as an Engineer at Vickers after 1911, was 2nd Lieut. Eric Moxey, another friend of Vivian's, born in Brazil and educated at Malvern College. He would survive the war only to be blown up defusing bombs in 1940 at RAF Biggin Hill, his bravery marked by the award of a posthumous George Cross, one of the first George Crosses to be awarded.

There were a number of public schoolboys among the first crop of subalterns including 2nd Lieut. Reginald Moore, a sub-editor on the *Sheffield Independent* newspaper, who had been at Harrow, and there were also representatives of the local gentry. One was William Clarke of Whiteley Wood Hall, who in volunteering for the City Battalion was joining his father's old regiment. He also brought his second gardener, Lewis Hill, along with him to volunteer, and Pte. Hill L. A. subsequently became 2nd Lieut. Clarke's batman.

So it is not so surprising that Vivian Simpson was not amongst that first group of junior officers, because he had not even been in the Sixth Form at Wesley College, nor had he served in the Territorial Force or had recent OTC experience. One suspects, despite his denials later, that he was not pleased to be passed over, but a second chance came after 10 October, when Colonel Hughes was replaced as the Commanding Officer of the City Battalion by a regular soldier.

The new man, Lt. Col. Charles Vaughan Mainwaring, had been commissioned into the Royal Inniskilling Fusiliers in 1883 and had spent most of his service in India, Singapore and Burma. When the Battalion first saw him, they reckoned he was going to be a stickler for discipline and hard work and so it proved. He was 52 when he joined the Battalion so there was always a question of whether he too would be fit enough to go on active service abroad. Like Colonel Hughes, he may well have just been appointed by the War Office to bring the Battalion up to proper army standards. Colonel Hughes was most probably disappointed to have to leave but he had done a good job in getting the Battalion started. He went back to his legal work, where unfortunately, when presenting a case in a courtroom in Essex in 1916, he suddenly had a massive heart attack and died almost immediately.

Vivian Simpson, who as a serious sportsman was as fit as most members of the Battalion, noticed how many of the men went sick, especially after the introduction of physical training was added to all the drilling. Drilling was often scheduled for six hours a day and then there were route marches around the hills of Sheffield and out into the West Riding and Derbyshire. He also felt that the inoculations they all had – one was for typhoid – had a tiring effect on him and he began to feel pretty exhausted at the end of the day. Virtually none of the Battalion was a manual worker and the routines they were being put through took a toll on them.

Reg Glenn found that being a signaller got you out of some of the hardest physical challenges. At an early stage, the Battalion began to identify specialists and Reg had put down that he could blow a bugle and knew semaphore with flags from his days in the Church Lads Brigade and the Scouts. The sergeant in charge of the signals and the Band sergeant both wanted him for their section, but the signals won out and Reg became a signaller for the rest of his service in the Battalion.

Initially this was a 'cushy' duty. While others toiled away on route marches, drills and attacking imaginary trenches in Norfolk Park, the signal section had a certain amount of freedom of action when operating on the flanks when they were on a route march, where they could take a rest when they felt they were not being observed. On one occasion on a fifteen mile march out to Bradfield, Reg got invited into a farm house after they had gone less than half way and was given a drink of fresh milk and some biscuits as he watched the Battalion disappear over the hill. Unwilling to catch up with them, he went back to the barracks and waited for them all to return exhausted and sweaty, while he had already got himself ready to go out for the evening with Elsie. He seems to have got away with this because the NCOs do not seem to have been able to keep a close eye on the signallers, who could bluff their way out of normal duties by claiming they were practicing as they waved their flags around violently. When they got into action at the Front, a signaller's job exposing himself using his flags or having to crawl out of communication trenches to repair cut telephone wires was a dangerous occupation, although, as Reg said, if he had joined the band he would have become a stretcher bearer when in action and they often were very exposed bringing in wounded men from No Man's Land while everyone else had their heads down in a trench or a shell hole.

Reg's company commander of D Company was Captain Albert Rudolf Hoette, a man who had had a colourful career to date. Colonel Hughes had selected him along with Captains Colley, Plackett and Armitage to command the companies of his new battalion. With the exception of Hoette, he would have known them all from their civilian jobs in Sheffield and from their Territorial Force experience. Hoette, on the other hand, from London, had volunteered his services when war broke out and was recommended to the City Battalion as a capable officer with two years of service in the South African War, where he had been first commissioned in 1901. In 1914, he was 44 years old and had led a roving life around the Empire and in Argentina, then regarded as almost part of the Empire. He had served in the Merchant Navy, been shipwrecked on his second voyage, farmed in South Africa, worked as a rancher in Argentina and as a sheep farmer in Australia. He was a man of action who inspired his men and he led his company well, until he was badly wounded on 1 July 1916 at Serre.

All Hughes's appointments to company commander were well into their middle age in 1914 and whereas they could cope with training at Norfolk Barracks and later at Redmires, they would all struggle with just surviving the appalling conditions in the trenches. The Battalion got a new adjutant at the same time as Hughes was replaced, with Eric Marples being promoted to major and posted to be the Adjutant of the 13th (Service) Bn. of the Northumberland Fusiliers, a regiment that raised more battalions than any other county regiment in the 1914-18 war. His replacement was Lieut. Eric Woodhouse, who Vivian knew from business circles, and referred to unflatteringly as 'Fatcake'. An unimpressed Vivian wrote to his brother:

> 'Fatcake has been appointed adjutant and he is full of beans. Of course he's the very man for the job, full of himself and his own importance, and that is the style the military believe in.'

With only a few obsolete rifles and a modern machine gun loaned by the Vickers steel works in Sheffield, the training became somewhat tedious and repetitive after a few weeks. Still wearing their civilian clothes in October, the Battalion received 600 Lee Metford rifles in the middle of the month and this gave a little more realism to their training and their drill. These rifles were still serviceable and could be fired on the range, but they had been in service with the British Army since 1888, when they had replaced the Martini-Henry. At that time, their bolt action, .303 ammunition and detachable magazine had been well ahead of its time and the Lee Enfield Mk III that replaced them after 1907 used many of the features found on the Lee Metford. Still only half the battalion could have use of a rifle and it was not until June of the following year that they received another delivery of 600 rifles, allowing everyone a weapon of their own, even if they were second best to the new Lee Enfield Mk 3 that the Army was supplying to its infantry battalions that were already at the Front.

Still, it was the lack of uniforms that most rankled with the volunteers. They had their first church parade on 8 November but to Reg it did not seem like a church parade as 600 men of the battalion sat in St. Mary's Church at the town end of Bramall Lane in their best Sunday suits. They sang good army favourites like 'Fight the Good Fight' and the fourth hymn on the hymn sheet turned out to be the National Anthem, whose second verse implored God, to scatter the King's enemies. After church they were marched by Major Clough, who had rejoined the

Battalion as Second in Command, on a circuitous route that took them all the way to the centre of town and back, when the Drill Hall was less than a quarter of mile away. They marched behind a band, not their own bugle and drum band, but the full blooded sound of a steel works band, aware that, although their marching was now up to speed, they looked an odd crowd in different coloured suits and a variety of hats.

When the long-awaited uniforms arrived in mid-November, they caused consternation. Expecting the new pattern khaki uniform, quite the most stylish, practical and modern in the world in 1914, they got a simple blue-grey design that

Reg and Elsie in late 1914, with Reg wearing one of the new blue serge uniforms that were a surprise to the City Battalion volunteers and universally derided.

Reg thought might have been made for an ambitious postman. It was universally disliked and the men were not mollified by being told that there was a shortage of khaki dye because before the war some of the main suppliers had been German companies. Vivian would not be seen out in the evening around the smart places in town in his uniform, especially as he was mixing socially with people who now had commissions and had paid for their own well-fitting uniforms cut by local tailors. Although made of blue-grey cloth, rather than '*Feld-Grau*', the London manufacturers had ironically produced a uniform with no breast pockets just low side ones, that looked as if it had come straight out of the German Army pattern book.

At around the same time, the volunteers got their personal equipment. Again, it was not the modern 1908 webbing pattern of the familiar five ammunition pouches on each side of a belt buckle. Instead they were each given two leather pouches positioned on a leather belt either side of the 'snake' belt fastener. The pouches were quite capacious and would each carry a fifty round cotton bandolier, but they looked old fashioned and again Reg, and many of the others, felt they were not being kitted out like 'real' soldiers and maybe still not being taken really seriously by the army.

The officers too had to endure a little ribbing from officers in other units, because one of the new colonel's idiosyncrasies was to insist that his officers did not wear their Sam Browne belts with a diagonal strap across the tunic. Instead he insisted that they wore two leather straps, one over each shoulder and straight down to their belts. When Mainwaring left the Battalion a year later, the officers very quickly reverted back to the normal style, that was later copied by almost every army in the world prior to the Second World War.

In November, the Battalion route marches had included treks up to Redmires where the volunteers could see the progress being made by the City Engineers on the huts that would be their new camp. The first time Vivian's company marched there they were caught in a wet mist and their clothes were pretty well soaked right through by the time they got there, as Vivian told his brother:

> 'The chaps took the conditions awfully well and larked about the whole of their spare time like a lot of two year olds. But we did enjoy the lunch of a hot cup of tea and a sandwich provided by Arthur Davy and Sons, which was very acceptable.'

The men were pleased to know they were going to proper quarters at last, where they could properly gel as a fighting unit, but some must have been concerned that this was where they would spend the winter – way above the snowline.

There was one more important visitor before the move up to Redmires on 5 December and he was the General Officer Commanding Northern Command,

Lieut. Gen. Sir Herbert Plumer. It was an especially significant visit for him, not just because he was inspecting one of the new Pals Battalions but because it was a battalion that was part of his old regiment. Plumer had been commissioned into the 65th Foot in 1876 and that Regiment became the 1st Bn of the York and Lancaster Regiment after 1881.

What Plumer did not know, when he visited the Battalion and said how impressed he was with them, was that a third of the men on parade that day would not survive the war. 161 of those initial volunteers would be killed serving with the battalion on the first day of July in 1916, the opening day of the battle of the Somme, when the battalion's total losses numbered 248 dead, including 87 who had joined the Battalion after Lieut. Gen. Plumer's inspection.

Chapter 4

'Gosh, it's freezing cold up here!'
5 December 1914 – 13 May 1915

On a Saturday morning in early December, lashed by appalling wet weather, Reg and Vivian paraded with the rest of the Battalion for the last time at Norfolk Barracks. They were about to start their real soldiering with a march up to their new camp at Redmires five miles away, where they would begin their more advanced training in field craft and musketry. The Battalion had expected to move into their new quarters a week or two earlier, but bad weather had slowed down construction of the huts and there were still no finished paths or roads, just acres of mud.

The Battalion moved off at precisely 1.30pm led by their new drum and bugle band, with Colonel Mainwaring on his horse leading them as they formed a long column that wound its way through the city centre and then out along Glossop Road heading for the moors around the Redmires reservoirs. Vivian Simpson found himself marching past his old school, once Wesley College, now King Edward VII School, and as they passed the rear of the school building, Old Edwardians in his company broke into the school song, while others further down the column were heard chanting Latin verbs that had been drummed into them on doldrum days in seemingly endless lessons.

After the column passed through Crosspool, the rain turned to sleet and the Battalion arrived at their new home soaked to the skin. Redmires lies 1,000 feet above sea level and is as bleak a place as you are likely to find that also lies within the boundary of a major city. However, it was perfect territory for toughening up the troops, had generous space to allow company manoeuvres and set up ranges for the men to be given some basic instruction in firing their rifles. Less than a couple of miles away was the tram terminus at Nether Green and the men soon realised that they could get into town fairly regularly and see their girlfriends or family after they had finished training in the late afternoon. For those who did not fancy the long journey into Sheffield, the camp was almost immediately adjacent to two pubs, the Sportsman and the Three Merry Lads, that had until now enjoyed a remote moorland location but now found many customers among the members of the City Battalion. The two pubs are still there now and they are still in a remote place but in the age of the car that is not such a disadvantage.

Reg wrote of his first impressions of the camp:

'When we got there we found the huts were unfinished, there were no roads in the camp just muddy paths and there were no beds. We went over to the Quartermaster's stores and were given a bag which we were told to stuff with straw and that was our bed. There were no proper beds at first in our hut and I had to sleep on the floor on that straw bag, that the army called a palliasse. We were given a couple of blankets and the hut had a coke stove in the middle which we had to crowd round to keep warm.'

Nevertheless, some men, despite arriving soaked right through and despite the continued wet and windy weather, took advantage of a leave pass to go back to town that evening and enjoy themselves with friends or girlfriends in their favourite pubs in town. Later some had to walk the five miles back to camp after the trams had stopped running, following the route they had taken early in the afternoon, avoiding the guard on the gate because they had spotted a hole in the wall through which they could sneak into camp. One is impressed at their stamina if not their common sense, but these were young men whose training to date had made them pretty fit and they were full of confidence, as well as a fair amount of ale.

To add to the discomfort of the new arrivals, there was thunder and lightning all night, but the men did not care. Some would be away from the family home for the first time in their lives and the excitement of the occasion and the banter of their mates would easily make up for the hardships that surrounded them. They had marched through town feeling like heroes already, with hundreds lining the roads to wave at them as if they were conquering heroes who had won a great victory. All the way during the march up to Redmires, young lads had run alongside them and the band had played intermittently, helping to boost their pride in their unit, and their own self-esteem, even higher. They felt like proper soldiers now, not part timers who went home in the late afternoon, even if they still had two months to wait before they got their proper khaki uniforms and almost a year before they were all issued with a Lee Enfield Mk III rifle, the standard British rifle of the First World War.

There had once been a racecourse on the site of the new camp but it was now disused, so the City Council decided to build the camp at Redmires, not just because it was remote and close to open country, but because the land had already been secured by the Sheffield Artillery Territorials whose colonel, Lt. Col. Henry Stephenson, later Sir Henry and MP for Sheffield Park, was a Liberal councillor and a former Lord Mayor. Council workmen had erected the huts to the standard army pattern, choosing to build them in wood, when in some camps they had to make do with corrugated iron, or even asbestos sheeting. The accommodation

A group of men including Reg Glenn (back row third from left with signal flags) outside a typical hut that had been erected at the new camp at Redmires.

huts were 60 feet long by 20 feet wide, raised off the ground on wooden posts and lit by gas. They were designed to accommodate 30 men, although at Redmires there were usually fewer men to a hut than the maximum. In Reg's hut there were only 20 men and that gave them a fair bit of personal space. The beds, when they arrived, could be folded back in half to create more space during the day, whilst down the middle of the hut was a line of very basic trestle tables and benches where the men ate their meals fetched from the cookhouse. The hut also served as a social space and many an evening would be spent playing cards or listening to music on gramophones that some of the men in the hut had brought from home. Once all the windows were in place and the vagaries of the single stove had been mastered, the hut could be quite cosy and it is clear from the memoirs and letters written by the men of the Battalion that they enjoyed their time at Redmires, even if the winter of 1914-15 was unusually cold.

Reg and his mates were amazed to find that they were not only expected to lay the paths, but also to quarry the stone in nearby redundant quarries. The stone was then broken up with sledge hammers and turned into chippings to form the surface of the roads and paths. In a normal battalion, most of the other ranks would have been used to hard manual labour, but it came as a bit of shock to men of the City Battalion that they had to swing a pick and use a shovel to create some basic infrastructure in the camp. When the roads and paths were completed, they appear from the photographs of the time to have been very competently built, with solid stones along both of the kerbs to keep the stone chippings in place. Until then there was mud everywhere and men carted it into their huts as well as finding it sticking to their boots and puttees and adding to the discomfort of the early days at Redmires.

Reg remembered that, as the smallest man in his hut, his size came in useful when there had been a particularly heavy fall of snow:

'On several occasions snow drifted against the building and blocked the door. I was then shoved through one of the windows with a shovel and sent round to clear the snow away from the door so the rest of lads could get out.'

The huts did not have washing or toilet facilities, nor would anyone in 1914 have expected them to. These were housed in separate buildings constructed of corrugated iron laid over a timber frame that Vivian Simpson found rather Spartan, writing to his brother:

'We get up at reveille at 6.30am and dash across to the wash house through a sea of mud and go through our ablutions in a shed that is open at both ends. I regret to say the chaps who strip are in a minority, because the water is chilly to the last degree.'

He went on to describe the routine after reveille and ablutions:

'After ablutions and dressing we make our beds and different chaps are told off to their various duties. Some as mess orderlies bringing breakfast back to our hut by 8am, others are orderlies in the officers' mess and they disappear for the day. One chap has to go and pump gas, three fetch potatoes and carrots to peel and one of our chaps has to act as an officer's servant for the day and another one as a groom for the Colonel's horse.'

Those remaining, he went on to say, tidy up the hut and polish their buttons and clean their rifles and are ready on parade when the bugle sounded at 8.45am. He thought that despite the weather and the intensive training, after a while they all felt pretty comfortable at Redmires and that the food was excellent, a view shared by Reg, who appreciated the generous helpings of porridge for breakfast and the stews that were the staple diet at lunchtime.

Perhaps it was acting as an orderly in the officers' mess, or being an officer's servant, or a groom to Colonel Mainwaring's horse that caused Vivian Simpson in January to revise his view about becoming an officer himself, after he had turned down the invitation to apply for a commission in the late November just before they moved up to Redmires.

Not included in the initial selection of junior officers, he had been recommended by his company commander, Captain Jarrard, to Colonel Mainwaring, who had endorsed the recommendation. No doubt by now Vivian had demonstrated his all-round competence and as an older man, he would have been an obvious choice for commissioning even among a company of bright young men. He thanked the Captain and the Colonel for their kindness, but they were no doubt dumbfounded that he had refused them and the Colonel was none too pleased.

It was not a spur of the moment decision and he had discussed the pros and cons with May, and she supported his decision:

'I have been told by chaps who have applied for a commission that you need to spend £80-£100 above your pay to be able to live comfortably as an officer. If the war lasts 6 months, or even a year, I want to come through all serene and have some money in the bank for a rainy day. May is entitled to ask for it because when we marry we will need the money to help settle down, and she is already having to wait because of me joining up.

'There is another point apart from the financial side, and that is that all one's spare time will be taken up cramming for this "business". Being an officer is a profession like anything else and to be qualified in six months, means hard and continuous work. As we are training at Redmires and not at a camp miles away I shall naturally spend all the spare time I can with May, as she has few friends and it is rather dull at home for her.'

However, when the Battalion got to Redmires Vivian was made a Lance Corporal within a week of arriving. This convinced him that he could be just as useful as a junior NCO as he could be as a commissioned officer, especially one who could not give his full attention to his duties as he would have half his mind on his forthcoming marriage and finalising the purchase of their house on Hagg Lane.

He also said several times that he thought the war would not last too long and may well be over by Easter. 'I do not think that holding a temporary commission as a Second Lieutenant will give you any permanent standing after the war,' he wrote in another letter, believing that all the effort involved would produce no social advantage but would have considerable financial disadvantages.

Despite this, he allowed his name to go forward again just before Christmas but found Colonel Mainwaring was quite unsympathetic this time.

The Colonel commented testily. 'This man was offered a commission several weeks ago and refused it. I see no reason for offering him another one.'

When telling Vivian the bad news, his platoon commander had told him that none of the officers had heard the Colonel speak a civil word to anyone. In a letter to his brother sent on Christmas Eve Vivian said that he had the strong impression that the 'officers hated their Colonel like poison'. No one in the family need worry, he wrote, because he was quite happy being a lance corporal, although he hoped they would not be upset that he was just an NCO when many of their friends in Broomhill, like May's brother Percy, had been commissioned already.

Probably as a compensation for his rejection, his platoon commander promoted Vivian to full Corporal on 7 January and he was accepted for a commission on 27 January, three weeks later. Vivian believed that his case had been pressed on the Colonel by Sir George Franklin who knew Vivian well, and who continued to have influence with the Battalion that was still financed by the City Council.

So all Vivian's brave talk and reasoned excuses for not becoming an officer were abandoned, and it is clear from his letters and later correspondence that he now felt that in his circle being a subaltern was beginning to count for something socially. At Wortley Golf Club, many of the members with whom he had played regularly were being commissioned, several in the 5th Battalion (Territorial) of the York and Lancasters, and just having two stripes did not quite seem to measure up.

Why Vivian, and many others in the Battalion, thought that the war would soon be over is something of a mystery. The war by December 1914 had reached stalemate on the Western Front and Tsarist Russia's vaunted military strength had proved illusory after their defeat in East Prussia in August, and their later reversals in Galicia and Silesia. The only way that the stalemate on the Western Front would lead to an Armistice was if the German Army agreed to withdraw from its conquests in Northern France and Belgium, as they eventually did in November 1918, something that would have been politically impossible for the Kaiser and the German High Command at the end of 1914. As well-read, educated young men, the members of the City Battalion must have kept abreast of news from the Ypres Front where the German offensive had started on 19 October. The bitter, desperate fighting lasted a month as the German 4th and 6th Armies attempted to capture the town and drive through to the northern Channel ports to deny them to the British. This German offensive had caused massive casualties on both sides and these losses included the deaths of very many German university and technical college students, who, in a mirror image of the City Battalion, had joined up en masse in a tumult of patriotic fervour. After a rushed eight weeks of training they were slung into the Ypres battle at Langemarck in November, to be slaughtered in an attack the Germans called the '*Kindermord*'.

The only conversation that Reg ever had with Colonel Mainwaring was when he was out with the signallers one day following the companies on a route march. The Colonel rode up on his horse and peremptorily demanded of Reg if he had taken the number of a car that had just passed them on the road. Not realising that was part of his job, Reg admitted he had not spotted it and received a ticking off for not being observant enough.

Perhaps the Colonel felt the signallers needed a bit of a 'fizzer' because as Reg describes their life at Redmires, it was again relatively easy compared to the intensive training of the rank and file riflemen:

'There were ten of us and nobody loved us because we had so much free time, and not even the RSM could touch us. We trained separately from the rest of the companies most of the time under the genial eye of our signals sergeant called McCloud who came from Coventry. He would take us away to a nearby farmyard where we were out of sight and we could practice with our flags undisturbed. We also now began to use the heliograph but there were many days we could not practice with them up at Redmires because the weather was so foul and there was no sun. When there were route marches, that often covered eight to ten miles, we had to keep up with the companies if we were attached to them. If on the other hand we were the "receiving" signallers we stayed close to the camp, so when the column had finally disappeared from view the Sergeant took us all into the Three Merry Lads pub to relax and await the return of the others.'

This relatively easy routine enabled Reg to get over to Hillsborough regularly to see Elsie in the evenings. Passes were generously available until 10pm and any latecomers always knew they could sneak in through the hole in the outer wall and avoid the guards. Many evenings though there would be entertainment in the camp after the YMCA hut had been opened on 30 December. Reg was a regular patron of this warm, spacious hut complete with proper chairs, small tables and a welcoming homely atmosphere. It served as the unofficial Other Rank's mess, offering the same sort of facilities that the NAAFI organisation would later offer to the servicemen in camps all over Britain, as well as many a far-flung location across the globe. A number of wealthy church-going supporters of the Battalion had seen the need for such a facility and they had raised the finance to get it built. The Lord Mayor and other dignitaries came for the formal opening and they named it the Lord Roberts Memorial Institution in memory of Britain's most famous soldier of the pre-war period, Field Marshal Lord Roberts of Kandahar VC, who had just died in France in November. The YMCA was much appreciated and was well patronised with its canteen offering tea and snacks, a quiet room for writing and reading the daily newspapers, and a decent space, where on many evenings there were formal and impromptu concerts around the piano. Reg remembered:

'The lads could play cards or dominoes but there was a ban on gambling in the YMCA. Taken as a whole they were a decent crowd and there were no roughs among them and no one ever got drunk.'

On Sundays, Reg went to the regular Church service that was held in the YMCA and there was also a post office within the hut that was very popular. Soldiers in the First World War were very good correspondents, anxious to keep in touch with their families, and at Redmires they often got letters back the next day. All in all, the YMCA was a pleasant place outside the rigours of normal service life and discipline and gave the ordinary soldiers a little of the relaxed comforts of home that the Officers and Sergeants enjoyed in their messes.

There were other important developments once the Battalion arrived at Redmires. The City Battalion, always under the auspices of the York and Lancaster Regiment,

York and Lancashire Regiment Cap Badge.

was now given its official title by the War Office. Henceforth it would be called the 12th (Service) Battalion, The York and Lancaster Regiment (Sheffield) as the War Office began the process of creating new brigades and divisions from the new volunteer battalions that had been raised in the Autumn. These new divisions were intended to be Kitchener's Fifth Army when their training was complete and would be sent to France to bolster the ranks of the BEF who had suffered so many casualties in the running battles from Mons in August to Ypres in October and November. The Sheffield Battalion was not now working in its own bubble; it was further recognition that the Army was taking the Pals Battalions seriously as the City Battalion, now the 12th York and Lancaster, were brigaded with the two Barnsley Pals Battalions, the 13th (1st Barnsley) Bn. and the 14th (2nd Barnsley) Bn. of The York and Lancaster Regiment. The fourth battalion of the Brigade was initially the 10th (S) Bn. The Lincolnshire Regiment – nicknamed the Grimsby Chums – which had originally been formed around a large number of volunteers from one grammar school in the town. Like the Sheffield Pals and the Barnsley Pals, the initiative for raising the 10th Lincolns came from the Mayor and the Town Council and all four battalions continued to be financed by their Councils while they were still waiting to being taken over by the War Office.

The Brigade really only existed on paper. Although the two Barnsley battalions were training in the same camp at Silkstone, the men of the other battalions had no contact with each other, except through their Commanding Officers and other senior officers who would no doubt have planning meetings with their new brigade commander, Brigadier H. Bowles CB, who set up his headquarters in offices on Bank Street in the middle of Sheffield.

The new Brigade was initially numbered 115th Infantry Brigade and was part of the 38th Division, but in April it was renumbered the 94th Brigade, one of three brigades that would form the new 31st Division and became part of the Fourth Army. This renumbering downwards was because the losses in the BEF had already reduced the number of up-to-strength divisions and brigades that the British Army could put into the field, despite the huge number of volunteers. The Brigade still comprised the three York and Lancaster Regiment battalions, but the 10th Lincolns were re-assigned and the 11th (S) Bn. of the East Lancashire Regiment took their place. Known as the Accrington Pals, they have become quite famous in recent years after featuring in a successful play based on their wartime experiences. Although Accrington claimed to be the smallest borough to raise a Pals Battalion in 1914, only one company actually came from Accrington, the others were from Burnley, Chorley and Blackburn. But this applied to all Pals Battalions to some extent and there were many volunteers in the Sheffield City Battalion who came from the Penistone and Chesterfield areas, with most of them serving in B Company when the Battalion was at Redmires.

The 31st Division, when it was officially formed on 15 April 1915, was basically a Yorkshire division, apart from the Accrington Pals and a Pals Battalion of the DLI – the 18th (Service) Battalion (1st County) Durham Light Infantry. The 92nd Brigade was known as the Hull Brigade and contained four Pals Battalions, the 10th, 11th, 12th and 13th (Service) Battalions of the East Yorkshire Regiment, whilst the 93rd Brigade drew on the Leeds Pals, and two Bradford Pals Battalions that formed the 15th, 16th and 18th Battalions of the West Yorkshire Regiment, plus the one DLI battalion. This all helped to reinforce the local character of the Pals Battalions, so that when they went into action they would not just be fighting with pride for the honour of their city and their local regiment, but for the 'Broad Acres' of the whole county of Yorkshire as well.

By Christmas 1914 the Battalion was well settled in at Redmires and now part of the official structure of the British Army, even if they were still dressed in their blue uniforms. Despite hostile weather, the training had been going well and the men were ready for what they hoped would be the Christmas break. Reg was one of the fortunate ones who got leave to join his family and Elsie in Hillsborough, but it was to be his last family Christmas for three years and he would have been even more surprised if he had known that his next Christmas would be spent on a troopship off Gibraltar. The other half of the Battalion had to stay in camp, and L/Cpl Simpson V.S. was one of the unlucky ones. The Battalion, however, had made its own Christmas preparations and some huts had been decorated with all the usual trimmings to compensate for being away from home. The Army tradition of a substantial Christmas dinner for the troops, served by their officers, was honoured up at Redmires, but Vivian really wanted to be back in Broomhill enjoying Christmas with his fiancée at the Belcher's mansion on Broomfield Road. It was one thing having a Christmas dinner with your mates in the platoon if you were in another part of the country, or if you were abroad, but it was another thing altogether if your family celebrations were going on four miles away and you could walk there in just over an hour.

Later in the day, visitors from the town came up to the camp, many in their motor cars, bringing greetings and presents from relatives. Vivian recalled:

'I got a lock up kitbag from Ma Belcher and a blanket sleeping bag with its own small hold-all from May, while Pa Belcher gave me a very Sheffield present, a ripping soldier's knife with my name engraved on the blade'.

One can also reasonably assume that there were a fair number of the men who got cameras for Christmas judging by the many photos taken of life at the camp, while the comfortably well-off parents of most of the volunteers would make sure there were plenty of cakes and buns, coffee and spirits for their sons and their friends who had to stay in camp over the festive season. Indeed, the 'Coffee and Buns boys' was the nickname for the Sheffield Battalion coined by the lads in the two Barnsley Battalions, no doubt meant as a bit of mild ribbing but with something of a barb, suggesting the City boys were 'posh' and a bit soft compared to rugged Barnsley lads.

New Year's Day, on the other hand, was to be celebrated by a long route march, but after the column had set out, the snow defeated them as the drifts were impossible to march through and the continuing sleet and snow drove them back to camp. In Reg's Company the extra time gained was filled in by their company commander, Captain Hoette, giving them a talk about his life in various parts of the world, working on farms, ranches or sailing boats from Argentina to the Cape and on to Queensland.

Training in January became even more intense and newly promoted Corporal Simpson found himself worked off his feet:

'Corporals do the hardest jobs because the Sergeants pass everything on to us that they want doing, including officers' requests to them for action. On top of that we have hundreds of fatigues to supervise as well! And all that for only 1/8d a day, only 8 pence more than I was getting as a private!'

There were a regular number of manoeuvres, including some night manoeuvres that were held in the early evening after 6.30pm when it was already dark. Vivian recalled one recent one in a letter to his brother:

'We were sent out to attack B Company and I was the NCO in charge of the point section. I evaded detection and got into B Company's position and managed to give the alarm to our chaps before we were detected and they captured me. They didn't half dust me up when I was caught, but the night ended in our company's favour although the Colonel was rather vague about who had won.'

On another occasion, in mid-January, the task of his platoon was to evade capture while the rest of the company searched for them on the moors above the camp. Vivian spent from 6.45 until 9.15pm doing a 'fine impression of imitating a stone' while 140 men searched for 40 who were hiding. All but three were captured but Vivian was one of the three who escaped detection. It seems from his correspondence that he was rather good at the tactical side of soldiering and enjoyed the fun of it all, where no one actually died as you charged around on manoeuvres firing blanks and pretending to shoot men who were the 'enemy' on that particular day.

But in February there was a reminder for all of the men in the Battalion that death could come out of the blue. It was not because anyone was accidentally killed, rather it was the death from pneumonia of a popular fellow in A Company, a victim of the harsh weather conditions at Redmires that winter. Private Charles Haydn Hanforth was one of the many former pupils of King Edward VII School in the City Battalion who had enjoyed an impressive career at the school before winning a History scholarship to Keble College, Oxford, in 1913. He did a year at Oxford but did not go up for the new Michaelmas Term in 1914 but joined the City Battalion instead. He had been a Sergeant in the school OTC and if he had lived, he would most certainly have been commissioned, as so many of the Battalion were later.

He died in the 3rd Northern General Military Hospital on Collegiate Crescent, a building that until the previous summer before had been the Sheffield Teacher Training College. He was given full military honours and A Company provided the bearer party and a hundred men who followed the coffin from the Hanforth home in Nether Green to the Cathedral, where the funeral took place. Charles Hanforth had been a leading chorister in the Cathedral choir and to add to the pathos of the occasion his father was the organist at the Cathedral. As a tribute to his dead son, he played the hymns and anthems that day during the funeral, which must have been a particularly desolate and heart-rending duty.

Whilst not a death that had taken place at the Front, it was still a stark reminder to many in the congregation that lives could be snuffed out with little warning and to have died whilst still training seemed so pointless and sobering. Later in the month there was a second death, when Private Charles Ortton died of peritonitis at the same military hospital. A former pupil at the Charity School on Psalter Lane, he was only 19 and had worked as a clerk at George Senior's steel manufacturing works at Ponds Forge. He was buried with military honours in the City Road Cemetery on the east side of Sheffield but there was less pomp and ceremony than there had been with the Hanforth funeral.

The newly named 12th Battalion were allowed a special shoulder badge that not only indicated their regiment but included the name of their city. This was a special honour that was not offered to most other Pals Battalions.

At the beginning of February, the Battalion finally got a supply of the modern pattern khaki uniforms. Not everyone was kitted out immediately and for two months there were some platoons in khaki and some still in the old blue uniforms. Even when wearing the new khaki uniforms, the old blue forage cap was often worn, probably because it was more convenient when training and it also allowed the service cap with its stiff brim to be kept in pristine condition in the huts. The men now felt really part of their regiment with the regimental cap badge on their service caps, and brass shoulder markings that read Y&L Sheffield.

After the severe weather in January, when the ground had been frozen hard, the Battalion could once again fully concentrate on their intensive training as well as constructing elements of a modern trench system. Thanks to the generosity of a couple of local landowners, Mr. William Wilson of Beauchief Hall and Mr. Wilson Mappin, the Battalion was allowed to practise digging trenches on their moorland property and prepare for war 1915-style. Deep trenches with sophisticated support and communication lines were the state of the art of modern warfare now, after the last open ground in Flanders had been closed off by the middle of October 1914. The battle of the Aisne in September had settled the central front north of Paris, so in the next month, the Germans and the Allies had tried to outflank each other in north-west France in what became known as the 'race to the sea'. By the time of the First Battle of Ypres, the western line of the Allies ran due north for a hundred miles from the River Oise to the North Sea at Nieuport. Despite German offensives in 1914 and 1915 at Ypres and later Allied offensives in 1915, 1916 and 1917, that line would become a permanent feature of the Flanders and Picardy Front for almost three and a half years.

In the face of the ferocious efficiency of modern artillery and the devastation that could be caused to infantry in the open by medium machine guns and co-ordinated rifle fire, the armies had no option but to go underground or they would have been rapidly decimated. So when the volunteers of the City Battalion were digging trenches, they were learning the essential rudiments of survival that they would need when they eventually got to the Front. Their training included the basics such as filling sandbags and then laying them correctly, and constructing parapets, loop holes and fire steps on the front side of the trenches, and parados on the rear side of the trenches they dug on Quarry Hill and Roper Hill. They were drawing on the experience of the regular and territorial battalions who had learnt the hard way in 1914 and the men knew what they were learning was crucial knowledge about war as it was now actually fought.

The trenches the men of the City Battalion dug in early 1915 are still there in outline on Hallam Moor to the west of Sheffield. The great majority of the trenches on the moor were most probably dug later by the Royal Engineers based at Redmires camp, who ran thirteen-week training courses for new Sapper recruits between September 1915 and March 1918. However, the initial trenches were dug by the City Battalion and today they are protected under the Ancient Monuments Act of 1979. Many local people still visit them and find a connection with the men of the City Battalion who trained for the brutal requirements of modern warfare on those bleak moors over a hundred years ago.

Vivian Simpson, newly commissioned as a Second Lieutenant, returned to Redmires on 18 February having been on a three-week initial course for new officers to learn the ropes before being let loose on a platoon. The course most probably concentrated on the etiquette, bearing and main duties of a junior officer rather than too much intensive training, but he will have been introduced to the course work he would have to undertake and the examinations he would have to sit on a regular basis while still running a platoon and carrying out company duties. He was posted to the new E Company under the command of his friend, Captain George Beley, whose new company was established to accommodate the recent volunteers who had to start their training from scratch. The change of heart by Colonel Mainwaring, that seemed so out of character, was probably driven by the need to find new officers for this new company and from all sides people were pressing Vivian Simpson's name on him. As there was absolutely no need to look for officers outside his Battalion because he had so much latent talent on hand, Mainwaring was really spoilt for choice in deciding who he would promote.

Moving to a new company was virtually obligatory for an officer promoted from the ranks, so Vivian did not have to face his old mates in A Company but even so, returning to your old battalion, or just meeting your new platoon for the first time, is a daunting prospect in any new subaltern's career. Vivian must have also been concerned how he would be received in the Officers' Mess, although he knew some of the officers socially and he had worked well with Captain Jarrard in A Company. He wrote to his brother four days later:

'I went back to camp on Thursday and everyone was very decent and until the new quarters are finished I am occupying Colley's quarters while he is away on a course. My first exam was the following day on Friday on "the Battle" and I did all serene having diligently worked for it while I was away. The exams take place weekly usually on a Friday but I can normally get away on Saturday afternoon if I am not supporting the lads playing for the platoon or company at football. One Sunday in three I have to stay in camp and it is rather difficult getting away in the evenings during the week as we only finish mess at 8.45. I understand my new uniform will be ready on Wednesday and I think Parkin's have made an excellent job of it.'

In the same letter, he thanked his brother for the 10/- note he had sent him, his share of the partnership's profits. From now on he continued to receive monies from the firm, though he felt somewhat guilty about it, as he was not playing any part in the firm's work and the war had slowed down business. However, it was money that came in handy to cover the cost of his mess bills that by convention you paid with a cheque.

During the following week, he served his first stint as Orderly Officer, wandering around the lines looking important, while keeping a check on standards and taking complaints. He would look in at bayonet practice – the Battalion practiced a lot of bayoneting of straw filled dummies – and observe with a certain detachment the squads who were suffering doing PT on the parade ground. He said of his day as Orderly Officer:

'I visited the cookhouse and checked on the distribution of bread and meat and I had to be on hand when the men were eating, theoretically to take complaints but probably more just to look decorative. I made regular visits to the guardhouse to check on the guard both in the day time and especially at night and throw all women out of the camp by 5pm.'

He seems to have had a fair amount of spare time. Meeting up on Saturdays at the King's Head in Angel Street for lunch with May, playing golf at the Hallamshire Golf Club just half a mile down the road from Redmires – his 'personal training' he called it – and on some Sundays he got over to Wortley and played a couple of rounds there before returning to camp. On one Sunday there he played the Earl of

Wharncliffe, the President and founder of the club he nicknamed the 'House of Lords' and got beaten closely in the morning by 2 and 1 but was hammered in the afternoon round by a considerably older man.

Vivian was full of admiration for George Beley and the way he inspired his new recruits in E Company. Not given to allot praise easily, Vivian must have really appreciated his guidance, because new subalterns in the Battalion learnt on the job and he was essentially an apprentice learning from more experienced older officers. Vivian in return showed a real enthusiasm and aptitude for training, so much so that he got a reputation as an excellent training officer and in the near future this would mean that he was stuck with training new recruits while the rest of the Battalion went off to war. He would even miss the biggest challenge of all, the first day of the Somme in July 1916.

He also got on well with William Colley, still commanding B Company and now back from his course and sharing his quarters with Vivian. Colley played golf at Wortley too and Vivian would have played him in medal matches before the war, but Colley had also been a City Councillor for Broomhall and was a man of some importance in the cutlery and edge-tool trade in Sheffield. His seniority in the Battalion came because of his twelve years with the West Riding Royal Engineer Volunteers where he had held a final rank of major. A well-travelled man, he had experience of the European continent and parts of Asia, as well as remote parts of South America and South Africa which he had visited on sales missions for his firm. He probably was one of the wealthiest men in the Battalion but like George Beley, he was well into his forties and a winter up at Redmires with all the out of doors activities, including all the long route marches on most Fridays, must have been difficult for him over a period of time. Among the several languages he spoke was a fair understanding of German and he had once won a case in a German court when his company's Sheffield brand was being fraudulently used by a firm in Solingen.

Made welcome by the other officers, Vivian enjoyed life in the Mess, but he spent as much time as he could with May. They visited the Cinema House in Barker's Pool some Saturdays and had afternoon tea in the new basement cafe that he was delighted to see was proving such a success. On these occasions they could lay plans for their wedding that they hoped would take place in the summer, assuming Vivian had not been posted to France. Also, they could discuss the details of the final purchase of the house on Hagg Lane that was intended to be their new home when they finally got married. The surveyor had put the value of the house as £600 and Vivian considered that a bit steep, but he managed to get a mortgage from the bank and also bought out the leasehold on the land; when spring came he gave some personal attention to the garden that had been left to grow wild over the winter.

At camp, Vivian fitted in to his officer's role as if he had been doing it all his life. The Colonel, who was keen on sport, saw him as the obvious choice to be the officer responsible for sport in the Battalion and he was tasked with organising a major athletics meeting for late April. This event was to be a sports day on the grand scale that the Colonel envisaged as a form of farewell to the city, with civic dignitaries being present and relatives of the men and the general public invited. He also wanted as many men in the Battalion as possible participating and the invitation went out to other units in the area to send athletes as well. So alongside his weekly examinations, where Vivian claimed he was averaging an 80 per cent pass rate, he had to collect all the entries, organise the heats and schedule the events of the Battalion sports day. He was also involved in representative football matches and played in an inter-platoon game when his side was short. This turned out to be a bad decision because his leg, injured when playing for Wednesday eight years previously, let him down three times during the game and he had to come off before the final whistle. After a particularly exciting match between his E Company, the new recruits, and A Company, that the latter won by the odd goal, he hit on the idea of writing to the captains of both Wednesday and United asking them to enlist in the City Battalion. He suggested that they encourage other team mates to enlist as well, as some professional football teams had already done – the Heart of Midlothian FC players in the Scottish League had done just that when they formed the 16th Bn. of the Royal Scots in Edinburgh in September 1914. Vivian had an ulterior motive as the new recruits would join E Company and most probably be in his platoon, giving his lads quite a competitive edge over the other companies in future matches.

The Battalion was full of local sportsmen of note, including several well-known amateur golfers as well as a professional, Private Fred Taylor, who was on the staff at Sickleholme Golf Club at Bamford. Corporal Ralph Wever had played hockey for the North of England and there were professional boxers, water polo players, motor-cycle champions. Private Haydn Taylor would gain fame in 1935 when

2nd Lieut. Vivian Simpson (centre on the front row) with the members of No. 20 Platoon at Redmires camp in May 1914 shortly before the 12th Battalion left for Cannock Chase.

he swam the Channel, in those days seen as a superhuman achievement bringing instant national celebrity status.

The great event was finally held on 29 April, just two weeks before the Battalion left Sheffield for good, and Vivian had processed 1,000 entries including some from the two Barnsley Pals Battalions and the 15th Bn. of the Notts and Derby Regiment, with whom the City Battalion had already built up a sporting partnership. Visitors flocked up to Redmires to see the event, the local press claiming that there were 10,000 spectators, and it says a lot about the public's affection for the Battalion that so many people came on the day. From Mainwaring's point of view, it was a way for the Battalion to show its worth in a spectacular manner, as well as a chance to say thank you for the help and support they had had from so many people in the city, especially from members of the volunteers' own families. It was a glorious sunny day that many who were there never forgot, but there must have been anxiety too among many family members. Private Eric Carr of A Company, soon to be commissioned, carried off the Victor Ludorum Prize as the best athlete of the event and the inter-platoon mile between teams made up of 16 men and their platoon commander and carrying full kit weighing 50 pounds, was won by No. 16 Platoon led by Second Lieutenant Arnold Beal. Both Carr and Beal would be killed within minutes of each other at Serre on the first day of the Somme battle, as would many others competing that day.

Colonel Mainwaring will have known at the time of the Athletic Sports that a move from Redmires was imminent. It was time for the four battalions of the 94th Brigade to be training together and that could not be done at Redmires or anywhere in the South Yorkshire area. For the Battalion as a whole there was excitement when the order came to move to Cannock Chase in Staffordshire, where the army was developing a huge camp for training large formations. For Reg and his signaller pals, it was seen as a definite step towards a move abroad and finally being involved in the real war. For Vivian Simpson, it brought disappointment. On 9 May he wrote to his family to tell them what was afoot:

'We've received orders for the Battalion to move to Cannock Chase near Stafford on Thursday next with the exception of E Company and poor Beley is fed up and nearly sobbed. I do not know yet whether I will be going or staying, but at any rate I have been told that I will go with the Battalion when they go to the front. I feel sorry for this because E Company were just settling down and they feel being left out very much.'

In the event, Vivian stayed at Redmires with E Company, whose members never felt really accepted by the old hands who had volunteered in the previous September. To add to their sense of difference, they were still dressed in the blue uniform whereas all the other companies were now fully kitted out in khaki, even though Reg and the members of D Company had not got their khaki uniforms until early April. Reg along with others got leave on the last weekend to say a proper goodbye to his parents and Elsie; they promised to be there when the Battalion marched down from Redmires on the Thursday morning on their way to the station.

He also called in on old colleagues at the Education Department and his old Headmaster, J.W. Iliffe in the Central School next door. It turned out that Mr. Iliffe had just discovered a problem. At short notice he needed someone important to present a bouquet of flowers to the newly crowned May Queen in a big Sheffield extravaganza held once a year in the Albert Hall in Barker's Pool. Reg's visit provided him with a solution and he grabbed Reg and persuaded him to do the honours that afternoon at the Albert Hall, which was Sheffield's premier concert, events and political meeting auditorium. So on cue, Reg went up and presented the flowers to the May Queen and for that moment he represented the City Battalion in the minds and hearts of all those who were present and they applauded him to the rafters.

Training continued unabated in the last week with an all-night operation followed by two field days that lasted from early morning to late afternoon. Vivian was not told until the last minute that he was not going to Cannock Chase, but he urged his family to be there to watch the march down to the Town Hall, encouraging his brother to bring his lad, Gordon, 'to see the "entertainment" as it would be something for him to remember'.

Nor was the promise that Vivian would be with the Battalion when they went abroad and went into action kept. Instead, he found himself sidelined into training new recruits for over a year and was only recalled to the Battalion in the field fourteen months later, after eighteen of the officers of the City Battalion were either killed or wounded at Serre on the first day of the Somme battle.

He was right that the march down to the Town Hall was going to be a great spectacle for the Sheffield public, but at the last minute, plans had to be radically altered and many Sheffielders probably missed the parade outside the Town Hall. Late word came that the railway company could not organise trains at 11.30am as everyone was expecting; instead they could only find space on the lines if the two trains carrying the battalion left at 8.25am and 9.25am respectively.

Reveille on the 13th now sounded at the unearthly hour of 0430 hours and everyone was ready to march off at 0615. They had prepared all their gear the night before, so all the men were primed and waiting to go on time. Watched by a disconsolate E Company and a rather wistful Second Lieutenant, they swung out into the Redmires Road and headed for the centre of town leaving behind a camp in good order with the Union Jack still flying from the flagpole. That flag had been presented to the Battalion in March by the Ecclesall MP, Samuel Roberts, after the original one he had given to the Battalion earlier was slowly shredded into mere strips of fabric by the gales and sleet of a Pennine winter.

Elsie and the Glenn family were waiting near the city centre for the column of the companies to reach them. As the men marched into town, cheering citizens turned out of their houses to applaud them all along the route. Those that had flags flew them from upper windows and at the Royal Engineers Drill Hall at the start of West Street, they were saluted by a presentation of arms by an honour guard, as the Engineers' and the Hallamshires' bands joined the column, augmenting the music from the Battalion's own drum and bugle band that had led the way down from Redmires. Unlike the December day when the Battalion had marched up to Redmires in the driving rain and sleet, this was a crisp late spring morning and as the crowds along the way grew thicker, wives, sweethearts, sisters and little brothers dashed into the column to hug and kiss their loved ones. Marching discipline was only restored as the companies got close to the Town Hall, when everyone appreciated that the last couple of hundred yards had to be done with a bit of swank and swagger and show the civic party – perched somewhat precariously on a newly erected wooden platform outside the side door of the Town Hall – just what they were made of.

It was a scene that in 1914 and 1915 would have been repeated in cities and small towns from Breslau to Bordeaux, from Salzburg to St. Petersburg, from

Colonel Mainwaring leads the cheers of his Battalion outside the Town Hall in their final parade in the City, before they marched down to the railway station and entrained for Cannock Chase.

Winnipeg to Wellington and all points in between. It is a most poignant part today of our iconography of the First World War, the image of cheering crowds; beaming, waving soldiers; proud but anxious parents, wives and sweethearts; as the farewell parade of the local 'boys' unfolds.

The Lord Mayor, O.C. Wilson, said all the expected things:

> 'We know you will do credit to yourselves in France, or Belgium, or Germany. We know you will take care that the honour of Sheffield is safe in your hands and we all wish you God Speed and a safe return.'

The Battalion was lined up in companies the length of Surrey Street, with members of the public estimated at 5,000 squeezed in behind them. It was only 7.35am when they first arrived outside the Town Hall and the formal ceremony did not take too long. Before calling for three cheers, Colonel Mainwaring, a man of few words, replied on behalf of all the Battalion finishing with this pledge. 'I need only say that we shall do our best to deserve all your good wishes and do credit to Sheffield.'

The Battalion then marched down the hill to the Midland Station, the bands still playing well-loved patriotic tunes of glory. A and B Companies were on the first train and left at 8.25am prompt, with C and D following an hour later. The Battalion would never formally parade in the City again. There would be leave for individual soldiers and they all got leave before going to Egypt. But Elsie, the daughter of a dead soldier of the Boer War, despite all the optimistic hubris of the occasion, must have thought that she was not just saying good-bye to Reg for the foreseeable future, but perhaps forever.

So it was a suddenly silent group of relatives and friends who walked back over the bridge into the station yard that early Thursday morning in May, and quietly dispersed to their different places of work in a now seemingly empty city.

Chapter 5

'When will we get over?'
Advanced Training 31 May - 21 December 1915

When Reg Glenn and his mates arrived at Cannock Chase, they were unimpressed that their camp on Penkridge Bank was unfinished, even though Major Hoette and an advance party of 100 men had been there for a couple of days doing basic preparation for the Battalion's arrival. It was like being back at Redmires in December except now it was warm weather not the arctic blizzard that had welcomed them back then. They had made Redmires their neat, comfortable and familiar home and now they seemed back to square one. The first few days were spent finishing off the huts, clearing stones from the parade ground and laying new stone chipping paths between the lines. They also soon started work on digging a protected 100-yard-long rifle range with secure butts for targets and markers, because getting their musketry up to standard was one of the most important imperatives for the men at this stage of their training. Meanwhile one soldier, skilled in the art, was detailed to recreate from pebbles, bits of red brick, coal and sandstone, a new mosaic of the Tiger and Rose regimental badge that mirrored the one they had left outside the guardhouse at Redmires, so enabling them to put their own identity on this nondescript groups of huts.

They knew why they had made the move. Redmires was fine for training a new battalion but these days the army fought in Brigades and Divisions and the units that made up those formations needed to be trained together, enabling their commanders to become familiar with handling such large formations of men. So new training grounds had been sought and thanks to the generosity of Lord Lichfield, the owner of the Cannock Chase estate, the army was now building a number of camps on the Chase that would eventually be able to house the equivalent of two divisions and have room for their training requirements.

Penkridge Bank, part of Rugeley Camp in the central part of Staffordshire, was one of the first to be constructed, another was Brocton camp a few miles further west nearer to Stafford, a camp where Vivian Simpson would spend November 1915 with the 15th Battalion, and later during the early months of 1918 training cohorts of young conscripts who would serve on the Western Front. Penkridge was one of the highest points on Cannock Chase and one of the bleakest, although now it was summer, Reg and the others were not too concerned about that. Rather, their problem was moorland fires and often in June they were organised into fire piquets and spent the day on the moors putting out small fires, or digging up the gorse that covered the Chase to help prevent fires spreading.

Today, Cannock Chase is forested and there is little sense of the wide-open spaces that were so ideal for training large formations of troops in 1915. The area had still been serving its medieval purpose as a deer hunting chase before the war broke out and Reg and his mates often saw herds of deer when they were out practising their signalling or on the frequent route marches across the Chase to one of the nearby towns.

There were still the usual rounds of training activities, more straw dummies were bayoneted, more concentrated practice on the rifle range using their Lee-Metfords that had finally been delivered in sufficient numbers, even if they were obsolete, with some unsafe to fire on the range. There was more PT, more trench digging and more parade ground drilling as well. On 24 May, when they had been at Penkridge for just over a week, there was a formal parade of the whole brigade, four battalions drawn up in parade order in what must have seemed an awe-inspiring display of strength to men who usually had only operated in companies and platoons. They were beginning to have more formal and social contact with the Barnsley lads and the East Lancashire Pals, and a needle football match between the Barnsley Pals and the City Battalion was keenly contested, finishing in an honourable 2-2 draw.

Reg also met men from the other battalions at the rather well-appointed YMCA hut that was already up and running when the City Battalion arrived. It was situated just across from the Battalion's lines and replicated all the comforts of the Redmires YMCA, including four billiard tables, social areas and quiet rooms where soldiers could write letters home. Reg sent letters off regularly to Elsie and his parents as the army postal service was most efficient (some 1,000 letters a day were sent and received from the City Battalion alone) and he could no longer pop back home every now and again as he had been able to do when they were at Redmires. They were not, however, confined to barracks and a sizeable number of the Battalion got leave every weekend starting at mid-day on Friday. Reg and his mates would then get themselves to Stafford where a train at 1pm would get them back to Sheffield later in the afternoon. Reg did not have to be back at the camp until Sunday evening so for a couple of days he could live a normal life, have a decent bath, perhaps take Elsie out to the cinema on Saturday evening and be up in time for Matins at Wadsley Church on Sunday morning as he had done in peacetime. Sunday lunch would follow before returning to Midland Station and an afternoon train back to Stafford.

At Penkridge Bank Camp, Reg was introduced to the new Morse telephone sets that became standard use for the army in the first part of the war. These sets needed an earth return connection and their messages could 'leak' into the ground and be

Reg Glenn (left) at Penkridge using the new Morse telephone.

read by German listening posts if the right geological conditions (clay and chalk were the most effective) were present. To Reg this was the arrival of the signalling twentieth century style. The flags and heliograph they practiced on would have been familiar to Wellington's army, even Marlborough's as they slogged across central Europe to Blenheim two centuries earlier. They seem so primitive to us now and it seems amazing that they were being considered fit for modern trench warfare in 1915.

A good signaller like Reg could manage twelve words a minute with his blue and white flags, but only if using lightweight silk flags. The usual material caused the signaller to be slower and was even more difficult to manoeuvre if it got wet. On the modern battlefield, Reg must have realised you would not be able to expose yourself to wave your flags and so much of their training must therefore have seemed to be pointless. A shuttered Morse signal lamp beamed through a trench periscope and viewed by a powerful telescope resting on a tripod, could be used safely in the trenches and Reg would have had considerable training on the use of the lamps at Penkridge and Ripon, where he finally received his coveted crossed flags badge (worn on the lower left arm) as a qualified signaller.

A week after the Battalion arrived at Cannock Chase, every man in the Battalion received a Bible and several soldiers got their mates to sign their names on a blank inside page. Reg instead used a new Prayer Book he had been given to record everywhere the war took him and at the end he had recorded 131 locations, starting with Redmires and including Egypt, the Somme, Vimy and the Aisne. There were also the names of places in England, such as New College, Oxford, where Reg was based when he was training to become an officer and later entries when he was wounded.

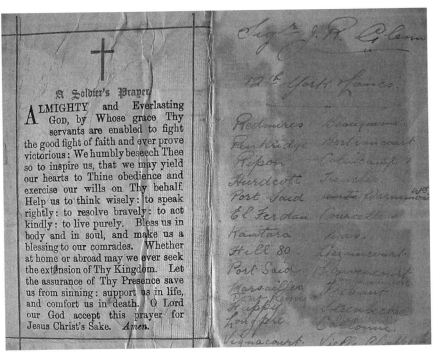

The inside first page of Reg Glenn's prayer book showing the names of all the places war took him to in Britain and abroad.

Wednesday at Penkridge was usually route march day and the Battalion, honed to a high standard on the hills around western Sheffield, usually acquitted themselves very well. The Battalion was marching for Yorkshire now as they swaggered through the nearby Staffordshire towns and they adopted 'Ilkla' Moor Baht'at' as their favourite marching song, even though it is reported that some of them did not grasp the meaning of the dialect words and had to have it explained to them. We can be sure this caused the Barnsley lads to be somewhat scornful of their 'posh' comrades, but they might be forgiven because there was no published version of this traditional West Riding song until 1916.

People in Rugeley, Milford and Hednesford must have been very apprehensive about this sudden influx of thousands of young men from the great urban centres of Britain, but the Battalion seems to have behaved itself in the nearby small country towns and rural villages and was often cheered by the locals as they marched through.

Reg recalled the reaction of one particular enthusiastic local man:

'On one march we passed a road sweeper who must have been an old soldier. He looked up and then did a marvellous present arms with his broom, and our officer returned the salute.'

When the City Battalion left for Ripon at the end of July, the Rugeley Urban District Council passed a formal resolution of thanks to the Battalion and wished them good fortune when they got over to France.

Some of the Battalion were now beginning to wonder when that would ever be. Most had signed up in September 1914 assuming they would be in action by the end of the year and here they were still marching, practising musketry and bayoneting, doing manoeuvres, that by July had increasingly involved the whole brigade in rolling attacks and protected defensive exercises, with battalions learning to support each other as they changed from reserve to leading formations.

At least there was some progress in their status, because two months after they arrived at Penkridge they were finally adopted by the War Office on 15 July. There had been some delay while Government and Sheffield City Council officials worked out, even haggled over, how much expenditure the Council had incurred financing the Battalion as they squeezed the extra revenue out of the Council budget to provide for uniforms, pay, equipment and accommodation for ten and a half months. To Reg and the other lads, it meant a kit inspection to rival all kit inspections. On 13 July Reveille had been blown at 6am and they were told that by 7.15 they had to get a replacement from the quartermaster's store for any kit lost. Never had a kit inspection been more thorough, as they had to account for every item and after inspection in their huts they were paraded outside in full marching order for several hours until the senior officers were satisfied everything was accounted for. Another parade two days later formally marked the handover from Sheffield Council's Organising Committee to the War Office, with the Organising Committee deservedly receiving official thanks for a job well done. For the men, there was no real difference in their military lives by this change of status, but not a few hoped it would mean that they were now much nearer to going into action and would soon be going over to France or Belgium and putting their training into practice.

Instead, they were sent to the 4th Army's training centre near Ripon for more advanced training. But before they left, there was still time for one more route march. It is not clear who ordered it, because Colonel Mainwaring was unwell and the Battalion was under the command of Major Clough, but it seems a very irresponsible decision even if the standards of the time were designed to push men to the very limits. The march, undertaken in extreme July heat, was a 16-mile round trip to Lichfield in full kit that ran into serious problems of heat exhaustion. Eighty men are reported to have dropped out and one of Reg's pals describes the men as dropping out like flies, while another called the march complete madness, and no doubt a few other epithets as well. The column had to make numerous stops and it was six hours after leaving in the morning that the Battalion got back to their huts with most men close to exhaustion.

There was no rest for the wicked, or the exhausted, it would seem, as the men now had to pack up all their kit for the overnight train journey to Ripon. But first, they had the extra exacting trial of a four mile march to Rugeley station before entraining. It says much for the Battalion's discipline, fitness and esprit de corps that the men managed the day's challenges, but it was a foolhardy use of authority that could have had fatal consequences, a stubbornly thoughtless order at odds with a genuine concern for the well-being of the troops.

Meanwhile 'back at the ranch', Vivian Simpson had stayed on at Redmires with E Company after the rest of the Battalion had left for Cannock Chase. This created space in the camp for a new company named F Company to be raised to train further recruits for the 12th Battalion. Initially, Captain Beley was in charge but he was replaced at the end of June by Captain William Jarrard, the former Sheffield university lecturer, who returned from Penkridge Camp and was put in command of both companies. The two companies stayed at Redmires until late July when a Northern Command Order (No.1228 dated 9 July) directed all training companies of the locally raised battalions of the same regiment to join up at one camp and be under the command of one senior officer. The 13th Bn (the 1st Barnsley Pals) had been based at Silkstone camp west of the town, and the 14th Battalion (the 2nd Barnsley Pals), who were quartered in the town, used Silkstone for their training, so the decision was taken to concentrate the training companies of the three York and Lancaster Battalions at Silkstone with Vivian moving to new quarters there.

There was one advantage for Vivian being based at Silkstone, he was near to Wortley Golf Club. So, in the summer of 1915 he managed to play a fair amount

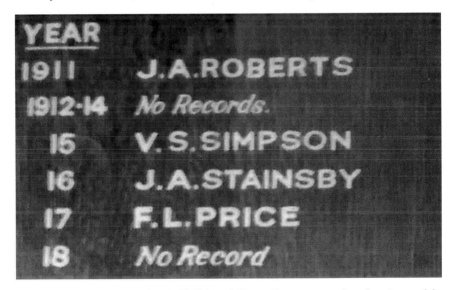

The Honours Board of Wortley Golf Club with Vivian Simpson named as the winner of the prestigious Captain's Cup for 1915. The Honours Board is still in place in the clubhouse today. (Photograph courtesy of Wortley Golf Club)

of golf there and must have been on good form because he won the club's most prestigious trophy, the Captain's Cup, which was a match play tournament played over several rounds.

While still at Redmires in June, Vivian also took advantage of being left behind in Sheffield to finally arrange his wedding. Though Vivian and May had been engaged for some time, the wedding seemed very rushed and a much pared down event from what would have taken place in peacetime. In normal times, a wedding of two such well–known and respected Broomhill families as the Simpsons and the Belchers would have been a major social event, with most of the people who counted in Sheffield civic and professional life being invited. But this was wartime and it was all rather hasty and definitely low key, although the wedding was held at St. Mark's Church, the parish church of Broomhill, just a few yards across the road from the Belcher's Rossleigh House.

A letter Vivian wrote to his older, married, brother George, on 16 June fully describes his minimalist plans for how the day should go:

'I have fixed matters up now for 9.45am Saturday next, the 19th instant, at St. Marks Church. I have got the licence and the ring and everything is serene. We should leave by the 10.54am train to Colwyn Bay. If Percy Belcher does not come I would be awfully glad if you could act as best man. I did not ask you in the first place because I understand it is normal at these affairs to have unattached gentry as best man. The affair will be very quiet with no invitations, but if there is anyone you want to bring just drag them along.'

How far May went along with these plans is open to conjecture, but it was hardly a young lady's 'greatest day of her life'. One can understand a need to rein in the cost and the ostentation in wartime but catching a train an hour after the start of the service is a bit extreme in anyone's estimation. There was time for a family photograph taken on the ample front steps of Rossleigh House, but perhaps that was taken before the wedding to save time.

Vivian was married in uniform, as was the fashion in both world wars, but there were no arches of swords to greet the newly married couple as they left the church, although Percy Belcher, May's brother, and now a lieutenant in the Royal Artillery, did get back in time. He features on the photo along with some members of the Simpson clan, but not all of Vivian's brothers and sisters had managed to get back to Sheffield. There was no one from the Regiment at the wedding or any colleagues from his pre-war legal world, but Vivian may have had to revise his train departure because it would be almost impossible to get through a wedding service and then get to the Midland Station in sixty-nine minutes.

Before E and F Companies moved to Silkstone in July, Vivian had been sent on a one month course of intensive training for temporary junior officers that was based

The wedding party in front of the Belcher's house Rossleigh on 19ᵗʰ June 1915. Percy Belcher, the best man is on the right and May is in a dark dress which she may have hurriedly put on after the service to enable a quick get away to catch the train to North Wales.

at the Staff College at Camberley and at Royal Military College Sandhurst. In the autumn of 1914, Kitchener had foreseen the need, not just for new armies and the recruitment of thousands of men, but for a much-expanded officer corps to lead the platoons and companies of the new battalions. It soon became clear to him that this was going to be a long war and particularly costly in lives of junior officers who, it was popularly believed, only had a life expectancy of six weeks at the Front. The officer corps of the Regular Army and the Territorial Force would be totally inadequate to cope with the demand for new subalterns and there would be a need for a process to identify suitable candidates for a commission and give them some training in their duties and responsibilities in a very short period of time. Vivian's training to date while serving with the 12th Battalion was one of expedience aimed at producing junior officers quickly, but Kitchener felt that there must be something more organised to prepare young men for such awesome responsibilities and reach acceptable standards of professionalism. Most of the course was held at Sandhurst but, as the RMC was still training its normal quota of 'Gentlemen Cadets', there was no spare room at the college to provide accommodation. The temporary officers on this short course were therefore accommodated a mile away at Camberley Staff College, which had been closed in August 1914 so that all the staff and students could return to their battalions, brigades and divisions to put their training into practice now Britain had entered the war.

The first course was started on 27 November 1914 and the new officers were formed into three companies designated M, O and P with sixty temporary officers and three instructors from the RMC in each company. These one month courses ran till April 1916 when they were replaced by a more thorough three month course; still a rushed military education compared to the eighteen month course that cadets usually took at the RMC in peace time. So when Vivian joined the course in July 1915, the instructors had organised seven of these courses already and had got over the teething problems of turning amateur volunteers into officers capable of leading men in the most ferocious war in history.

Vivian was quartered at Camberley and he was put into O Company, where most of the officers came from northern regiments. Among his sixty colleagues were officers from the East Yorkshires, the West Yorkshires, the King's Own Yorkshire Light Infantry, the Durham Light Infantry and some well-known Lancashire regiments, as well as some Canadians recently arrived in Britain. In a letter home, he wrote:

> 'There are some very decent chaps on the course, but some of the other kind as well. You do not make many new acquaintances because people stick with chaps from their own battalions and brigades.'

Vivian shared a room at Camberley with Lieutenant Charles Elam, son of a well-known Sheffield physician, who had been amongst the first City Battalion officers commissioned in September, and a 'youth' in the East Lancashires, who was presumably one of the 'other kind'.

It is not clear why Vivian had been selected for the course when many others in the City Battalion had not, but it may have been because he was older than most subalterns and the course may have had a secondary purpose of identifying, at an early stage, those who might be suitable for a captaincy and be capable of taking command of a company if losses continued to run at a high level. Vivian wrote to his brother:

> 'They keep us pretty busy here. From 7-8am we do physical drill or a run, 9.15am -12.45pm lectures, 2-3pm revolver practice, 6-7pm more lectures and Mess at 8pm. We mess at three long tables in one great room decorated with big game trophies and paintings of famous generals. The corridors are all stone paved and the walls on the ground floor are panelled with the names of all the staff college graduates from the commencement of the College in 1860 to the present day, and you can find the names of most of the present day generals when they passed through here.'

The course consisted of instruction in tactics, military engineering, military law, military organisation and hygiene. There was time given to signalling instruction and practice and one lecture on the role of the fledgling Royal Flying Corps given by an RFC officer. There was a considerable intellectual element to the course, including military history and a balanced syllabus of political analysis covering the rivalries of the major powers, the Balkan ethnic entanglements that led to the start of the war and an understandable desire to give these temporary officers a moral justification for Britain going to war in August 1914. In the latter element of the course, the lectures were titled 'Germany's hope of world domination' and 'The Germans conviction of their racial superiority', issues the British would never have considered applied to themselves.

There were other advantages to being at Camberley for Vivian.

'There is a very decent cricket ground behind the main building with tennis courts at the rear and the front, where there is a path leading down to a large lake whose banks are planted with old English flowers. A mile away through the woods is Sandhurst where everything is ripping! It also has fine buildings and playing fields. As well as a revolver and rifle range and a riding school.'

Best of all for Vivian was the discovery nearby of the new Camberley Heath Golf Club that had only been opened in 1913, ironically by HRH Duke Albert of Schleswig Holstein. He spent much of his spare time on the course, beating one of the local committee members 8 and 7 on one occasion, pocketing a 5/- stake. He also arranged for May to visit him for one weekend and she was put up at a hotel nearby. They walked over to Farnborough through the pleasant country lanes on the Saturday and were impressed by two huge airship sheds and the workshops for building planes. On the Sunday Vivian played golf, beating a local member in the morning, and then an East Lancs officer in the afternoon. 'So I won a free lunch and tea and so had an enjoyable day for "Maykins" and myself!'

By the middle of August, Vivian was back with the 15th Battalion at Silkstone and wondering why he was not being promoted to Lieutenant and getting a second star because he was doing all the company planning. The other subalterns, including the new ones he called mere 'children', initiated very little and were happy to follow his training schemes and schedules and it was Vivian who lectured the NCOs twice a week. He thought he deserved the adjutant's job and the promotion, perhaps a captaincy, that went with it. He also was less than impressed with the quality of the men who were now volunteering for the City Battalion. He considered them far inferior to the men who had volunteered earlier and was concerned that 'although the 4th Army would be one of the best when it went into action, later Armies would be full of very poor stuff'. He was also not very impressed by being served in the mess by former Barnsley colliers, who he considered were a bit short of the social graces and delicacy of touch needed for the job of waiting at tables.

Still there was always nearby Wortley Golf Course and May joined him again for another golfing weekend in mid-August, staying at the clubhouse while Vivian bashed out a couple of rounds a day. The weekend was extended for the Barnsley Feast as all the members of the Battalion got an extra day's leave to enjoy the festivities in the town if they wished.

May and Vivian made some important decisions in September about the new house they had finally bought on Hagg Lane. May had little wish to live in the house by herself in a remote part of Sheffield away from her family and friends, even while Vivian was at Silkstone camp but rarely free to join her. So, through the good offices of George, they put the house up for leasing at an annual rent of £50 (payable in advance) and by early October they had a tenant. It was a sensible plan, giving May a useful lump sum, while she moved back in with her family in Rossleigh. There she would not only have company, but when their first child was on the way she would have her mother's love and care and servants to help and support her. It was fully understood that they would ultimately re-occupy the house when the war was over.

Among those at Silkstone camp there were a couple of men who had recently returned after experiencing the fighting on the Western Front. They made it clear that they were glad to be back, whilst Vivian was keen to hear what war was really like not just the 'guff' in the papers. He wrote home:

> 'They say the Saxons hate the Prussians and the Bavarians like poison and let our men know when the Prussians are going to advance. In some places the trenches are very close and the Germans seem to know most of the English regiments. They call over and ask whether the Staffords, who the Prussian Guards won't face, have come into the line and there are other regiments they seem afraid of. They say that our lot give men rum before a bayonet charge and they think it is doped as the men don't know what they are doing for about half an hour afterwards. They take few prisoners on either side and if you are left wounded on the battlefield you're "done in" without so much as a chance of a back word.'

Vivian found all this sobering, but not something that he would communicate with the recruits, who either were still full of bravado or had little imagination and all professed they were keen to get at the 'Hun'.

When Reg and the rest of the 12th Battalion got to Ripon in the middle of the night, they still had a march of a mile to South Camp where they would spend the next eight weeks. Reg described the night as so black that you could only see the pack of the man in front as you marched along, and when they eventually reached their huts, they were totally exhausted having been on the march, or travelling, non-stop for twenty-four hours. Fortunately, the Fourth Army's Ripon camp was already well established, and the Sheffield lads did not have to undertake any extra work to get the huts and the lines up to scratch this time.

Five days after arrival, they were inspected by the Commander of the Training Centre, Gen Sir Bruce Hamilton, and a week later the Deputy Chief of the Imperial General Staff, Maj. Gen. Sir A.J. Murray, did a similar inspection. Reg and his pals wondered why there were so many inspections that on the surface seemed just formal and cursory, when a General, followed by a posse of self-important looking officers, wandered through the lines occasionally asking a simple routine question. More important for them was a visit in early September of the new commander of their 31st Division, Maj. Gen. Robert Wanless-O'Gowan CB, who, although they did not know it then, was the General who would take them to war. Their new General had first-hand experience of the Western Front having previously commanded the 13th Brigade (5th Division) in France and Belgium and had seen desperate action at Hill 60 in the Ypres Salient. He would lead the 31st Division at Serre and stay with the Division until 1918, after the 12th Battalion had been disbanded in February of that year.

Although most of the facilities at South Camp were up and running by the time the 12th Battalion arrived, the men had to dig out another rifle range for their own use and soon after they finally got a supply of 80 Lee Enfield Mk III rifles, one for each NCO, that could then be used to train the men on the rifle they would use when they got to the Front. Reg and the signallers did less musketry practice because they were concentrating on their own specific training, but Reg always claimed that he soon proved to be a good shot.

On Friday 10 September, the Battalion had the day off to celebrate the anniversary of the formation of the Battalion in Sheffield the year before. Half the Battalion got leave for an extended weekend and half stayed in camp and took their leave the following week. Reg stayed in camp and took part in a concert organised by the padre in the YMCA with Sergeant Wilson proving something of a virtuoso on the piano, as a number of officers and men undertook solos and teamed up to belt out choral numbers and popular songs of the day. Many men afterwards would recall that happy afternoon ten months later, when so many present, including Sergeant Henry Crozier, who made a particular telling contribution to the entertainment, did not survive the 'walk' up the slope at Serre on the first day of the Somme.

The YMCA proved once again to be a godsend to the Sheffield lads. Some evenings there were band concerts as well as informal sing songs and Reg and his friends found other leisure opportunities including swimming in a nearby river and visiting the cinema in Ripon, where they saw the D.W. Griffith epic American film *Birth of a Nation*, a film that raised the aspirations of the modern cinema above slapstick and crude melodramas. Some of Reg's mates visited the Cathedral, where later there was a church parade for the Battalion, and some of them even went over to see Fountains Abbey some way due west of their camp.

Just before leaving Ripon for the south of England, there was one more General to inspect them. A mere brigadier this time, as Brig. Gen. G.T.C. Carter-Campbell DSO took over 94th Brigade from Brig. Gen. Bowles. To Reg and the lads, he was just another general, who with his clipped moustache looked identical to the last one and would be with them for a while and then be whisked off somewhere else. In fact, Carter-Campbell would stay in command of the Brigade until January

1918, although he was sometimes away because of illness, including the vital first day of the Somme battle. Like Wanless-O'Gowan, he had considerable experience of the Western Front having been wounded at Neuve-Chapelle in March 1915. A Scotsman commissioned originally into the Cameronians, in March 1918, he was given command of the famous 51st Highland Division and served out the war with them.

The Battalion now moved to Hurdcott camp on Salisbury Plain and Reg recalled that they had an eight-mile march to the camp after they reached Salisbury station at 7am on Sunday morning, 26 September. But, at least when they got to Hurdcott Camp, the huts were properly kitted out and ready to be occupied. There was a strong feeling among the men that the move south meant that they would soon be going over to France and joining in the fighting.

The five Service Battalions of the York and Lancaster Regiment that had been raised by the War Office (6th, 7th, 8th, 9th and 10th Bns) and were not Pals Battalions, were all now in France with the exception of the 6th Battalion that had left in early July to go to Gallipoli. In September, the 10th Battalion was engaged in the major British offensive at Loos, yet Reg and his mates were still practising routines that they had done so many times before. A four hour drill session for the whole battalion was particularly not appreciated and the regular route marches just seemed like filling in the time while waiting for orders to go to France.

Coming back to camp after another seven mile route march two days after arriving at Hurdcott, they were passed by a car leaving the camp carrying Lt. Col. Charles Mainwaring, whose eyes were downcast – deliberately not looking at the troops. On arrival at camp they discovered that their Colonel had been replaced and, presumably unable to face a formal goodbye, had driven off quietly when he hoped few of the Battalion would be around. At 52, he was officially judged 'unfit for military service' and had been replaced by a younger CO, who it turned out also had medical problems.

Reg and the others took a different view of Mainwaring than Vivian Simpson did. They expected Colonels to be strict but fair and set high personal and professional standards. They understood and admired the way their old Colonel had got the Battalion up to standard and there was a genuine sense of loss and sympathy for him that he could not lead them in France. For Charles Mainwaring, the decision must have been devastating though hardly a complete surprise. He had been occasionally ill at Redmires and Ripon and after thirty-one years' service in the tropics (he had been born in Madras [Chennai] in 1863) he would always have found a northern European climate a challenge and virtually impossible to survive in the trenches. As a regular soldier, his greatest ambition would have been to lead his battalion into action, yet now he was never going to achieve that. No wonder he could not look his men in the face that afternoon as he drove away from Hurdcott Camp and into retirement, although he remained on the Active List of Indian Army Officers until December 1918.

Lieut. Colonel Joseph Crossthwaite who was the Commanding Officer of the 12th Battalion from 28 September 1915 until 30 June 1916.

He had a real pride in this rather unusual battalion and in a speech to the men he had made at Ripon, when he probably knew he was going to be moved, he had told them, 'I have never known of a unit who went so long without a single court-martial.' Perhaps something of a back handed compliment, but for him a real tribute to the self-discipline of these 'middle class amateurs' who had so embraced the military life and become a very enthusiastic and efficient battalion.

His replacement was a Regular Army officer, Lt. Col. Joseph Crosthwaite of the Durham Light Infantry who took over officially on 28 September. A younger man (44) who had served in France since September 1914, initially as second in command of the 2nd Bn DLI. He had taken over command of this regular battalion in January 1915 and led it through some of the fierce fighting in the Ypres Salient before being wounded. In July, he briefly served as the CO of the 1st Bn Somerset Light Infantry but became ill and had a period in hospital before being judged fit again and sent to Hurdcott in late September to take over the 12th Bn York & Lancaster from Mainwaring.

He was the Battalion's third CO in just over a year but now the men were serving under Battalion, Brigade and Divisional Commanding Officers who had seen considerable service on the Western Front, whereas all other veterans in the Battalion – officers and NCOs – only had experience of the Boer War or colonial campaigns, which were hardly the same thing.

In the middle of November, the Battalion matched ten miles to their fourth camp, Larkhill, north east of Hurdcott. Along the way, Reg and his mates passed Stonehenge, somewhere they would have all heard about but never seen. But when they got to their new camp, where they would be based for two weeks for an intensive musketry course, it was the dirtiest and least hospitable camp they had yet experienced. They moved into huts that had recently been vacated by a Canadian battalion and they found that on top of all the other inadequacies there was no coal to heat any of the buildings. That might not have worried a Canadian unit too much, used to living in tents during their training in the snow filled wastes of Ontario, but the 12th Battalion was unimpressed.

Nevertheless, their performance in Parts 3 and 4 of their musketry training was impressive and they always came top in their brigade and won four out of the five competitions that were held at Larkhill. They now all received their own individual Short Magazine Lee-Enfield Rifle, the SMLE Mk III and this boosted their enthusiasm for practising on the ranges that was always a popular duty because it did not require the exhaustive efforts of long drill or PT sessions, route marches or field exercises. They also became familiar with the Lewis gun and the Vickers MMG, the Army's standard medium machine gun, with some of them detailed to become specialists on these two key battlefield weapons.

Reg knew the Canadians had left Larkhill for France and so he and the rest of the Battalion expected that their departure for the Western Front was imminent. This seemed confirmed when a 31st Division advance party went across the Channel at the end of November, with Captain Arthur Cousin representing the Battalion. Yet no sooner had they landed than they were sent back because the orders had changed and the distribution of a solar topee sun helmet to every man confirmed that they were off to the Mediterranean, possibly to Gallipoli, where British, French and ANZAC forces had been waging a bitter, desperate and unsuccessful assault on the peninsula since April. They did not know, as November turned into December, that the decision to withdraw from the Dardanelles had been already taken and that the evacuation would start on 18 December. However, they were still destined to go to the Middle East, but now were sent to defend the Suez Canal against a resurgent Turkey who might be encouraged by their victory at Gallipoli to go on the offensive against the British Empire.

The Battalion made its final preparations back at Hurdcott Camp, and on 20 December, Reg and his colleagues entrained for the journey to Devonport where the SS *Nestor* was waiting to take them to Port Said. Generals came from miles around to say farewell and make one final inspection and there was a message from George V wishing them God Speed and telling them, 'I am confident that the high tradition of the British Army is safe in your hands ... and you will maintain the unceasing efforts necessary to bring this war to a victorious ending.' It was probably a letter he had sent to every Division going overseas, but he did usually inspect Divisions in person. The war had helped George V to create a proper and popular role for a constitutional monarch, especially one who was trying to fully establish his British credentials. Unfortunately, he had fallen off his horse on a recent visit to France and was no doubt genuinely disappointed that he was too injured to visit the Battalion before they left for the Middle East.

On 21 December the Battalion embarked on the SS *Nestor* at the Keyham Dock, Devonport, and, with crowds cheering them all the way past Plymouth Hoe and out into the Channel, they at last set off to war.

Chapter 6

Standing Guard – Just East of Suez
1 January - 10 March 1916

Reg and most of the Battalion had never been abroad or been to sea. So, when leaving England, cheered on as heroes, he felt the true exhilaration of something that was still a great adventure. Inoculations for cholera and typhus, the first in the arm but the second one, more painfully, in the breast will have brought him down to earth, as would trying to sleep in a hammock within the closest proximity to your mates in a fetid lower deck. He had also noticed that first day that the destroyer escorts were rolling and pitching as soon as they were in the Channel, whilst the 14,500 tonnes *Nestor* was still reasonably stable, but soon the excitement of ocean travel would wear off.

The *Nestor* was not some battered old hulk requisitioned for the war, but a very modern liner that had made her first voyage to Australia in 1913. She had then been hailed by the Melbourne press when she docked in Victoria as the largest merchant ship to have yet entered an Australian port. She was intended to be a luxury liner for wealthy passengers from Britain to Australia, but she also had third class accommodation for poor immigrants and that is where the men of the 12th Battalion were accommodated.

On the second day there were many who missed breakfast, but Reg

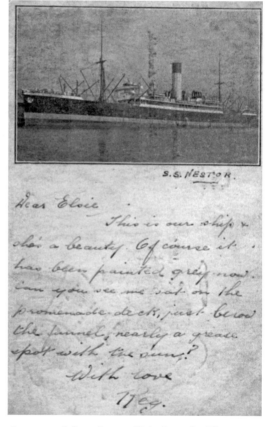

A post card from Reg to Elsie from the SS Nestor, a luxury liner that was turned into a troop ship and carried the 12th Battalion to Port Said at the end of December 1915.

considered that the food on the ship was some of the best he ever had during the war and initially he enjoyed his breakfasts on board. However, it was not long before the *Nestor* was in the infamous Bay of Biscay, whose reputation even landlubbers in Sheffield had heard about. The Bay did not disappoint and there were soon many sick soldiers on board. It was not much better when they passed Cape Finisterre off the north-west point of Spain, where they now got the full force of the Atlantic rollers and the seas at times were powerful enough to come over the Nestor's bows and soak men daft enough to be still on deck.

Out of sight, but in a line of progression to Gibraltar and into the Mediterranean, were other ships carrying other battalions of the 31st Division, each one of them a prime target for lurking U-boats. Reg took his turn on piquet duty, searching with binoculars for a sight of a U-Boat travelling on the surface, as they tried to keep up with fast merchant ships turned troopships. When the Captain felt there was any danger, they zig-zagged, and on one day before reaching the Gibraltar area he startled everyone by firing off the rear gun, albeit as a practice shot.

Christmas Day was spent at sea somewhere out in the Atlantic near Gibraltar. There was no special Christmas dinner for the troops, just another stew which Reg promptly lost over the side of the ship. They should have passed through the Straits during the day, but the ship sailed around in slow circles off the African coast because of reports of a U-Boat off Tangiers. They came north again when it was dark and sailed into the Mediterranean during the night, passing the lights of Gibraltar, with the fierce beams of the searchlights on the Rock sweeping the Straits for interlopers, whilst on the other side were the lights of small hillside villages along the Moroccan coast.

The following day started with a wonderful deep orange and purple sunrise and a calm sea of an intense blue, but on the 27th, they turned round and headed back towards Gibraltar. Although the Sheffield lads did not know it, a British ship had been torpedoed and sunk in the vicinity and the Navy was taking no chances with the precious lives of troops who could afford to arrive a day later; or so they thought. This lost day at sea would later cause a furious sense of injustice amongst survivors of the 12th Battalion, because when they finally arrived at Alexandria – part of an official war zone – a day late on New Year's Day 1916, they were later deemed not to have qualified for the 1914-15 Star. This prestigious medal showed among other things that you had volunteered for the army early in the war and had not waited to be conscripted, but it could only be awarded to men who had been in an official war zone overseas by 31 December 1915, and sailing through the Mediterranean, even in danger from U boats, did not count.

On the 28th, they were sailing east again and enjoyed fine views of the distant mountains along the Algerian coast. The voyage was more like a pleasant cruise now, enjoying the warm December sunshine, the cobalt sea and the azure sky, despite the need to still do look-out duty watching for U-Boats that might well have been Austro-Hungarian, sailing out of their Adriatic ports. The calm continued on the next day as they sailed past northern Tunisia and into Valetta harbour.

Reg was struck by the majestic splendour of the Grand Harbour with its high walls, fortifications and warships riding at anchor. Like everyone else on board, he would remember throwing coins to small boys who would dive in and catch them before they sank too far. Some even caught them with their toes, which impressed the Sheffield lads, as did the Maltese gondolas that flitted across the harbour offering a ferry service to the locals and British officials. Some of the officers were allowed ashore but the men had to stay on board which was much resented. Reg, however, was lucky as the Colonel and a few senior officers had to be at a meeting in Valetta and took Reg with him in case they needed a signaller. Reg later said he could not remember much about Valetta except the Victoria Cafe and the Crown and Anchor, but within two hours he was back on the *Nestor* and was sailing again due east for Alexandria.

Despite the relaxed atmosphere on board, there was another serious U-Boat scare on 31 December. The ship zig-zagged from 11am because of the fear of a U-Boat on their tail, always attempting to present their stern to the enemy submarine, creating a much smaller target than a broadside. Eventually they outran the U-Boat, but later it got near enough to fire a torpedo at the SS *Ionic*, the troopship carrying the 11th Bn East Lancs, but missed. At 9.30am on New Year's Day, the SS *Nestor* entered Alexandria's massive harbour filled with merchantmen of all nations and the grey warships of the Royal Navy. Reg, along with most of the Battalion, was on deck taking in his first sight of the Orient, staring in wonder at the intriguing and beguiling sights of the city's waterfront behind the docks; on the quay plaintive Arabs beseeched the soldiers at the ship's rail for money, then scrambled about pushing aside their colleagues to rush to collect the coins when the soldiers deigned to throw them any.

In the evening, the Battalion entrained for a thirteen-hour night journey to Port Said at the northern entrance of the Suez Canal, but there was little sleep for the men as the seats were wooden slats and very uncomfortable. The journey took so long because there was no direct line to Port Said through the marshes and lakes, so the train had to go round by Ismailia, the nerve centre of the Canal operation. So, as dawn broke, Reg could see that they were travelling due north alongside the fabled Canal, that along with Gibraltar, Singapore and Hong Kong was one of the great icons of British Imperial pride and strategic power. Also exciting and novel were glimpses of Egyptian life, of deserts, camels, palm trees and Arabs – the men in many coloured robes, the women all in black with only their piercing eyes showing. To a generation brought up on Bible stories and Sunday School lessons, this was both dramatically new and appreciably familiar.

When they reached Port Said, they found English ladies waiting with mugs of tea, before they marched off to their nearby camp where they found they were expected to sleep fourteen to a tent. Some men actually got passes to go back into Port Said that night, a town of two very different halves. West of the canal was the Egyptian town where soldiers were warned not to go, but on the east side of the canal was the European Town that surprised them by its attractive boulevards, gracious houses with verandas, smart shopping streets, open air cafes and vibrant night life, even though they had arrived on a Sunday. Most of all, whilst Ismailia had been full of soldiers, British, Indian and Australian, the people here came from many European countries and clearly enjoyed a Mediterranean lifestyle, as if they had transported it from the Riviera or the Italian littoral.

Reg and his tent mates lived somewhat less luxuriously, as he reported in a letter home:

> 'It was very hot in the day and very cold at night, we had not expected that. We were surprised that the sand got very cold and then the floor of the tent got very hard. We had to snuggle up to one another in the tent to keep warm. On top of that the camp did not have a name.'

While they were at Port Said, camping on the strip of land to the east of the town alongside the Mediterranean, they could go swimming in the sea and had generous leave from 2-8pm when they could visit the European Town where local Egyptians were barred from entering, as was custom and practice right across much of the Empire.

On 5 January, Reg's D Company travelled south by rail in a violent gale that blew fine sand into their faces, before detraining at El Kap station, a position ten miles south of Port Said on the west bank of the Canal. Here, they were deployed for the first time in what, in theory, was a front line position. This was serious soldiering now, although in reality there was no immediate Turkish threat, and yet the men must have felt a certain frisson as they took up their defensive positions ready to repel invaders, rumoured to be heading their way across the Sinai Desert. This was not such an unlikely event because the Turkish 4th Army under Djemal Pasha – but really led by the German General Kress von Kressenstein – had attacked the Canal a year previously and on 3 February 1915 had actually got two companies across the Canal at Ismailia, before being forced to retreat back into the Sinai desert, losing 2,000 men including 700 prisoners.

While the riflemen dug shallow trenches and built sangars – breastworks above ground – with sand bags, Reg and the signallers were kept busy running out telephone lines to platoon and company positions and setting up a signal station that would link D Company to Battalion Headquarters back at Port Said. Reg also found that in the bright sunlight the heliograph could be seen at a considerable distance; he even claimed that in the flat desert its messages could sometimes be read thirty miles away.

Meanwhile, A Company, and later C Company, spent January defending the Mediterranean coast road due south east of Port Said, where there were important oil company facilities along the old caravan route to Palestine. The land behind their positions had been flooded for miles to create a natural barrier against a Turkish flanking movement, and here the Battalion shared duties with a battalion of the East Yorkshires of the 92nd Brigade. In February, the Battalion was assigned the defence of a section of the canal further south, around El Kantara and El Ferdan, nearer to Ismailia. Here Reg found there already was an existing signal station and among the units he had to provide with telephone lines was the Mysore Lancers in positions three miles away.

Reg, and many of the other lads, got on well with the cavalrymen from southern India who were very friendly towards their British comrades in arms. They had been out in the Middle East since October 1914, when Indian regular forces were drafted in to defend the Canal against an expected Turkish attack. They helped see off the Turkish assault in January/February 1915 and later were part of Allenby's victorious campaign through Palestine and Syria

A group of 12th Battalion signallers in Egypt with Reg in the middle row on the right.

12th Battalion Signallers with three different forms of equipment. The soldier standing is using his flags to send a semaphore message, a field telephone can be seen on the left and the sergeant in the centre is using a telescope to read distant heliograph messages.

in 1917-18. Reg admired their personal bearing and their esprit de corps, but he drew the line at their curries; that was a culinary step too far for a lad from Hillsborough at that time.

The 12th Battalion companies now had well-constructed defensive positions six miles out in the desert and on one occasion a patrol of the City Battalion saw a Turkish patrol at a distance, but they seemed in no mood to engage and would only be a reconnaissance patrol checking on British positions. Later, Reg would help lay down wires and create a signal station at Hill 80, about as far to the east as the Battalion got in the time they were in Egypt.

For leisure activity, the troops swam in the Canal, using a moored barge as a diving platform and there were impromptu swimming races against the Barnsleys with the Sheffielders claiming they always won. To cross the Canal, they had an iron boat with a continuous static rope that the passengers used to haul the boat across from side to side. Reg recalled:

'One day we thought we could beat an oncoming Liner and get across before it reached us–but we didn't! The taut rope was still high in the water and got entwined in the propeller of the Liner and we started to be pulled towards the hull of the ship and disaster. Fortunately, the rope snapped and we were all tipped into the Canal and had to swim for the bank. Fortunately at the edge it was not very deep and we could walk out and scramble up the side. The Liner never knew and certainly did not stop, and we didn't get into trouble because no-one in authority saw what had happened!'

The Battalion stayed in the central area of the Canal, north of Lake Timsah, until they got their orders to sail to France in early March. The temperature during the day was now considerably warmer and their serge uniforms could be stiflingly hot during the day. Whereas Reg and the others could take off their tunics, they could not remove their trousers, and so they were relieved when the order came to cut the trouser legs and make them into a pair of shorts. At night, when it was cold again, this still did not seem such a good idea, but the real fault was with the Army that had not provided them with lightweight khaki drill uniforms before they left England, only a solar topee. The sight of some of their officers wearing their new lightweight uniforms that they had got Port Said tailors to run up for them, did not improve their mood, even if many of the officers only got their lightweight uniforms delivered just as the Battalion was leaving for France.

On 28 February, an Advance Party left for France and the men knew it was just a matter of time before they were off. The 11th Division, recently returned from hard fighting at Gallipoli, was gradually taking over their positions and among their battalions was the 6th Service Battalion The York and Lancaster Regiment. They would stay on in Egypt to recuperate and reorganise until early July but would be long gone by the time of the next Turkish offensive across the Sinai desert in August, an offensive that was repulsed at the battle of Romani, 25 miles south east of Port Said, leading to another Turkish withdrawal and one that decisively marked the end of the attempts by the Turks to capture the Suez Canal.

Once the Battalion was back at Port Said awaiting embarkation, Reg had time for some shopping for souvenirs and swimming, but on the night of 10 March, the platoons were ferried out to their troopship at anchor in the harbour and settled in. Their new ship, HMT *Briton*, was a Union Castle liner that had taken troops out to South Africa during the Boer War but she could accommodate around 2,000 troops. So she sailed for France with two companies of the 14th Bn York & Lancaster and two companies of the 18th Bn (2nd Bradford Pals) West Yorks, as well as the City Battalion.

Reg had enjoyed his time in Egypt, seen something of the fabled Middle East and there had been no one killed in action, although one man, a reporter on the *Sheffield Daily Telegraph* who came from Rotherham, was left behind with appendicitis and unfortunately died in hospital on 17 March. They had also had their first court-martial in mid-January when a sergeant was reduced to the ranks, but Reg never found out why.

The first day out in the Mediterranean there was rough weather and choppy seas and many of the men were sea-sick again. But for Reg the bigger tragedy was that someone, he assumed a sailor, had stolen a precious leather belt studded with the cap badges of many of the regiments and corps that Reg had met up with during his time in Egypt.

The Egyptian interlude, though, was something he would never forget. This was 'Join the Army and see the World' soldiering just like in peacetime, but where they were now going was an altogether different prospect. As they sailed westwards Reg and many others must have wondered if they would still be alive at the end of 1916, as everyone by now knew about the grim reality of the Western Front, even if you could not imagine how bad it really could be until you were actually there.

Chapter 7

'Worry? I never worry!!'
March-June 1916

Reg, on the other hand, always said he was not worried by what lay ahead. Certainly in later years, when asked what contributed to his incredibly long life, he always emphasized that he never worried, and maybe he was lucky enough throughout his life not to be faced with the worries and fears that assail most people.

Standing by the rails, enchanted by the beauty of the southern French coast, as the HMT *Briton* sailed closer to Marseille on the morning of 15 March, Reg's thoughts were for the moment far from the battles to come. Once inside the harbour of one of the world's great ports, where the shipping of many nations lay at anchor, he looked on spellbound at the grandeur of the scene, where the mountains formed a majestic backdrop to the panorama of the city dominated by its great Basilica of Notre-Dame de la Garde and its formidable guardian fortresses. This was more tourism than soldiering, seeing romantic sounding places for the first time, intoxicating for a lad who three months earlier had never been out of England, indeed had not often been out of Yorkshire and the next door counties.

The band of the West Yorkshires played the Battalion in to their dock, with a selection that Reg and the lads thought was pretty impressive. After the *Marseillaise* to pay respects to their French hosts, there were current favourites, including Ivor Novello's great new hit 'Keep the Home Fires Burning' that the Battalion had adopted as their signature tune, because it so encapsulated their thoughts and longings while they were overseas.

A change of orders meant that they had to remain on board at the quayside for twenty-four hours until their train was ready, so the men had an uncomfortable night kipping down anywhere they could because they had handed in their hammocks. Reg was less than pleased when so many officers were allowed ashore while they were cooped up on board, but in the morning, there were other interesting things to see such as their first sight of their 'enemy'; German prisoners of war in their shabby field grey uniforms working on the dockside. Most of the Battalion would never have met a German before the war, although Reg probably knew German shop keepers in Hillsborough, but all who saw those German prisoners were impressed with their manly appearance and bearing. Reg thought many of them looked cheerful, no doubt happy to be out of the war with a very good chance of surviving and one day returning to Germany, but others looked sullen and miserable.

German Prisoners at Marseille who helped unload equipment from Reg's ship. This was the first time almost all of the men in the 12th Battalion had seen an enemy soldier and it was a curious, if not eerie, experience.

A shock awaited Reg when they finally marched through Marseille to the station. There were one or two coaches on the train that would be carrying over 2,000 men of the 31st Division, but they were reserved for officers and NCOs. Reg and his pals found that they were allocated to a goods wagon that stated blatantly on the side *40 Hommes/8 Chevaux* and could only offer a dirty straw-filled floor as an amenity but no seat, no toilets or any cooking facilities. It was how the French Army transported its men around France and the 'Tommies' were not going to get anything better, just because they were English.

The journey however turned out to be a tourist's delight, and in Reg's wagon the large door (to accommodate the passage of *huit chevaux*) was kept wide open so everyone could see the magnificent countryside and towns they were passing through. First, they went along the Mediterranean coast then turned north up the Rhone Valley, with the Alps on their right hand side, through fabled cities like Arles and Avignon before stopping for tea at Orange, where they were treated as conquering heroes again. Perhaps these were the first 'Anglais' the locals had seen, proof of their ally coming to the aid of La France, and more than a few Sheffield men got kissed by local girls. There was no doubt of the warmth of the welcome in other towns up the line, unlike in Marseille where the locals had scarcely seemed to notice the newcomers.

Travelling through the night, they passed through Lyon and the next time they stopped it was for breakfast at Macon, where Reg discovered there was one advantage to being on a train:

'When the train stopped we took our billycans to the engine driver who gave us hot water from the engine's boiler, so we could make our tea. We had no idea that it had chemicals in it but it didn't seem to do us any harm, but we must have drunk some muck in the time we were in France. We went for hot water every time we stopped after that.

'Breakfast was no great picnic, nothing hot, just the basic rations we had been issued for the journey, mostly biscuits and corned beef. Also there were no toilet facilities on the train, so we had to wait for a halt and then line up along the side of the track!'

Stopping at Dijon, they all got a reality check. On the opposite line at the station was a train full of seriously injured French soldiers, swathed in bloody bandages and with a fair number of recent amputees among them. Those of the Battalion who could speak French soon found out that they had come from the battle at Verdun, where the German offensive was almost a month old and where the French losses were already astronomically high.

Another uncomfortable night on the train brought them through Versailles and round the west side of Paris, then north through Amiens and a glimpse of the great cathedral. This was British Army territory now and men in khaki uniforms were everywhere. At each station and in fields alongside the line Reg could see British encampments and equipment, the retinue of an army of over one million men getting ready for comprehensive warfare, twentieth century style.

Finally, at 3pm on 18 March, they reached the rather nondescript small town of Pont Remy and detrained. The bridge that formed part of the town's name was over the Somme, a river that at that time meant little or nothing to the lads of the 12th Battalion, but soon would become embedded in British history as firmly as Agincourt, Trafalgar or Waterloo. This was not to be their final destination after two days on the train, for soon they were off again for a seven mile hike to Huppy, a very pleasant French village full of whitewashed houses with bold red roofs, where many of the women dressed in black with large white hats. It was a place that Reg, and so many in the Battalion, took an immediate liking to, finding the surrounding countryside familiarly like England, and they settled down for a week at Huppy finalising their training before their first spell in the trenches on the Somme Front.

On 25 March, the Battalion joined the rest of the Brigade for a four day march east to Bertrancourt, 70km away. Now they were closer to the Somme battlefield where the new British Fourth Army was holding the southern extremity of the British sector of the Western Front, a line of trenches that ran from the Ypres Salient in the north down to the River Somme in the south. An advance party under Major Hoette, comprising 10 officers and 40 NCOs had an easier journey when they were bussed to Courcelles, from where they were then taken into the trenches opposite Serre on 28 March. There they met up with a Territorial Force battalion, the 1/8th Bn Worcesters, who were holding the section of the line that was to become very familiar to the Sheffield men over the next few months.

Reg did not go with this advance group but when the Battalion eventually arrived in the area, he did go into the front line with a group of signallers to learn the ropes of trench routines.

'We got to Colincamps where the Brigade HQ was located behind our trenches. We had seen it taking a pasting the night before from the relative safety of Bertrancourt. We were a bit jumpy at first, every time we heard a shell come over we ducked even if it was miles away. We went up to the line at night and in the communication trench we could hardly see where

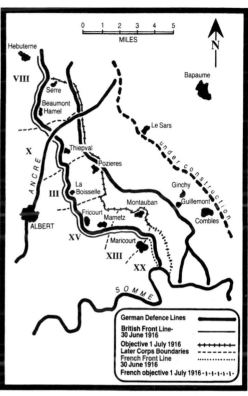

(Left) The British front line prior to 1 July 1916. (Right) The objectives for the Somme area on 1 July.

we were going so we just followed the chap in front who was following the guide from the Worcesters. When we got to the front line the advice from the soldiers there was always keep you head down and if you wanted to go to the latrines always go on your hands and knees. That was apparently so that Jerry cannot see a group hanging about waiting for their turn and send over a shell or a minenwerfer bomb. We signallers were shown where all the dugouts were and the communication equipment and where the telephone wires were laid. It was a very helpful visit but when we came out the next night, we were pleased to be back.'

The Battalion relieved the Worcesters on the night of the 2/3 April and the forward companies stood to at dawn on the firestep, peering through periscopes at the German line up the slope at Serre. They now had new items of equipment, as each man had already been given the 1915 pattern gas mask that was a primitive affair that fitted loosely at the bottom and was stuffed into a soldier's shirt. The other new item of equipment was the Brodie pattern British helmet, probably the most symbolic piece of equipment that any soldier in the First World War possessed. Designed as the answer to the unacceptable number of head wounds, it had taken the Army thirteen months to decide to give soldiers this very basic protection. Based on the design of an English medieval archer's helmet and universally known as a 'Tin Hat', when improved by Sheffield's Sir Robert Hadfield's process of adding 12 per cent manganese to the steel it gave good protection against falling shrapnel, flying stones and cascading earth. The French had produced the first helmet in summer of 1915 and the British and Germans soon followed with helmet designs that were so distinctive that it was easy to identify friend or foe. Reg and the others were given a helmet each on the night they took over the Worcester's trenches. When they came out of the line, they had to hand them over to the relieving battalion because there were not enough helmets available in the Fourth Army for everyone to have their own at that time. Later, Reg would recall:

> 'The trenches were in a good condition, with duckboards in the bottom, but we found that when it rained they soon became flooded and you were stood in water. The trench was about 6 foot deep and 3-4 foot wide and you couldn't pass anyone without scraping against them.'

Reg, like the other members of the Battalion, soon became familiar with the geography of their sector of trenches. The front line ran from 'John Copse' to beyond 'Matthew Copse' and the support line was called 'Rob Roy' trench, with communication trenches called 'Nairne', 'Jordan', 'Le Cateau' and 'Excema' and the reserve, or third line, called 'Campion'. There were 4th, 5th, 6th and 7th Lines as well, so there was some considerable degree of defence in depth if the German ever changed their strategy and attacked.

> 'There was a lot of wire in front of our trenches and wiring parties used to go out regularly and repair any damage from German shells or bombs. There were sections of the wire that could be moved so patrols and wiring parties could get out into No Man's Land at night. The German wire did not seem like ours and seemed to have no breaks in it and we found that out the hard way on the 1st July.
>
> 'One of the reasons why our trenches were in good condition was because they had once been the German front line, but they had pulled back up the slope some time before we arrived, but they left their dugouts intact and they were far superior to the ones we constructed. The dugout where the Colonel was at Battalion Headquarters was as good as my cellar at home with wooden walls and comfy beds and down a steep flight of steps. Unfortunately, they were the wrong way round for us. Dugouts were always built on the side facing the enemy to stop random shells, mortar bombs or

rifle grenades flying in and at least twice when we were at Serre people were killed in the dugouts because this happened.

'I didn't get to live in the dugout, even though I was now attached to Battalion Headquarters. I had to kip on the fire step near the dugout, so to provide a bit of protection you were allowed to dig an alcove (some called them funk holes) about 18 inches under the parapet. Sometimes when it rained hard we would put groundsheets over the trench to try and keep dry.'

For the first three days, D and C Company were in the front line trenches with A and B Companies back in reserve. The 12th Battalion covered a front of 1,300 yards, quite long by Western Front norms, with a battalion of the KOSB (King's Own Scottish Borderers) to their left and the 14th (Barnsley) York & Lancaster Battalion to their right. On their first morning, the Germans put on a robust 'Hate' session, firing a substantial number of shells, bombs and rifle grenades into the City Battalion's trenches, presumably intended to unnerve the newcomers to the line. After that, life returned to normal in the trenches with little activity during the day, but a lot of heavy work repairing and improving the trenches and the wire during the night. Especially hard work was making sure the right angle traverses along the length of the trench were strong and fully intact, so that they could stop blast and shrapnel from an explosion in one section of the trench going very far before it reached a solid wall.

Nevertheless, on the first morning in the trenches the Battalion suffered its first fatality when Private Alexander McKenzie was killed by a rifle grenade that came over the parapet and landed right where he was standing. He was the son of a regular soldier, Sergeant McKenzie, who was lately the instructor to the Sheffield Territorial Artillery, and he had been a clerk with Moss and Gamble Brothers before enlisting. That night, a burial party took him to the rear and Major Hoette helped carry his body, He was buried in the cemetery at the old sugar factory, whilst distant gunfire and exploding star shells created an eerie background as the Padre conducted his funeral. His death had a sobering effect on all the Battalion but especially on Reg's D Company who knew him best.

Yet within a remarkably short period of time Reg and the others got used to the routine and difficulties of trench life.

'We started with lice as soon as we got into the trenches. You itched all over and when we were in the rear you could hear them crackle when we ironed them out. We used Keating's powder when in the trenches but the lice were difficult to shift and soon came back any way. Rats were another horror of trench life. They grew large on the bodies of dead soldiers and all the rubbish that was around in No Man's Land. As ammunition did not seem to be rationed we used to shoot them. I once woke up and found a rat on my chest only inches from my face trying to gnaw through my haversack to get at the biscuits.'

Rations would be carried up the communication trench at night and Reg like everyone else had to do this duty at some time.

> 'We frequently got stew which was very nourishing and easy to prepare and distribute, plus tins of biscuits that were very hard but tasty. Sometimes we would crunch them up and make a sort of porridge. We also had tins of corned beef and cans of Maconochies, plenty of cheese and tins of jam, almost always apple and plum but very occasionally strawberry, in fact we always had plenty to eat but very rarely got any bread in the line. To make tea we would soak a sandbag in paraffin and set it alight to heat the water in our billycan, although water was in short supply and sometimes I shaved using cold tea I had saved because it was the only liquid available.'

Reg and the signallers avoided a lot of the routine work in the trenches, but they had plenty to do ensuring communications were maintained between Companies and Battalion HQ and also between the Battalion and the Brigade. One of Reg's jobs was copying out all the new codes that came in Morse and tabulate them for the Orderly Sergeant, who would issue them out to the companies and platoons. Another of his jobs was sending Brigade HQ the details of the rations required by the Battalion in Morse, and although his work was now mainly dealing with telephones and keeping the many wires intact, Reg still had his two semaphore flags with him should the need arise for sending visual messages, as he explained:

> 'We had to ensure that if the wires were cut we mended them as soon as possible. We had to go out over the top at night and find any breaks that had been caused by shelling and fit the two ends together. We found our way around by trial and error but after a while I knew the area between our trenches like the back of my hand. There was so much rubbish strewn around that it helped you identify where you were. Sometimes we would just lay a complete new line to save time rather than hunt about for breaks. The frightening bit was if you were ordered out to mend the line in daytime and you were out of the trenches crawling about certain that German snipers could see you. But you just had to do it!'

On 12 April, after a nine day baptism in the trenches, the Battalion handed over to a battalion of the East Yorkshires, when 92nd Brigade took over the Colincamps sector of the line. The lads were glad to be out, happy to have survived and maintained their spirits on their first tour at the Front. They sang all the way back to the huts at Bertrancourt but they had lost another couple of their comrades and some of their number were showing signs of shell shock. They had often been deluged with rain during their period in the trenches and when they got back to

Bertrancourt, there were large vats of lukewarm water that could accommodate eight men at a time and Reg luxuriated in a long soak that helped to restore some sense of normal existence.

While Reg was in Egypt and then back in France, Vivian was still stuck with the 15th Reserve Battalion, moving round every so often from one camp to another. In November, they were at Brocton Camp, one of the camps on Cannock Chase close to where his parent battalion had been until the end of July.

Then in December, when Vivian was still hoping he would be recalled to the City Battalion who were clearly about to go abroad, probably to France, he was again overlooked. When they went to Egypt instead just before Christmas, he must have felt unwanted. He certainly felt unappreciated, especially as he was always in command of a company yet the powers-that-be could not even give him a second pip, let alone the captaincy that he felt he deserved. He found out later that Captain Beley, whom he considered a friend from civilian life, had written in a report that Vivian was not up to the job and he felt sure this had blocked his promotion. He found this particularly galling because he believed he had run Beley's Company for him when they had served together at Redmires after the main body of the Battalion had left for Penkridge in May.

The one consolation was that he could occasionally get leave and see May, who was now several months pregnant and only too pleased her husband was still in England and not at the Western Front, or even the Suez Canal. Leaving a wife and family was a burden that so many in the army had to face up to. Many would be killed before seeing their child born, but it was not in Vivian's character to want to miss the action abroad because of these family considerations, painful and distressing though a parting would have been.

By Christmas 1915 Vivian and the 15th Battalion had moved to Colsterdale Camp, seven miles west of Masham high up in the Yorkshire Dales. This was the camp built on Leeds Water Department land that had been first used as the base for the Leeds Pals (the 15th Bn West Yorkshires) and was probably even bleaker than Redmires. Certainly, it was remote, with no convenient towns or villages nearby, nor two pubs on the doorstep as the Sheffield Pals had enjoyed at Redmires. Vivian found it pretty uncongenial, with constant snow during that winter adding to the discomfort of the place and the frustrations of the job.

There was leave for the men starting just before Christmas until the middle of February, but Vivian missed out on the prized Christmas leave and so spent Christmas away from his new wife and his family. Instead he did the honours of carving several turkeys and serving the men in three of the huts and standing the sergeants drinks when he visited their mess. Before lunch, there had been a church service in the dining hall and then he had refereed a Sheffield-Barnsley football match that Sheffield won, although in Vivian's estimation they threw away at least ten opportunities to score more goals. For amusement after the Christmas lunch, there was a rifle shooting match with the Barnsleys which ended up in a tie and to round off the festivities, Vivian got into a long argument with the Padre that ended about 2.30am in the morning.

Boxing Day was another day off duties and Vivian took the opportunity to practice riding a horse but fell off and was later 'as stiff as a poker'. He had written to the family to tell them not to bother with presents but had bought himself a revolver for £3 10/- which he thought was an absolute bargain, although one would have assumed that as an officer he would be supplied with the standard Webley. He did write and say he would like a diary and he explained why in the letter:

'Because I have a lot of things to think about. I have 249 men on my present strength and I think the City "Worthies" ought to raise another Battalion, if Barnsley can manage two why can't Sheffield? Acting in loco parentis to so many men is enormous. I shall never fear the task of clothing, feeding, and acting as a father confessor to a large family after the experience I have had. Of course, some company commanders put the fear of God into their men but that is not my idea of an officer's job. One thing they impressed on us at Camberley was that you should be a friend in need to all of the men and I have found that they never take advantage of it and that just shows how bloody marvellous are the majority of the men we have.'

Vivian would remain at Colsterdale till the middle of March, until the day the Battalion marched twenty miles over the hills to Hipswell camp that was part of the huge complex being built at Catterick to house an expanded British Army after conscription had been introduced in January 1916. Hipswell was just a staging post for the Battalion and after a week they moved on to Newsham Camp at Blyth on the south Northumberland coast. Here, they continued training drafts for the three York & Lancaster Pals Battalions but the Battalion was also tasked with guarding the harbour and the coastline either side of the mouth of the River Blyth.

Vivian had many complaints about how the training was organised but when guarding the harbour and the coast, he felt they were making a real contribution to the war effort. After all, a German Battlecruiser Squadron had raided the north east coast in mid-December 1914 and done a lot of damage at Hartlepool, Whitby and Scarborough. He wrote to his family:

'Our principal job is guarding the harbour which is used as a busy submarine, torpedo boat and destroyer base. At present we have ten submarines and HMS Talisman in harbour. The Talisman is an oil driven destroyer that has an official speed of 35 knots but is really capable of nearer 50. It is most interesting watching these boats practising and how they can turn round and hare off in the opposite direction at terrific speed.

'My Company guard about 300 yards of coast with a fairly substantial trench running along the length of the position. It is our job to improve it and the barbed wire entanglements. There are twelve guard posts in my sector and it can take hours to get round them all. The other night I started at midnight and by 3am I had only inspected the posts on one side of the river.

'I am responsible for the safety of the Customs House, the coaling staithes, the dry docks and the river banks (the latter to prevent the landing of undesirable aliens) as well as the submarines and the destroyers. We also put a guard on all ships that come into the harbour as no one is allowed ashore without a pass. Most of the ships are Norwegian, a few Swedish and there was a Russian ship in recently. We have two ships that are under arrest. One arrived back without the captain and mate and we think they were pushed overboard and we found that the other had an important spy on board.'

Although he felt he was undervalued by the Battalion hierarchy, Vivian never had any doubts about his own competence. He considered his Company was the best in the Battalion but he did not think they were a patch on the earlier volunteers and later he was pretty scornful of the quality of the new men that he had to train after conscription was introduced. When Major General Montgomery, the GOC in command of all of the Tyne Garrison, inspected the Battalion, he was directed towards Vivian's Company, the only one to be closely inspected. This convinced Vivian that his Company was regarded as the best by the CO, although he was not prepared to recommend him for promotion. Vivian complained in one letter to his brother:

'If I had known what I was in for I should never have stuck to running a Reserve Company in the 15th Battalion. It is very heartbreaking work to put your utmost into training the men and then find that they are taken for the Barnsleys when sent to France. The two will never mix and part of the problem is that the Barnsleys' training companies are not turning out good enough men. So my men get chosen to make up the numbers.'

Vivian was also aware that the Sheffield men were very unhappy about being sent to the 13th and 14th Battalions. They had joined the Sheffield Pals and expected to serve with the Sheffield Pals but like many recruits by 1916, they got sent to whatever battalion or regiment needed them. Their plight made the Sheffield papers and the City Council also made strong representations, so that the 15th Battalion thereafter made some attempt to accommodate these concerns, but the demands for reinforcements of whatever battalion took priority.

On 31 March, at 3am in the morning, the Battalion was told to find 100 men for the 12th Bn immediately, another 100 for the 13th Bn and 200 men for the 14th Bn, and in the middle of April, Vivian had to find another 120 men from his company with half of them going to the Barnsleys. As the CO came from one of the Barnsley battalions (before the war he had been an Alderman and Chairman of the Education Committee on the Town Council), he probably got wind of Vivian's attitude towards their two battalions and this cannot have increased his enthusiasm for promoting his Sheffield company commander. There was always going to be some friction between the men from a large city and men from a smaller neighbouring town and there was also the social divide between a middle-class battalion and one that was predominately working class. It is surprising that there was not more trouble, but Vivian was not the sort of person to keep his views to himself and he probably did not help create much harmony in the camp between the different companies.

In a letter to the family in the middle of June Vivian wrote despairingly, 'I think promotion is permanently off as the powers-that-be regard officers in Reserve Battalions as either wash outs or lead swingers or both'. However, he found some solace on the golf course. He discovered south of the river a pleasant links course at Newbiggin and got his clubs sent up from home. He had a regular partner in one of the other officers and he found the course a pleasant distraction, especially as it had some dramatic greens perched on the cliff tops. Although even here he had some complaints which he mentioned in a letter home:

> 'The course is amusing for the first ten holes but the remainder is spoilt by the public wandering up and down the fairways regardless of the possible consequences. It reminds you of the problems they had at the Sheffield municipal course.'

He was also concerned about his nephew, Gordon, who was his brother George's son. He had just gone to Winchester College in Hampshire, a school that was something of a cut above Wesley College where Vivian and his brothers had been educated. Clearly the family had ambitions for the next generation, although the bad news was that Gordon was not settling in at all well at Winchester, something that was not uncommon at famous boarding schools whose traditions were firmly fixed in the Victorian era.

More important though than all of these travails was the news on 4 May that May had given birth to their son, a boy they called John Vivian, who one day would be a captain himself in another desperate and equally horrific war. Although his father will have seen him several times, John Simpson himself would have no memories of Vivian for he was just under two years old when his father was killed at Vieux Berquin in April 1918. Vivian would always be 'the man in the photograph who was my father', as happened to so many children whose fathers did not come back from the Front.

Reg, and the rest of the 12th Battalion, were back in the trenches for three more tours before the great assault of 1 July. Twice in May and once in the middle of June the Battalion returned to the line opposite Serre and on each occasion their arrival was met by a heavy artillery concentration from the Germans opposite. On 2 May, they relieved the 14th York and Lancaster and the German shelling went on all through the morning and again in the afternoon when they concentrated their fire on the extreme left of the Battalion's line at John Copse.

On the second day back a disaster that was waiting to happen, did happen. A *minenwerfer* bomb flew into the open door of the company telephone dugout where C Company were holding the line. It killed six men inside, including one of the Battalion's great personalities, CSM Joe Ellis, a veteran of the Matabele and Boer Wars who had served with the 2nd Y&L in India and Malta and ended his military career as an instructor with the Hallamshire TF Battalion. He was familiar to many of the Battalion from his civvy street job, where he was a formidably

Vivian in the garden of the Belcher's house with his son, John, born May 1916.

impressive commissionaire at Walsh's department store on the High Street, the fashionable place to shop and take afternoon tea for Sheffield's middle class. Reg, like all the Battalion, would have been saddened by his death and chastened by the fact that the explosion took place in a telephone dug-out where he could have been himself at the time. To add to Reg's despondency, one of the dead was a signaller he knew well, Private Percy Richards, who had worked at the Town Hall.

On 6 May, the Battalion was relieved by the 12th East Yorkshires and went back to billets five miles back at Bois de Warnimont, far enough away from the danger to relax. This quiet, undamaged village was a beautiful place full of wild flowers and majestic tall trees, where villagers were still working in the fields harvesting their crops. But they were not there for long as the 12th Battalion were soon back in the trenches on the night of 15/16 May when they relieved the 1st Bradford Pals Battalion, the 16th West Yorkshires. This time, the German artillery started in visceral intensity before the handover was complete and the trenches were already being knocked about and caving in before the Battalion was fully deployed.

This was more than the usual hate session to welcome a new unit to the line, because the German regiment opposite had more ambitious plans for the evening. At around 1am, a large German raiding party was seen outside C Company's position at John Copse heading toward its main target, the 4th Royal Berkshires in the next set of trenches to the north. The bombardment had cut the British wire in several places and the German raiders got into the Berkshires' trenches and caused them to fall back to their support trench causing many casualties, including around 40 killed.

Their withdrawal from the front line left the 12th Battalion exposed on its northern flank, already a weak spot because of the right-angle bend in the British front line at John Copse, and some of the German raiders got into the Battalion's communication trench and attacked C Company from behind. This put the Sheffield lads in a dangerous position but cool leadership by two lieutenants, Middleton and Grant, temporarily in command of B and C Companies, held off the attackers and eventually forced them to retreat into No Man's Land and back to their own trenches, no doubt with one or two terrified Berkshire lads dragged along as prisoners. Meanwhile, German bombs and shells rained down on known command positions and No 11 post was obliterated, with many men being buried alive and others killed outright by the shells or suffocation.

This was the first time the Sheffield men had seen Germans face to face in action and they acquitted themselves well; seven men would be awarded the Military Medal for their gallantry that night, including Sergeant Henry Crozier, who had so charmed his audience by his singing at the farewell concert at Redmires, an event that now seemed a lifetime away.

Reg's job that night and the following day was to go out and repair the telephone wires and restore contact between Battalion HQ and all the command posts, dangerous work when shells were still falling and when snipers had a clear view in the morning. The bombardment ceased about 0230 hrs but the damage it had done was evident in the chaos of the Battalion's trenches. The front line scarcely existed on C Company's front and the communication trenches of Nairne, Le Cateau and Excema were badly damaged as was Rob Roy, the support line. Many men had rushed to dig out their comrades while a fierce bombardment was continuing. Among them was Private Robert Mathews, a medical student at Sheffield University before joining up, who was killed by artillery fire whilst trying to dig out a comrade who had been buried by an earlier shell.

Altogether, the Battalion had 15 killed and 46 wounded that night. When they went back into the trenches on 14 June, they experienced another difficult time as the Germans were subjecting the Battalion's line to regular bombardments. They knew a major British offensive was coming and they wanted to disrupt the preparations. After their four tours of the trenches from April to June, the Battalion had lost 39 men killed, with another seven dying of their wounds later. By the standards of the Western Front in 1916 these were almost light casualties. There were also 68 wounded and twelve men were diagnosed with shell shock, something the High Command was very ambiguous about. But the Staff, who may have had years of colonial soldiering experience, would never have had to undergo such intensive artillery bombardments as were now commonplace. Men could not only be rendered speechless, deaf, blind, some also shook uncontrollably, clearly losing any control over their mental faculties, becoming totally paralysed and unable to react at all. What is more amazing is that after hours of bombardment, the shelling did not drive the majority of the men insane, especially if they had been buried by explosions and seen their comrades blown to smithereens.

Reg, fortunately for him, was one who escaped the effects of shell shock and his equilibrium was quickly restored on the many occasions when he left the front line. In late June, when it was clear that massive preparations were being made for the coming offensive, he took a day off for some family business. He later recalled how his sister, Edith, had sent him a letter telling him that her boyfriend was in France serving with the 8th Battalion of the KOYLI and if he saw him give him her love. Reg knew Dan Edwards, the boyfriend, because they both worshipped at Wadsley Parish Church and he was a mate from back home.

'As a signaller we were responsible for telephone communications and being connected to Brigade it was surprising what you got to know about. When times were slack you could pass the time talking to the chap on the switchboard and I asked him if he knew if the 8th KOYLI were in our area. He soon got back to me and said they were camped at Albert, one of the main towns behind the Somme lines.'

So Reg took the opportunity of a free day to cycle over to Albert from Bois de Warnimont some distance away, uncertain whether he would be blocked by security checks and asked some awkward questions by the Military Police. He explained later:

'I borrowed a bike, put on my blue and white signaller's armband denoting I was on duty, stuck a standard brown envelope in my belt to make it look more official and headed off for Albert prepared to bluff it out if I was stopped by the MPs.'

L/Cpl Dan Edwards of the 8th Bn KOYLI, a friend of both of Reg's sisters who was killed on the First Day of the Somme offensive.

As Reg rode along the back roads towards Albert, he was amazed by the scale of the British Army's preparations. Everywhere he looked, the number of wagons, guns and horses was staggering as were the huge numbers of khaki clad soldiers, seemingly from almost every regiment in the army and the Dominions.

He found Dan Edwards without too much difficulty and spent a pleasant afternoon with him reminiscing about Hillsborough and Wadsley and passing on Edith's love and best wishes. He left to go back to Warnimont and they wished each other all the best for the 'Big Push' due any day soon.

He never saw Dan Edwards again. When the 8th Bn KOYLI went into action on 1 July, Dan was killed in action along with so many in his battalion. Later his name would be included on the memorial plaque in Wadsley Parish Church. Dan was listed among the missing for several months, his body no doubt lost somewhere in No Man's Land but when it was confirmed in early 1917, his death must have been absolutely devastating for Edith and also for Ada, who regarded Dan as a good friend. Edith remained single throughout the next decade although she did eventually get married to the Rev. Samuel Snell in 1932, but Ada never married.

Chapter 8

'You will have to stick it!! You must stick it!!'
Serre, 1 July 1916

On the morning of the attack on Serre, Reg shaved as usual. He always shaved when in the lines and saw no reason why he should not do it before the forthcoming offensive, the most serious challenge that the 12th Battalion had ever faced. 'If I was going to be killed then I wanted to be clean shaven. I used a cut-throat razor of course, and every time a shell went over or exploded, I nicked myself,' he wrote later.

Already by that time nothing seemed to be going right, and the start of the attack was still several hours away. Firstly, the Battalion had expected the attack to be on 29 June, but terrible weather conditions had delayed it for two days. Under his original orders, Reg was expecting to be kept back at camp at Bois de Warnimont with around 200 men of the Battalion under Lt. Middleton, who would form a cadre around which the Battalion could be rebuilt if all went very wrong with the 'Attack'. During the afternoon of 30 June, Reg's orders were changed and he was ordered to move up to the front line to be part of the team operating out of Battalion HQ, based in dugouts at John Copse, arguably the most exposed place on the Brigade's section of the line.

Although he was no longer safe behind the lines, Reg was philosophical about his new duties, right in the heart of the action, recalling, 'I did not know if I was pleased or not. Most of us just accepted the orders we were given. You did not bother with the why and wherefore. You just got on with it.'

As if the Battalion's task was not difficult enough, on the morning of 30 June, the CO of the Battalion, Lt. Col. Crosthwaite, finally went sick and left the Battalion never to return. He had been struggling during the weeks in the trenches with ill health, most probably a result of his injuries at Ypres the year before and had been given periods of sick leave to help him get fit again. If the attack had been on 29 June as originally intended, Crosthwaite would still have been in charge, but it is fair to assume that no British colonel would willingly leave his men at the moment of their most dangerous and critical operation when clearly many were going to get killed or wounded.

This would have been a major setback for the Battalion, but colonels got killed in action in the First World War and automatically the second in command took over. But Major Clough had himself gone sick at the beginning of June, finally succumbing to a problem of synovitis of his left knee, which may have been middle age wear and tear exacerbated by the demands of trench duty, even in summer conditions at the Front. A former secretary of the Yorkshire Rifle Association and crack marksman, he had been the second in command of the 12th Battalion from the very start in Sheffield, and as such was a familiar figure to the men when deputising for absent infirm colonels, whether Mainwaring or Crosthwaite.

The Battalion now found themselves on the day they most needed cool professional and inspirational leadership feeling rather like a team in a Wembley Cup Final who have had their captain and most experienced player withdraw from the side on the morning of the match. The Brigade sent for Major Plackett, the former branch bank manager from Hillsborough, who had initially commanded B Company and had Boer War experience during his years as a volunteer officer with the Imperial Yeomanry, the 4th York & Lancaster Volunteers and the Yorkshire Dragoons.

He too was expecting to miss the battle on 1 July because for seven weeks he had been the Chief Instructor at the 31st Division's school where specialist techniques were taught to unit instructors. The first that Reg and the others knew of these changes was when Major Plackett appeared and took the parade of the Battalion at the Bois de Warnimont camp on 30 June, to hear the words of inspiration from no less a figure than the Corps Commander himself. Lt. Gen. Sir Aylmer Hunter-Weston KCB DSO who was known, not necessarily sympathetically, as Hunter–Bunter to his troops, did his best to say all the right things to encourage a sense of certain victory and limited personal danger. Perhaps he believed what he was saying, or maybe he knew there was a disaster in the making down the road in less than twenty-four hours. He gathered the men around him, barking:

> 'The Battalion is fighting for the highest of ideals. Fighting for the defence of home and of Empire. Your lot is a very heavy one, and a huge responsibility is shared equally by every individual. No individual soldier may say he has no responsibility. You are Englishmen and now you have your opportunity to shine. You will stick it! YOU MUST STICK IT!! I salute each officer, NCO and man!'

It is not clear what the men of the Battalion thought about his stirring words. All general officers looked the same to them with their smart uniforms, polished brass and leatherwear, and especially the regulation military moustache. It was right, though, that the Corps Commander came and said his piece, but the Battalion had been preparing for this attack for almost two years and they were certainly ready for the fight. Nor did Hunter-Weston's assumptions about the devastation caused to the

German trenches by the massive British bombardment they had witnessed for the last six days seem implausible. Since they had been in France, the Sheffield men had seen the British wire cut to pieces by German artillery, their front line trenches obliterated and many of their comrades entombed in collapsed dugouts and trench walls.

Major Alfred Plackett, listening to the speech, must have been wondering about his own state of preparation for the 'Big Day'. He had not been involved in the final planning for the assault. The specific orders to company commanders will have been worked out before he returned to the Battalion and they were quite complicated.

The Battalion's front had been narrowed to 300 yards running from the northern end of Mark Copse to John Copse. The other lead battalion in the 94th Brigade was the 11th Bn East Lancashires and they held a similar area of frontage south from Mark Copse to Matthew Copse. Around 700 officers and men would be in the 12th Battalion's four assaulting companies, only 70 per cent of the total strength of the Battalion, and the lead companies would be A Company on the right led by 24-year-old Captain William Clarke, and C Company on the left commanded by 47-year-old Captain William Colley. Colley had recently been fortunate in getting home leave, where he feared he was seeing Yorkshire for the last time. As a more mature man, he could weigh up the chances of a company commander in the 200 yard advance to the German front line and realise he was not going to make it, whilst younger, and perhaps less imaginative, men felt death could not possibly happen to them. Unfortunately, for many this optimism proved to be no defence when faced with the reality of war.

The two forward companies, A Company on the right (next to the 11th East Lancashires) and C Company on the left, would advance before the British barrage

stopped and take up positions half way across No Man's Land, thereby shortening the distance to the German front line. They would form the first two waves and each wave was made up of two of the company's platoons. They would be followed by B and D Companies whose start lines were 400 yards further back at Monk and Campion trenches and they would move forward at 7.29am to be ready to support the two leading companies.

Captain William Colley, a former Sheffield City Councillor and well-known businessman, who had commanded C Company since the formation of the Battalion expected to be killed in the initial assault on the German trenches at Serre. He was right to be pessimistic as he was one of the first men to be killed in the attack.

Behind them was the 14th Bn. York and Lancaster who were one of the Brigade's back up battalions, who would follow C Company in file and form a defensive line on the flank of 94th Brigade's position facing north to meet any counter attack from the Germans south of Gommecourt. This deployment complemented the most significant part of the 12th Battalion's orders on 1 July that were designed to push the Germans out of Serre and then turn it into a British 'fortress' to protect the Fourth Army's northern flank against future German attacks. As the Third Army to their immediate north would play little part in the 1 July offensive, the 12th Battalion would be defending what could be seen as a vulnerable salient, where German attackers could break through and drive a wedge into British positions, thereby undermining any gains made further south on the Somme battlefield.

Reg remembered:

'It was about 7.30pm when we finally set off from Bois de Warnimont for the front lines and it was quite dark by the time we entered the communication trench system at Colincamps except for the vivid flashes of the artillery lighting up the sky. It was a real struggle moving down the communication trenches loaded up as we were. We signallers had a lot of extra kit to carry on top of our greatcoats, packs, rifles and webbing. I was carrying a telephone and a reel of wire and we had to splash our way along the flooded trench because with that weight we would have found it

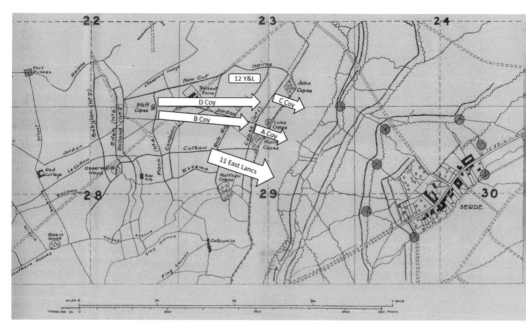

The map above shows attack by 12th Battalion on 1 July, led by A and C Companies.

impossible to climb out and go over the top to our assembly trench. As the going was so difficult, we took a longer time then was expected and only arrived in position at first light.'

The Germans were in no doubt about the day of the attack; they had been observing the British build-up for weeks and how the countryside opposite was now full of men clearly waiting for an assault. They had sent patrols out during the night and among other things found the marker tapes that the 12th Battalion had laid down to indicate the start lines for their attack. What they did not know was the time of the advance and assumed it would be at first light or shortly afterwards and so at 4.05am they opened up with their own very accurate counter barrage, aimed not just at the front line but later at the support trenches, especially Monk Trench, 500 yards to the British rear, to disrupt the deployment of B and D Companies, the third and fourth wave of the assault and prevent their easy passage forward. When the attack started, the Germans wanted to keep them back in the support trenches while their front-line machine guns and musketeers dealt with the first wave of attacking troops of Captain Colley's C Company and Captain Clarke's A Company.

The British plan for 1 July all along the front, but especially relevant at a *schwerpunkt* (strong point) like Serre, was predicated on four assumptions: that the massive bombardment would cut the German wire in very many places, therefore allowing troops rapid access through into the German lines without vulnerable bunching and 'queuing' for a chance to cross the wire; that the bombardment over so many days would have destroyed the German trench system so completely that they could not be defended and British troops would just cross the German first, second, third and fourth lines with comparative ease and could leave mopping up to support troops; and that German troops who had been more in the front line would be either dead, entombed or driven insane by the intensity of the bombardment, and therefore would be in no state to offer a coherent defence of their position and would retreat in the face of superior forces if they still could.

There was an unwritten fourth assumption, articulated in the final written message to the 94th Brigade by their relatively new temporary Brigadier, Hubert Rees DSO, their old Brigadier, G.T.C. Carter-Campbell, having gone sick and only returned to the Brigade on the 2 July, when he wrote, 'Englishmen have always proved better than Germans when the odds are heavily against them'; a viewpoint that is not particularly borne out by the events of history, but to men brought up in what still seemed to be the full glory of an Empire that covered a quarter of the globe's surface and a quarter of the world's population, English superiority was really taken for granted.

Nobody in the Battalion knew the time for the attack as only the Company Commanders had been informed. They also assumed it would be at first light when they would have been emerging out of the darkness heading east towards the German trenches. Reg had now arrived at Battalion HQ at John Copse and was relatively safe in the deep dugout that served as their HQ. Outside, men looked for any protection they could find, some in hastily constructed bombardment slits – more like Second World War slit trenches – just somewhere to hide until the hour of the attack. Reg recalled later:

> 'You can imagine how hectic Battalion HQ was at that time. Everyone rushing here, there and everywhere, officers making last minute arrangements and everyone more than a little nervous but determined to put on a good show. The intensity of the German barrage was unexpected. This was intended to be our hour when the British artillery plastered their trenches, and somehow the City Battalion men hadn't expected to be worrying about the enemy bombardment just their own personal preparation and their private thoughts. Funny thing about the barrage was that you were more worried about showing you were scared in front of your mates than actually being hit. The least amount of cover gave you some sense of security, even a sheet of brown paper covering your head would have been welcome as protection against the shelling.'

Reg watched the first two waves of A and C Companies go out into No Man's Land at 7.20 am and lie down about half way across to the German wire. In the last minutes of the British barrage on the German front line they were relatively safe in No Man's Land even though the troops found it an eerie experience to be walking through the British wire in broad daylight. The wire had been cut in several places by a working party from the 10th East Yorkshires, who along with the other three Hull battalions of the 92nd Brigade were in reserve positions back beyond Colincamps.

The orders for all troops that day assaulting the German line, across the whole Somme battlefield, was that they would walk forward at a fair pace but not run. There were several reasons given for this. Firstly, the German front line defenders would not be capable of resistance after the mauling from the British artillery, therefore there was no imperative to get to their line as speedily as possible. Secondly, the amount of equipment each soldier was carrying, including extra Mills bombs for the bombing sections and full pouches and extra cotton bandoliers of clips of .303 ammo, a rigid entrenching tool hanging vertically down their back, four empty sandbags each and rations for two days, meant that they could not run very fast and would soon become exhausted if they tried. Thirdly, they would expect to be in action for several hours and therefore needed to conserve their energy for when it was really needed if they came into close fighting with the German soldiers.

This decision proved to be a fatal error, for when the British barrage lifted from the German front line as planned at 7.30am, the few minutes grace caused by the slow moving British infantry allowed the defenders of the 1st Battalion of the Infanterie-Regiment Nr169 enough time to emerge from their deep dugouts and strong points in their trenches and be ready for the 12th Battalion men. The Germans got enough men into position and had their six machine gun teams ready very quickly, and then looking out of the loopholes in their parapet they were amazed to see four lines of khaki infantry get up and, seemingly leisurely, set off from their temporary positions in No Man's Land and walk towards them.

Reg, who had a 'front row seat' at Battalion HQ in John Copse had watched Captain Colley's men walk out of the trenches and then lie down a hundred yards to the front. He then followed as far as the British wire, ready to use his flags to signal when given messages. Captain Colley had looked extremely strained. When one of Reg's mates had asked him the time, he noticed how much his hand shook when he pulled out his pocket watch. William Colley was clearly a man on the edge. Reg recalled:

'Zero hour was 7.30am, after one and a half hours of very heavy shell fire on the German lines. The Germans called it *"Trommelfeuer"* – drumfire in English – because it sounded like continuous fast drumming, not the usual intermittent shell fire when you could distinguish one shell from another, even usually make out whether or not it was coming your way.'

It must have seemed to Reg and the other City Battalion lads that it really was reasonable to suppose no-one would survive that drubbing, or at least be in a position to fight back and the generals had got it right.

'Then at zero hour the British artillery lifted off the German Front line and there was a moment of uncanny silence. I could even hear the skylarks singing. It was such a beautiful morning with the sun in a near cloudless sky, and some of us feeling parched already. The whistles blew at 7.30am prompt and the men got up in extended order and advanced towards the German wire.

'In a moment they all lay down again and I wondered why, thinking they had perhaps been tripped up by a wire in No Man's Land.'

The two-minute respite that the British had given the Germans was a disastrous error, not just at Serre but all along the 4th Army line. Pickets of the 169th Regiment who had stayed at sentry duty during the bombardment now yelled to their NCOs down in their deep, protected bunkers that the English were coming. A life or death race to get up the steps or ladders followed as German soldiers rushed to get into their front line, find a position and start firing their Mausers at the 'crazy' Tommies walking towards them. The six machine guns and the trench mortars were already causing chaos in the British ranks and the lines coming towards them were getting thinner and thinner as they approached the wire. Far from being cowed by the bombardment, most of the Baden lads could not wait to get into the open air, find a loophole and fire away at the enemy. They did not need to aim carefully as the British ranks in front of them were sitting ducks and when they got to the unbroken German wire, they were so close that it was impossible to miss unless their attackers flung themselves down into one of the hundreds of shell holes, many of which had been created that night. At that point, the Tommies were trapped and the Germans could now hold their fire until they saw any sign of movement and then they would let them have it. Some of the German troops felt so emboldened and high on adrenalin that they stood up on their parapet to get a better angle to shoot the enemy in shallow shell holes, unknowing, and unconcerned, whether their targets were wounded or not.

Captain Colley's premonition of death had turned out to be correct and he was killed by a shell after he had advanced only a little way. His remains were never found, the fate of so many Sheffield men that day. Brigadier Hubert Rees, observing from Brigade HQ, reckoned he had never before experienced such a devastating counter barrage against a trench assault, and it not only dropped on the men already in No Man's Land, but had a devastating effect on the third and fourth waves who had to come 'over the top' to reach the British wire. Later, it was estimated that half of B and D Companies had become casualties before they reached the British front line.

Reg had ducked back into Battalion HQ and was waiting for instructions. It was not that safe a place and, among others, Major Hoette, acting as the Battalion second in command, was injured whilst at John Copse. Unsurprisingly, Reg never got to use his flags and in fact never sent a signal all day. All the telephone wires were cut all along the Battalion's position and Reg became a runner instead, carrying messages to platoons and companies from Major Plackett's HQ, a dangerous and difficult task as the German machine guns were now sweeping the area around Rob Roy and Campion trenches trying to break up the later attacking waves before they got going.

Those members of C Company who actually reached the German wire found no gaps at all. Theoretically, parties of Bangalore torpedo specialists should now have come forward and cut passages through wire, but most of them were already casualties and to have crawled out just a few yards from the German parapet and try to calmly cut a way with wire cutters through the deep German wire would have meant instant death. So those who reached the wire now found that not only were they few in number, but if they did not take cover, they would all be shot. It was palpably obvious that with such reduced numbers they could not continue the advance even if they had found a passage in the wire, and most opted for lying quiet and praying for survival and helping a wounded comrade in the same hole.

Some gallantly still continued firing and throwing Mills bombs. Two Lewis gun teams continued to take the fight to the Germans that morning and inflicted some casualties, including killing the *Unteroffizier* in charge of the 'Adelbrecht' machine gun team and wounding the *Unterofffizier* in charge of another. Their attempt to take on the heavier Maxim machine guns saved some Sheffield lives that day. Advancing with A Company, a Lewis gun team that included L/Cpl Matthew Burnby, Pte. Herbert Arridge and Pte. Charles Garbutt had been forced to take cover but throughout the morning they kept up fire on the German positions until their ammunition pans ran out. The three of them survived to bring their gun back at nightfall. They were all subsequently awarded the Military Medal. Matthew Burnaby was promoted to Sergeant and in 1917 was commissioned into the Machine Gun Corps, whilst Herbert Arridge was later commissioned into the KOYLI, and in October 1917 he was attached to the Indian Army.

Private Bertram Corthorn was the sole survivor of a Lewis gun team in B Company who came up to support A Company. The initial plan provided for B Company to pass through A Company after the lead companies had already taken the first four lines of German trenches. B Company, along with D Company, would then capture Serre village itself. Instead, they were stuck outside the German wire on the right of the battalion front where there was a little more opportunity for some manoeuvre, because the wire had been more damaged on this side and small parties had slipped through. Bertram Corthorn kept firing his Lewis gun until it was hit by a sniper and put out of action. He then reverted to a rifle and fired round after round until his ammunition ran out at 7.50am. With both the Lewis gun and the rifle he had tried to concentrate his fire on the German machine guns and consequently saved a fair number of lives of his comrades. The one life he now concentrated on saving was Private Reginald Brookes, who was in a nearby shell hole where Corthorn took cover. Brookes was very badly wounded and could not move, so instead of crawling back when it became dark, Corthorn stayed with him through the night and into the following day. It was only after Brookes had died in the afternoon of the second day that Corthorn decided to crawl back to the Battalion's lines when it got dark.

This he did and dragged his damaged Lewis gun with him. He had been out in No Man's Land close by the German wire for over forty hours by the time he got back and on Captain Moore's recommendation he was later put up for a medal and received the prestigious DCM – the Distinguished Conduct Medal. Captain Reginald Moore, who was B Company commander, had tried to reach Corthorn and support him but he was badly injured earlier in the attack and was losing a lot of blood and had to be taken to an aid post, but he had witnessed Corthorn's courageous actions and so could recommend him to their Commanding Officer.

In the first half hour of the attack, two of the company commanders were killed and one seriously injured. Two CSMs were killed in the assault across No Man's Land, with a third, Acting CSM Herbert Atkinson of B Company, dying eight days later. Officers, in their different pattern uniforms and carrying Webley revolvers, were a prime target for German riflemen, as were NCOs rushing around outside the wire trying to gather what was left of sections and platoons before moving forward. These isolated groups searching for a passage through the wire and then onward into the enemy trenches attracted massive German rifle fire and were an easy target. Captain William Clarke, desperate to find a way through the wire, was shot dead looking for a gap and his body slumped onto the wire and hung there. There could be no more poignant image of the Serre attack than that of a gallant officer trying to carry out his orders despite the futility of the situation, after the attack had clearly lost momentum. Any forays across the wire and into the German front line could only be a gesture that would soon lead to annihilation.

Lt. Charles Elam, of A Company, is believed to have managed to get a group from his platoon through the wire and hold a section of the German front line for a while until he was counterattacked by a superior force. He must have then been killed because his grave was later discovered where the German second line had been in July. 2nd Lt. Philip Perkin, already regarded as a keen, plucky young subaltern, who had only joined the Battalion in April, was also seen trying to rally groups of men but they had nowhere to go and he also would be numbered among the dead that day. Who knows what terrors he suffered in those last few minutes of life, when he knew he had to lead – but lead where and how? Stumbling around in confusion it was only a matter of time before a bullet got him and any men with him.

There were many acts of courage shown by the Sheffield men rescuing their stricken comrades and tending to them in a shell hole while all hell went on overhead. There were others like Bertram Corthorn who would not leave injured mates when they could have crawled back to their own lines. There were others who continued the fight from their disadvantageous position. One was Sergeant Reginald Gallimore who stood upright, firing at Germans on their parapet and remained miraculously unscathed. He had spent almost two years preparing for this fight and so fight he intended to do. He was well known in the Battalion and had been a keen volunteer for patrols in No Man's Land, yet his actions must have been born of frustration as much as anything, because the attack they believed had been planned so meticulously had fallen to pieces within half an hour.

By 8.30am, the German commander of the 169th Regiment could report that no hostile British troops remained in German positions and that the attack had stalled, though he did not know if the assault would recommence when the Tommies had regrouped and deployed their reserve brigade. If he could have seen what Reg saw in John Copse and the front line trench that ran to Luke Copse and Mark Copse, he would have known his regiment had won the battle for Serre already. The trench was full of dead and injured, most of them from D Company caught in the open coming forward to pass through the British wire and into No Man's Land, but there were also stragglers from C Company, many of them wounded, stumbling and crawling back into the front line at John Copse.

Throughout the morning came exaggerated reports of British troops being seen in the village of Serre itself and even in the vicinity of Pendant Copse well behind the German lines to the south east of Serre, but there was no hard evidence for these stories. It was also reported that the Germans turned their artillery on their own front line; proof, it was hoped, of a sizeable British presence in their front trenches. There were also claims that around mid-day, the Germans shelled Serre village, giving rise to hopes that significant British forces had reached the village itself. But if 94th Brigade troops had got this far, which is unlikely, they cannot have been in significant numbers and would have been despatched by defending German infantry.

The only City Battalion men we can be sure got into Serre village were the four who were prisoners. They included L/Cpl Albert Outram, one of Reg's signaller mates, who would spend two years working as a PoW in Germany, mainly in salt mines; he would not be repatriated until early December 1918. Another was George Mulford of D Company, who had been a sergeant until June when at his own request he had reverted back to the rank of private. There was Private Frederick Johnston of C Company who was injured when captured, dying in a German Field Hospital on 10 July, and Private Thomas Leefe of A Company, who suffered a head injury and was blinded in both eyes, repatriated to Britain in October 1916 after an initial period in German captivity.

At around 1pm, the Germans appeared to allow a truce to enable British stretcher bearers to pick up their wounded in No Man's Land. It was all unofficial, and still highly dangerous, but shows that the Germans felt the fighting was over and that any British troops in No Man's Land were looking for wounded comrades, not preparing to renew the assault. In fact, Brigadier Rees had already called off the assault that had been planned for mid-day, because he seems to have been a humane man who could see that continuing to attack would be futile and could only result in further heavy casualties. A different brigadier with visions of glory in his sights might have been encouraged by Corps and Divisional superiors to have another 'crack at the Boche', but Rees, the son of a Church of England canon, knew his men had given all, tried desperately to do their duty and been completely thwarted by circumstances beyond their control. He was replaced the next day, when Brigadier Carter-Campbell returned to his command, in what must have been seen as a snub, even though he was soon given a new command. The acting CO of the 11th East Lancashires, Major E.L. Reiss, certainly thought Rees had been shabbily treated, and so he took the time to write him a most sympathetic letter on his departure from the Brigade on 2 July.

Reg had been expecting to be a part of this assault, so he was relieved when it was called off. Instead, during the afternoon, Reg was sent by the Adjutant with a message to the transport lines at Colincamps, detailing the severely reduced rations that the Battalion would now need. He went back along the communication trench with Private Colin Evans, as was standard practice if there were men available, so that if one man got hit the other could continue and deliver the message.

'As we got near to Colincamps we saw a barbed wire cage that had been constructed to hold the German prisoners we had optimistically expected to capture as we advanced over their defence lines and up to Serre. They were guarded by the Military Police who asked us where we were going and when they did not seem to like our answer they directed us into the cage. They said they were collecting stragglers to form into a reserve unit if a German counter attack came off in the afternoon. But like all military police behind an offensive they were looking not just for genuine stragglers looking for their units but for those who were considering desertion. They did not seem to understand that we were runners from Battalion HQ and had a legitimate message to deliver. However, when they were not looking we just breezed out of their cage, delivered our message and gave them a wide berth on our way back to what was left of our Battalion. When we got back it was soon apparent that the Battalion had taken a big hit. There seemed to be more wounded and dead than living in our trenches.'

If the Germans had advanced into the British front line in the afternoon, they would have found no resistance, just dying, injured and bewildered soldiers lying in the bottom of the forward trenches, incapable of any further resistance. Always the masters of the counter-attack, the Germans were fortunately only interested in restoring control over their own front lines, not sallying forth to take trenches that could serve them no purpose and were not part of their coherent and well-constructed defensive position.

During the night, Reg went into No Man's Land and helped look for some of the wounded. There were numerous soldiers, both official and unofficial, who were cautiously wandering around No Man's Land searching for the injured, and especially their close friends – even relatives – who they had seen shot earlier in the day. Reg was on the lookout for his best friend in the battalion, Leslie Vernon Morte, a clerk from Rotherham. He never found him, but his body was later identified from a dog tag and he was buried in Luke Copse Cemetery. Luke Copse Cemetery is a small linear cemetery lying not far ahead of what was the British front line, roughly where the men who assaulted the German positions were

Leslie Vernon Morte was Reg's best pal in the 12th Battalion. He was killed on 1 July 1916 and Reg spent the night looking for him in No Man's Land but to no avail.

killed as they emerged from their trench. In later years, when Reg went over to visit Serre, one of his first 'duties' was to go and 'say hello to Leslie' and pat his headstone and tell him he had come back 'to see him again'.

When darkness fell, companies of the two Barnsley Battalions took over the front line from the survivors of City Battalion and they moved back to Rolland Trench 900 yards behind the Front. They stayed there all through 2 July, while replacements came up including the men held in reserve and also fifty new untried men who now joined the battalion. It was not till 8pm on the next day that they were relieved when the 48th Division relieved the 31st Division, with the 1/4th Bn Oxfordshire and Buckinghamshire Light Infantry taking over the positions in the sector from John Copse to Mathew Copse. What was left of the Battalion now marched back two miles to Louvencourt where they all thought they would get a well-deserved rest, a bath and clean uniforms. Instead, in a final cruel twist, after all they had suffered, they were unbelievably made to march twenty miles to Longuevillette, where at least there was peace and quiet in a pretty village. They were now led by Captain Douglas Allen, who had missed the battle because he was another 12th Battalion officer who was away on a course at the 4th Army's School of Instruction. As the ranking officer he now took over on 4 July from the Adjutant, Captain Norman Tunbridge, who had been temporarily in charge after Major Placket had been evacuated with shell shock on 1 July. Captain Allen became the third commanding officer of the battalion in five days and would hold the position until the end of the month.

For Reg, who seems to have survived the battle unscathed, one of the few to suffer no wounds, the travelling was still not over and the survivors still had another long march of 15 miles before getting on a train at Frevent that carried them 40 miles north. Eventually they found a proper chance to recuperate, have a bath and sleep in decent billets at the attractive town of Merville on the River Lys, where they rested for almost a week.Here they could attempt to come to terms with their own traumas and the gruesome events of the last few days. They could swap information among themselves about those friends who had definitely been killed and those who might be dead or just missing and still lying out in No Man's Land, as one man, Private Arthur Stagg, did for fifteen days before getting back to the British line.

On 1 July, Reg and the others had finally come up against the grim ramparts of reality. They had expected victories and afterwards more cheering but instead, the Battalion had discovered its nemesis. They had been used to ecstatic cheering crowds from that first day of volunteering to the emotional farewell parade outside the Town Hall before they left Sheffield for good to go to Cannock Chase. It had all been one great delirious adventure with opportunities to see countries and places they had read about – Gibraltar, Malta, the Suez Canal, Marseille and the splendours of the Riviera and the Rhone Valley, all inevitably leading up to a successful conclusion as part of a great victory on the Somme that would shatter the German Army and shorten the war. The *Sheffield Daily Telegraph* caught the popular mood in a caption under a photo of Major Placket, referring to him as 'the man who commanded the boys in the local battalion who won glory in the great push on 1ˢᵗ July'.

Instead, at Serre on 1 July, the City Battalion and all of the 31st Division had suffered a total, unmitigated defeat. Apart from the many acts of individual bravery and loyalty to wounded mates and strangers, there was nothing to show for their efforts except a huge and unbelievable casualty list. Of the 747 Sheffield men who were part of the assaulting force, 240 ORs and 8 officers were killed in the brief action below Serre village. The full death toll was not known at the time, but bodies could be seen clearly from the British lines and almost all those who were missing at roll call on 2 July turned out to be killed, not wounded or prisoners. 249 men were wounded, of whom 17 succumbed to their injuries, whilst around 75 men were carrying less serious wounds, bringing the casualty total for the action, including the four prisoners taken by the Germans, to 576 men, more than two out of every three men who were involved in the attack.

The two Barnsley Battalions also had many casualties, but as the supporting battalions their losses were not so severe. Even so, with losses of 12 officers and 274 ORs for the 13th Battalion and 10 officers and 265 ORs for the 14th Battalion, the impact of these devastating figures on people in Barnsley would have been just as great as the City Battalions losses. The 11th East Lancashires suffered even worse than the York and Lancaster Battalions with 21 officers and 564 ORs being killed or wounded. The 93rd Brigade's leading battalions, the 1st Bradford Pals and the Leeds Pals of the West Yorkshire Regiment, had similar devastating losses, as they also recorded a gallant failure south of Mathew Copse.

Opposite them, the three battalions of the 169th (Baden) Regiment's casualties were only 14 officers and 577 men. These losses had been sustained during the bombardment and then holding off the whole of the 31st Division, and even units of the 4th British Division at the southern end of their sector. They had been supported by all arms fire from north of Serre, by the Infanterie-Regiment Nr 66 from Magdeburg, who, when they realised that there was to be no British assault in their sector, turned their weapons to support the battalions of the 169th Regiment facing the City Battalion. From now on, Infanterie-Regiment Nr 169 would be known as the 'Iron Regiment' for its defence of Serre on 1 July 1916.

By any reckoning, it was a clear victory for the German defenders on 1 July at Serre. They would never be forced out of their 'fortress' at Serre in 1916 and only relinquished the position in February 1917 when the whole German army in the Arras, Somme and Aisne sectors made a tactical withdrawal to the well-prepared 'Hindenburg' lines, (known to them as the *Siegfriedstellung*). This move was planned with the strategic purpose of shortening the German Front because of their comparative shortage of troops caused by losses sustained during the battles for Verdun and Haig's Somme offensive from July to November 1916. During the German offensive of March 1918, the Germans recaptured Serre and the battlefield where the City Battalion had fought so hard almost two years previously, but in the great British counter–offensive of the summer of 1918 Serre was finally captured by British forces on 14 August, and the village's moment in history was over.

'It was a sad time. Many pals had gone and we had to start clearing up the effects of those who would not return. It was a mistake to form a Battalion from such a small area, as there was a greater feeling of loss all round.'

Reg wrote this many years later, but by the time he reached Merville the full significance of the losses was finally sinking in. Apart from his close pals like Leslie Morte, there were so many familiar faces that were no longer there, even though there was still the hope that missing meant they could somehow be alive, hopefully as German prisoners. Reg would not know at that time that his sister's boyfriend, L/Cpl Dan Edwards, whom he had visited at Albert just before the 1 July offensive was also among the missing and later was confirmed as dead. Dan's body was never identified and he is remembered, like so many in the City Battalion, on Edwin Lutyen's great commemorative 'Memorial to the Missing of the Somme' at Thiepval.

Because the Battalion's volunteers had come from a certain section of Sheffield society, the loss was felt especially disproportionally in certain suburbs and institutions. Within less than a quarter mile radius of the centre of Nether Edge, there had lived eleven of the dead. 39-year-old, 2nd Lt. Charles Wardill and his brother Sidney, a private, of Violet Bank Road were two of those killed on 1 July, as was Private John Thorpe who lived at the end of Montgomery Road and Private Arthur Greensmith who lived on Kenwood Park Road. There were also Fred Hobson of Machon Bank Road, Stanley Mason of Briar Road, Eric Mountain, just nineteen years old, from Chelsea Road, Norman Bedford from Kenwood Road and Harry Wharton from the bottom end of Sandford Grove Road. The Gunstone brothers, Frank and William, whose family owned a well known bakery business and who lived at the bottom of Ashland Road, were two more brothers killed serving alongside each other on the fateful day. They lie buried at Luke Copse cemetery close by each other. Their family added at the bottom of both their headstones the words – 'Alleluia! The Lord God omnipotent reigneth'.

These local losses would be just as poignant in other communities across Sheffield and within the institutions that had contributed so many volunteers. The number of men lost who had formerly been students or staff at the University was one of the highest in the city and included the poet Alexander Robertson, a former university lecturer, but a corporal in A Company at Serre. Reg's colleagues in the Town Hall had also paid a high price for their patriotic enthusiasm on the slope up to Serre, while thirteen former pupils of King Edward VII School, including 2nd Lts Arnold Beal and Eric Carr, were killed on the morning of 1 July and at Central School, Reg's old school, the death toll was probably higher.

Only four officers who had been in the trenches during the battle were available for duty by the end of the day. One of them was the Medical Officer, Lt. Edward Cunnington RAMC, who established his aid station at John Copse and for three days worked tirelessly to save as many wounded men as possible. There are so many inspiring stories of the selfless courage, skill and sheer doggedness of MOs on the battlefield – one of them, Capt. Noel Chavasse, won a double VC, only the second man to achieve this amazing feat – that Cunnington's quiet heroism just seems par for the course. A graduate of Cambridge University, he had only qualified as a surgeon at St. Bart's Hospital in early 1915 and was a house physician there before he joined up in July of that year. However, he would never in his brief medical experience have had to face the sheer volume and complexity of the wounded now being brought to his post, whilst having to deal with each one in such primitive and dangerous circumstances as a front line dugout under shellfire. He is also reported as having gone out each night to help find wounded soldiers beyond the British wire and for his heroic efforts during those three days he received a Mention in Despatches. Sadly, Edward Cunnington did not survive the war. He was killed at Bullecourt, near Arras, having got a convoy of wounded away just before his position was overrun during the German offensive of March 1918.

The mood of the Battalion is difficult to judge from the reminiscences and the diaries that have been preserved. It certainly was still a long way from the world of Wilfred Owen, Siegfried Sassoon and Robert Graves and others who later set a hostile tone of criticism against Haig and his generals, denouncing the whole conduct of the war by the military and political leadership. In 1916, the vast majority of the men on the Western Front still believed in the British cause, even

Sgt. John Streets from Whitwell in Derbyshire, whose poems about his time at the front with the 12th Battalion are of the highest quality and deserve to be better known.

after the massive and unforeseen losses of the Somme. The morale of even badly mauled divisions held, and with amazing resilience battalions were reformed around the survivors, so that within a fortnight they could be back in an active sector of the line. Within a month, like the 12th Battalion, they could be once again holding positions in the front line.

One man who Reg must have known well because he was a Sergeant in D Company, was John William Streets, a miner from Whitwell in Derbyshire, known to his family and friends as Will. Like many men of that generation he wrote poetry, but his verses were of an altogether higher standard than the average tyro poets, and he deserves recognition alongside the most famous names among the war poets. Sergeant Streets was another of the great talents who were lost in the First World War when he was killed at Serre.

On 1 July, he had got back to the safety of his own lines, yet despite being wounded himself, he went back into No Man's Land, to look for one of his soldiers and was never seen again. What was believed to be his body was initially buried at John Copse cemetery, but when it was cleared in 1923, he was reburied in Euston Road No1 cemetery at Colincamps. There he has a headstone that says 'Sergeant J.W. Streets, York and Lancaster Regiment, believed to be buried in this cemetery'. The family inscription at the base is an amended couplet of one of his poems, 'An English soldier'. It reads:

'I fell. But yielded not my English soul
That lives out here beneath the battle's roll'

That epitaph, and the following fragment of one of his last poems, sums up the mood of volunteer soldiers of 1916, who did not regard the sacrifice on the Somme as worthless. Rather they believed that the struggle against Germany must be relentlessly pursued to a successful conclusion, no matter how long it might take to achieve it.

'I know that should I still and prostrate lie
Amid death's harvest there on France's plain
No false regret shall scorning wander by
And taunt me that my youth has been in vain.'

Chapter 9

'I'm serene now I am out here at last!'
August 1916 – March 1917

On 3 August 1916, Vivian Simpson finally re-joined the 12th Battalion in France as a replacement officer for the seventeen officers who had been killed or seriously wounded on 1 July. The Battalion had already had one tour in the trenches near Neuve Chapelle between 24 and 27 July, when Reg and his comrades had been back in the front line for the first time since Serre. They were covering a sector of the British line after another disastrous attack by the 61st Division and the 5th Australian Division at Fromelles, a diversionary attack aimed at keeping the Germans guessing where Haig's next push would be launched. It was the first action by the Australian Imperial Force (the AIF) in France and they regarded it as another British calamity like Gallipoli in 1915.

Vivian had arrived in France before the Battalion went back into the trenches, but he was first sent to the huge British base at Etaples, near Le Touquet on the Channel coast. Known as the 'Bull Ring' it was the major entrepot for new troops from England as well as for hospitalised soldiers and Vivian found himself being processed there for well over a week.

He wrote to his brother in some frustration:

> 'There are all sorts of troops here the finest looking being the Australians and the Scots, whose uniform sets them off against the more usual infantry outfit. We live in tents in the officers' lines and my first day here was fairly slack though we had to keep reporting ourselves to different officers. Yesterday we went through a gas trench to show how innocuous it all is.'
>
> 'I have no idea when I am going up the line, nor even whether I shall be posted to the Battalion. I hope at least I am posted to the Brigade where at least I will have some old friends. I do not want to go anywhere where I have no pals as I find it difficult to get intimate with new people. One has hundreds of acquaintances but few friends.'

He need not have worried, because at the start of August he was back with the Battalion and posted to B Company. He soon found that there were many missing faces and few of the officers that he knew. He had been away from the Battalion for over a year since they marched out of Redmires camp and he had been detailed to stay and train new recruits. He had missed all their raw, as well as their happy experiences; missed the disaster at Serre and the good days in Egypt and so he was something of a new boy again. At least in B Company he knew the Company Commander, John Middleton, now a captain, and a number of the other ranks who had survived the summer in the trenches, such as Reg and a few surviving volunteers from the now so distant days at Redmires.

There was a temporary CO, Major Clement Gurney of the 13th York & Lancaster (the 1st Barnsleys), who seemed popular with the lads and would serve again as CO of the Battalion before being given a battalion of his own (the 11th East Yorkshire), be promoted to Lieutenant Colonel and go on to win a DSO and Bar. With Major Gurney in charge, the Battalion went back into the line the day after Vivian had joined them. They still were not up to full strength and they joined up with the 11th East Lancashire to form a composite battalion and were given a long stretch of the line to hold. Vivian's B Company was particularly isolated, with both flanks open, but the five days they were in the line were relatively quiet and it gave Vivian a chance to get his bearings and familiarise himself with the reality of trench life without any high dramas or traumas. The companies suffered from regular trench mortar 'stunts' but had only one fatality, when a soldier was killed on the final day just as they were being relieved by one of the Barnsley Battalions.

Still officers came and went. While in the line, Captain Middleton was taken ill and was hospitalised. He never returned to the Battalion but joined the RFC and later in the war won a DFC (the Distinguished Flying Cross), the new medal for airmen of comparable status to the Military Cross. Norman Tunbridge, who had been the Adjutant since March 1915 and was one of the survivors of the Serre attack, left in mid-August to become the temporary second in command of the 11th East Lancashires, while subalterns regularly went off on this course or that.

Then, on 18 August, the Battalion got their new CO. Lieutenant Colonel Harry Fisher had originally been commissioned into the Wiltshire Regiment, had seen action in the Boer War and now came to the 12th Battalion from the 92nd Brigade where he had been Brigade Major. Major Gurney in the meantime stayed with Battalion and became the new second in command, so Vivian could have little quarrel with the leadership of the Battalion although he soon rated many of his fellow subalterns as not up to much, dismissing them as the 'common herd of one star people', while at the same time recognising that the best junior officers were the ones who kept the Army effective 'not the Majors and the higher ups!'

It was clear however that Vivian soon proved a very effective company officer, almost revelling in the life in the trenches and popular among the men who wanted good leadership in action from fair minded officers. The Battalion went back into the trenches on 26 August and were there for a lengthy spell of sixteen days until 11 September, holding a front of 700 yards. Unlike Vivian's first tour in the trenches, there was a lot more hostile bombardment this time, both from the *minenwerfers* and from German artillery although the casualties were surprisingly light.

Later Vivian would recall;

'I had a fairly good time in the trenches and I am becoming quite fond of being in the front line. The men are so decent one gets frightfully fond of them. We have got some old hands who are Regulars from the 1st and 2nd Battalions who have been here in France since the beginning in 1914 and it is most interesting to talk to them. They say their officers never looked after their welfare like we do and one morning they nearly dropped dead when I asked them if they had got enough to eat.

'The extraordinary thing is that I have far more nerves at home than I have here, and if it were not for the casualties the whole thing would be a scream as there are so many humorous moments.'

Two nights before the Battalion left the trenches, Brigade decided to stage a 'stunt' – a trench raid of two platoons strength and Vivian was selected to lead one of the raiding platoons while 2nd Lt. Thompson, also a new officer in the Battalion, was chosen to lead the other. During the afternoon and early evening, the British artillery and mortars pulverised the German wire to create enough gaps for the raiders, but, of course, they also alerted the Germans to the fact that something was afoot. Ostensibly, the main purpose of the raid was to grab a prisoner or two and gain general information about the enemy's dispositions. In reality the raid was undertaken just to keep the Germans on their toes and never allow them to relax in their trenches, whilst the chance of the raiders suffering several fatal casualties was very high.

Vivian recalled in letter written shortly afterwards:

'We started into No Man's Land before midnight and worked our way silently to the German wire. Thompson's platoon initially did not get any further because the wire in front of them was largely intact and I was left to go it alone. Zero hour was 1.30 am and we were quickly into the Boche front trench but found they had laid a trap for us. They knew we were coming so they moved their men back to a second line fifteen yards further to the rear, so we captured an empty trench. They had blocked the communication trenches on every side of us and then started hurling grenades at us and we retaliated. If Thompson's party had been able to reach their objective then we might have wiped out the "gentle" Hun, as it was we gave him a nasty knock and then retired.

'From 2am to 4.30am I was out in No Man's Land searching for any wounded and four men who were missing. I was unrecognisable when I eventually got back to our lines, all my clothes and puttees were torn to shreds and I looked like a rag and bone man. I did get a small piece of shrapnel that hit me on the behind and raised a lump, but these entertainments would be all right if there were no casualties. I reckon we killed about thirty Germans and I found it was all rather exciting.'

Actually, although there were congratulations all round from First Army HQ down to the new CO, the raid had cost the Battalion four dead, twenty wounded (one of whom died later) and four missing who were in fact taken prisoner. So the 'gentle Hun' got four prisoners but Vivian got none, seemingly a poor result for a lot of effort and bravery. Vivian was recommended for an award, but nothing came of it, yet he had clearly established his reputation in the Battalion as a plucky officer with strong leadership qualities. Later in the month, he became the acting company commander of B Company, although to his continual chagrin he remained a second lieutenant.

Once out of the line Vivian could catch up on family correspondence. He wrote frequently to his wife and of course asked about the 'infant' who seemed to be delighting everyone at home and was very good natured. Vivian was pleased that May had gone to Wortley Golf Club for an extended stay, believing that the change would do her good and she would be meeting old friends and getting in a round or two. He was also interested, as the current cup holder, to find out who would be competing for the Captain's Cup that year. He made it clear in his letters that he hoped victory would go to 'old' Bury rather than Dr Stainsby, but he was to be disappointed, because John Stainsby was the 1916 winner; two years later, working as a RAMC surgeon on a hospital ship, he was torpedoed by a German U-Boat and was drowned at sea. John Stainsby's name is recorded on the same War Memorial at Wortley Golf Club as is Vivian's and Vivian's brother-in-law, Percy Belcher.

Vivian also gave his elder brother George some advice over his concerns about his son who was still struggling at Winchester.

'Let him take an interest in games as they are the best education for ordinary life a man can have and they teach people to be sane. Games have saved the British nation in this crisis not brains of the Asquith stamp. Games have taught people to stick it and make a joke of tragedies!'

These were views that many a headmaster would be regularly promulgating from the platform at morning assembly, that officer selection boards also regarded as self-evident, that a chap who could race through robust tackling for a dazzling try, or bang a six yet never flinch from a fast bowler's bumpers, had the sort of dash and stoicism that would transfer easily into leadership at subaltern level. And who is to say he was wrong? Yet, although the Germans played neither rugby nor cricket, they too seem to have produced fine and courageous wartime junior officers.

At 6.14am on 16 August, Private James Haddock was shot by a firing squad provided by B Company. Neither Reg nor Vivian have left any recollections of this episode when the only member of the Battalion to be executed was shot. The execution took place at dawn on the same morning as the Battalion left the Neuve Chapelle area, moving four miles south to take up positions at Festubert, another village already famous in the Army and the British press after the battle in May of the previous year.

Vivian certainly would have been well aware of the execution and as an officer of B Company may well have been involved in the proceedings, although James Haddock was a stranger to all of them. He had arrived with a draft of 28 replacements on 9 August and RSM Polden had directed him to join B Company in the front line. When the new men reached the forward trenches, Haddock was nowhere to be seen and he had deserted again. Five days later he was picked up by the Military Police seven miles away, hiding under a tarpaulin on a farm wagon and arrested.

His Field General Court Martial that followed, held on 24 August, pronounced him guilty of desertion and recorded the sentence was 'to suffer death by being shot'. However, as was so often the case, they recommended mercy because he may have had shell shock, as several 12th Battalion members, including officers, had suffered recently and been evacuated back to England.

What made Private Haddock's case different was that he had form and was on a 'final warning'. Before the war, he had been a regular soldier with the York and Lancasters and had served for a time in India. However, he had left the army in 1912 but was still in the Reserves so that when war started, he was drafted into the 2nd Battalion of the Regiment and had been out in France since September 1914, long before any of the City Battalion men had seen the Western Front. But he had gone AWOL eight times and deserted once before and at his Court Martial in April he had been sentenced to 20 years penal servitude, later reduced to five years and suspended, at which point he was sent back to his unit.

The recommendation for mercy this time was not upheld, the final decision being taken by Haig himself, who, in the light of the continuing heavy losses in the ongoing battle of the Somme, decided an example should be made of James Haddock. If Haig intended to impress the men of the Battalion with the ultimate deadly reality of discipline, the effect on many of the Sheffield soldiers was rather one of horror and even sympathy for the unfortunate victim. Corporal Frank Meakin, whose platoon guarded Haddock overnight on 15 September, wrote in his diary; 'I was more shocked by this beastly crime about to be perpetrated than I have been at anything since coming to France.'

One could imagine that Reg might very well feel the same, but others will have felt that some ultimate penalty had to be used occasionally, otherwise so many would make the calculation that desertion and imprisonment was better than death.

Britain still had the death penalty in criminal cases and among the main combatants in the First World War, the 306 soldiers executed for 'cowardice and desertion' is a very low figure. Perhaps more amazing is the fact that no British serviceman was officially executed for these reasons throughout the Second World War, even though Cairo, Naples and London were full of deserters, whilst Nazi Germany and the Soviet Union executed thousands of their own soldiers for desertion, cowardice and other military crimes. Frank Meakin reported that Haddock went to his death smiling, perhaps he was just pleased to get the terrors of war over. Decencies, or hypocrisies, were observed and James Haddock was given a grave in Vielle-Chapelle New Military Cemetery with a headstone that is no different from that of any other dead soldier in France.

The Battalion went into the line at Festubert as soon as they arrived on 16 September and their first spell in the front line lasted eight days. Festubert was a relatively quiet section of the British front but a rather peculiar one with its own special dangers. Because the land was so wet, even boggy, normal trenches could not be dug and so the front was a series of breastworks which were formed by building a parapet above ground and giving all round defence. Each post was at least 50 yards from the next, but some had at least 150 yards between them, and the idea was that they could support each other with covering fire if the Germans raided the position. The obvious problem was that movement in daylight between the posts was impossible and German snipers were constantly on the alert. At night time when the Sheffield men moved around, the German infantry fired bursts of machine gun and rifle fire on fixed lines, hoping for a hit. However, despite a certain level of trench mortar and artillery activity, the Battalion's casualties were very low in a sector where no-one was very ambitious for action.

Vivian wrote home, saying:

'We have lots of amusements here and really life is fine. We've had no heavy bombardment yet and I shall have to wait till we get to the Somme for that. How the Hun sticks our artillery I do not know but I expect he retires into his deep dugout at which he is adept.

'We are badly bothered by snipers but I have been tremendously lucky and managed to spend a few hours observing their front line. They let me have it with a rifle grenade but it hit the parapet and their snipers have had no better luck. They are frightfully cunning and give nothing away and I have never seen a Boche expose himself in the trenches yet.'

He also found the conditions appalling as did everyone else and persistent rain made the situation worse. Vivian wrote home again asking for some thigh length waders:

'Could you order me some waders, ones that go over my own boots. I am wearing size 7 boots now. I do not want the sort of waders that you use instead of boots as they make a mess of your feet. We have to wade about through all sorts of stuff at times and continuous wet feet are not only unpleasant but you can get trench foot if you are not careful.'

The Battalion handed over their positions to the 14th York & Lancaster on the 24th and suffered their only fatality of the tour when Private Joseph Fairclough was killed as they were pulling out. Capt. Thomas Grant was also hit in the arm and the responsibility for running B Coy fell to Vivian, which he readily accepted, but could still only display the one star of a 2nd Lieutenant on his cuff.

Vivian constantly felt the injustice of his position, made worse by the fact that he was considerably older than the majority of the subalterns. Yet he was still a new boy in France and others had longer service, whilst Major Placket, with his shell shock, and other officers wounded on the Somme and recovering in England, were still on the Battalion strength and blocking promotions, as he wrote home to his brother:

'I was attached temporarily to C Company recently and Capt. Cousins had the grace to say that he picked my brains pretty considerably. I think without saying, that I can walk rings round any company officer and none of the companies are run as well as my company at Blyth. I do not know why I never get promotion. The Battalion received congratulations and thanks from the G.O.C. First Army for the raid I organised but nothing happened for me except that I get detailed for the unpleasant and difficult jobs. It is disheartening because the people at home must think I am a washout – however, I am used to it now.'

The Battalion was back in the Festubert Line on 1 October and Vivian was still in command of B Company. The tour was a short one of only four days and the action was as desultory and half-hearted as before, except for one disaster early in the morning of 3 October, when Lt. Col. Fisher, just back from a conference at First Army Headquarters, decided to do a tour of the isolated outposts that made up the Battalion front line. Leaving one of the island posts, he was hit by a sniper's bullet, possibly a random shot fired on a fixed line hoping for a kill or the sniper might have observed some activity as commanding officers rarely moved about by themselves, and so he got a shot off and killed Lt. Col. Fisher outright with a shot to the head.

Harry Fisher had only been with the Battalion for just eight weeks and was the first CO to be killed in action, but the Battalion was once more without a CO. Again, Major Gurney stepped up and filled the breach until a successor could be appointed when the Battalion had moved down once again to the Somme battlefield, near their old positions just north of Serre at Hebuterne.

The Battalion now re-joined VIII Corps as part of Fourth Army and was initially billeted in Marieux before moving on to familiar surroundings at Bois de Warnimont, but they did not go into the front line trenches until the very end of October. The 31st Division took over a sector of the front just north of the Serre battlefield where so many of the Battalion's dead still lay out in No Man's Land and where the stench from the decomposing bodies was almost unbearable. The Hebuterne sector, that was to be the Battalion's home until March1917, was just north of John Copse opposite the formidable defences of

Lt. Col. H.B. Fisher who was shot by a sniper during a night inspection of the Battalion's outposts. He was CO of the 12ᵗʰ Battalion only from 18ᵗʰ August to 3ʳᵈ October 1916.

Gommecourt and Reg and many other veterans of the Somme faced the prospect of a tour in this sector with foreboding.

Throughout the month, the Battalion received a large number of reinforcements that epitomised the changing face of the Army. There were four new drafts of men who had no connection with the regiment. There was a group 97 strong from the Northamptonshire Regiment, another of 93 men who were originally expecting to be sent to a battalion of the North Staffordshire Regiment, 48 men from the Lancashire Fusiliers and another 48 from the Northumberland Fusiliers. They were not particularly welcomed by the original Sheffield volunteers, partly because they were not local to the Sheffield area, partly because they were new, untried, and hastily trained soldiers who had not been through the horrors of the summer. Also, some of them were conscripted men who had not volunteered in 1914 and 1915 but had only joined the Army when they had no option, when they were called up under the Military Service Act of 1916. Richard Sparling in his 1920 history of the12th Battalion suggests that when they went into action, they proved their mettle on the whole, but perhaps, unsurprisingly, a barrier existed between the originals and the new arrivals.

Lt. Col. C.P.B. Riall, formerly with the East Yorkshire Regiment who was born in County Wicklow, son of a RN Commander, educated at Charterhouse and Trinity College, Dublin. He served as the CO of the 12th Battalion from October 1916 until 15 May 1917.

This was common in many units in most armies before the newcomers demonstrated their courage and endurance in combat and being worthy of the traditions of the regiment they had joined, even if they were only there because of an administrative decision to fill manpower shortages in badly mauled battalions. The division between the 'family' of old local soldiers and the newcomers was never fully healed, even when the newcomers eventually formed a majority of the Battalion. Indeed, after the war when the survivors formed the Twelfth Club, the new men who joined the Battalion after 1 July 1916 were not granted automatic membership, although they could be elected on a personal basis if they wished to join and were accepted.

One newcomer who did not need to be accepted was the new CO, Lt. Col. Claud Riall, a regular soldier with eighteen years' service with the East Yorkshire Regiment, who had recently been serving temporarily as second in command of the 13th Bn of the York & Lancaster. He soon impressed himself on the men after arriving on 12 October, by ordering a long route march and the following day undertaking a lengthy and painstaking inspection of every aspect of the Battalion, thereby familiarising himself at an early stage with the officers and men under his command. After so many changes at the top, the Battalion now had a CO who would serve in that position for seven months and one who would also be sympathetic to Vivian's hopes of a captaincy.

At least he made Vivian the temporary commander of A Company shortly after he arrived, and Vivian was certain that this was his chance to prove himself and finally get his captain's three stars as he told the family in a letter home:

'If I keep the Company for over thirty days then I am entitled to an acting captain's rank, although they usually shift you just before the thirty days are up. Anyhow I do not think they will have the face to do me a dirty trick after I have led B Company for a fortnight and now A Company and been in the trenches with them.

'We are now in a "warm" district although we are forbidden to tell you more, except that it is quite undulating like the downs and much nicer than the heavily wooded country where we were previously. I would like you to see the battleground, a complete waste of stunted trees and ruined buildings and no living soul, save birds that fly about quite unconcerned. It is really extraordinary to see no civilians for miles around and not a single place fit for habitation. I think everyone will appreciate home comforts when he gets back and I never want to see this horrible country again. The peasants hate the English troops like the devil and are as awkward as they dare to be.'

Vivian wrote again on 2 November while the Battalion was in the front line at Hebuterne:

'I have a few minutes to write after three strenuous days in the line during which I only got three hours sleep. We are holding a warm part of the front and yesterday the Boche put a shell into the HQ mess and the Mess Sergeant, the Cook and one orderly are no more. A minute or two later and I would have been in there myself. We are going through what the early men had to put up with and the mud is so bad in places that the men can get stuck for four or five hours. They often have to leave their waders in the mud and come out in their stocking feet, some even with no socks on. The water in places is three feet deep and you have no idea of the fearful exhaustion of dragging your legs out from the knees down after every step.

'One never gets used to artillery fire – the effect is so shattering. I was amused when you told me of W.H.R. back home who was suffering from shock after the Zeppelin raid on Sheffield. He ought to be out here and see what we have to go through all the time. Nobody takes any notice of MG or rifle fire, and on the whole trench work is not very interesting, merely nerve straining. Anyway nothing in civilian life will shake my nerves if I can get through this lot without getting shell shock. It is marvellous what men can go through and for the last few days the lads have been through hell, and even though we are keeping the Boche busy he is a tough foe and far from being beaten. The country should never forget what Tommy has done for her, we even get shelled by the Boche when we are back in our billets miles from the front and the incessant shelling in and near the line makes you nervy, however much you are prepared to put up with it.'

In the middle of November, the 31st Division put in a major assault on the German lines as part of the offensive that became known as the battle of the Ancre.

This time it was the turn of the 92nd Brigade to bear the brunt of the fighting and the lead battalions of the East Yorkshires suffered casualties comparable with those suffered by the City Battalion on 1 July. This time, the East Yorks did make some progress into the German trench system, because, critically, the German wire was cut in many places, but the supporting battalion on their flank did not and they were left vulnerable to counter attack and eventually had to withdraw. One of their men, Private Jack Cunningham of the 12th Bn East Yorkshire Regiment, won the VC in that attack when he found himself all alone yet took on a force of German troops in a communication trench with Mills bombs and forced them to retreat.

One has to question Haig's cavalier attitude to casualties in another failed attempt to capture German strongpoints at the northern end of the Somme battlefield in the Gommecourt-Serre area. It was also so late in the year, after the offensive on the Somme that had gone on for four and a half months achieving only limited gains along the Albert-Bapaume axis and nothing north of Beaumont Hamel.

The 12th Battalion took over the trenches from the East Yorks immediately after the battle and held the line for four days. It was while they next went into the front line trenches that Vivian's promotion to Acting Captain came through on 24 November. Although he had long coveted this promotion, it was difficult to argue that it was not deserved. He had led A Company for 36 days and had already done two tours in the trenches with them, even though he had a low opinion of most of the new men who had been drafted in. He wrote:

'We have 75% new men, aged and talkative, with the guts of a mouse. They are more trouble and bother than an infant's school. I had only four hours sleep in four days looking after them in the line.

'I am, of course, glad my Captaincy has gone through and I hope they will make it a Temporary Captaincy soon, if only for the sake of the family who must have been embarrassed that I was still only a Second Lieutenant. If I avoid being a casualty and my nerves do not give way one might go even further.'

Ironically, Vivian did go sick after another tour in the trenches, where he had told the CO that the Brigadier's orders for new dispositions for holding the line were all wrong and, as he knew the sector blindfolded, they ought to drop these new ideas and follow his guidance. He worked on the CO for two days before Lt. Col. Riall was convinced and then persuaded Brigade to follow Vivian's advice, which they did.

Only one day out of the line, Vivian was diagnosed with an abscess on his left tonsil and sent off to hospital at Wimereux on the Channel coast near Boulogne. The hospital was in the Casino and he clearly was considerably ill for some days. He found himself in a bed next to an acting major from his own battalion whom he seems to have thoroughly disliked, their acquaintance going back to meeting each other in business circles in Sheffield before the war, as he told in a letter home:

'I am in the next bed to this Captain, recently made an Acting Major, who you all know. How he gets sick I do not know. He never comes near the front line, the 3rd support line being the nearest he gets to the front. What a nut, I ask you, he has spent only three or four days in the front line out of his whole existence in France and they say brains are lacking in the army.'

Later in December, Vivian was sent to a hospital in England and when he was judged to have recovered he was discharged, but given enough leave to allow him to spend Christmas with May, John, and the Simpson and Belcher families back in Sheffield.

Reg, on the other hand, had never had a leave back in England until he was sent for officer training at Oxford in July 1917, when he had been recommended for a commission. Nor did he get the chance to enjoy his Christmas Day as the Battalion was on the move all day, and they only got to celebrate Christmas on Boxing Day at Sailly Dell when they had established themselves in new billets. Reg must have felt fated never to have a proper Christmas Day in the Army, as the previous year he had been at sea off Gibraltar throwing up his Christmas dinner over the side of the ship.

It is not recorded if Reg ever went sick while he was in France, but a huge number of the Battalion were ill and most of them hospitalised for a period. Between October 1916 and April 1917 there were 887 members of the Battalion evacuated to hospital, some no doubt going more than once. It is hardly surprising when you are asking men, despite their being young and very fit, to survive in trenches and dugouts during a northern European winter, where they are dealing with wet, freezing conditions, deep mud and regular flooding, not to mention snow and blizzards. It is amazing that anyone came through unscathed and for many the reason for hospitalisation was 'trench foot', caused by constantly having to endure wet feet in wet boots that made their feet swell to three times their normal size, be excruciatingly painful to move at all, and make the flesh so swollen that one could push a finger right into the foot and leave a hole in the bloated tissue. Reg claimed he never got trench foot because he changed his socks regularly, but all the time the men were at the Front they would have been nursing cuts and bruises, suffering diarrhoea and colds, even flu, yet remained at their posts. It was a very strange way to live and in past centuries it was the reason why armies went into winter quarters and accepted a virtual truce until the weather was warm enough to continue fighting.

Vivian was back in France before New Year's Eve, having met up with his sisters in London before getting the boat train from Victoria to Folkestone. Because his train went at 6.50am, he checked in at the Grosvenor Hotel, adjacent to the Victoria station complex and full of officers coming back from leave and due to sail for France in the morning. In the evening, he joined his sisters for a farewell meal at a swanky restaurant in the West End and thought the place 'rather flash and the people rather shoddy'.

'They gave us a fair dinner but the place was very cosmopolitan. Then some silly ass stood up and proposed a toast to "our boys at home and abroad" that met with a very weak reception.'

Vivian's sisters saw him off in the morning at Victoria on the early troop train, and like all war time partings they must have been thinking that this may be the last time they would see their brother. No doubt there were stiff upper lips all round, but Vivian had told them at dinner the night before that, in his opinion, the Germans were far from being beaten and that there was unlikely to be an end to the fighting in the coming year of 1917.

To celebrate the New Year, half of the Battalion went back in the line at Hebuterne on 1 January, occupying the left sector trenches. Vivian was the officer in charge of A and B Companies comprising his half of the Battalion and the tour although a long one went off without too much drama.

Vivian wrote to his family, and at the same time thanked them for the special Christmas festivities he had enjoyed at Sheffield. He got regular letters from many of them, while May wrote every day and he liked to hear of her life in peaceful Sheffield and how the 'fat lad' was getting on:

> 'The weather has been quite decent and often there was strong moonlight so that made one's duty much easier. Pitch dark is horrid out here as you feel your way along and you slip between trench boards, tear your hands against the wire revetments and fall down with great frequency. The waders you sent have been torn to shreds and let in water and are now quite useless, I am afraid.
>
> 'We still had plenty of artillery fire but with my luck I brought two companies out of the line after nearly a fortnight, with no casualties from enemy action. Leaving the trenches was a problem. The Boche artillery put a ring of shells round us for two hours, and I got a platoon out of the front line before he proceeded to knock it in. One shell landed on a big dug out where fifty men were sheltering but fortunately it was a dud. When we eventually got away he shelled the exit to the communication trench in a village behind the line. He usually does this hoping to kill a few on their way out of the trenches.
>
> 'I often think of Wortley and the chaps I used to play with when the sun shone and the only thing that mattered was whether you legged someone down or not. Those were days when you could give your brains a rest, we have none of that here as there is always something to think about even if it is quite a trivial problem involving one of the men.'

Later in the month, Vivian was sent on a Lewis gun course for three weeks, and when he got back in February he was asked to be the acting adjutant because Lt. Ward, the acting adjutant, was going off on a Staff course and Captain Tunbridge was still away on another course. Again, he told all in a letter home:

> 'I refused the adjutant's job, but the CO said the Brigadier had suggested me and when Riall told him I wasn't keen, the Brigadier insisted I do it. The CO did try and arrange it so that I would not lose my rank as I no longer would have a company, and that I would keep my three stars and my captain's pay.'

However, it was not to be. Regulations said that the adjutant was a lieutenant's job and so Vivian had to revert back to his substantive rank and take a loss in pay. He was not greatly pleased but then found that the adjutant's job was interesting and put him at the centre of things in the Battalion, as he virtually became the CO's right-hand man, and Vivian got on well with Lieut. Col. Riall and they trusted one another.

'I am getting along all right and the CO says I should make a very good adjutant. Which coupled with the fact that he has put my name forward to head the list of promotions is very satisfactory. I have had to take my three stars down so I am a 2nd Lieut. again. Thus the Army treats its sons. Makes them take up a more responsible position and then strips them of their rank in consequence. Fortunately I am only losing six pence a day so I am still quite well off financially.

'The adjutant's job is very similar to office work and I fell into it like a duck to water. I am all serene reorganising a lot of things and with inside knowledge I know some of the weak spots on company management. I shall go back to my company having had a very useful experience and also done the CO a good turn. I've done a lot of useful things for him without him asking and he has appreciated that. I've far more power to get things done than as a Company Commander and I haven't let the grass grow under my feet I can tell you.'

In the meantime, while Vivian was bemoaning his loss of rank, Reg was getting what must have been a long overdue promotion. On 13 February, he was made an acting unpaid Lance Corporal, a position that was confirmed as a paid Lance Corporal in early April. As Reg had been with the Battalion from the start, and not missed a single time in the trenches, it was surprising that he had to wait so long. Several of his signaller mates had been sent off to undertake officer training preparatory to being commissioned, as happened to Josias Jago who in July 1917 became a Second Lieutenant in the Notts and Derby Regiment (the Sherwood Foresters). Reg must have impressed as an NCO because in July he also was recommend for a commission and sent back to England for officer training and he would say goodbye to the Battalion and the Regiment for the rest of the war.

At the end of February, the Germans began their planned withdrawal back to their newly prepared and formidable positions that the British called the 'Hindenburg Line'. Any plans for a British offensive for the spring were now thrown off balance because the German defences that Haig had been planning to assault from Arras to the Somme were now relinquished. Although there was rear-guard delaying action in many areas, along with many booby traps left in the German trenches and dugouts to catch the unwary, the British now occupied land with unexpected ease, where they had expected to pay a high price in men's lives for attacking these same trenches in Spring 1917, with no guarantee of success.

Vivian wrote home, telling then of the unreal experience of strolling around the German positions at Gommecourt, defences that they had been viewing through trench periscopes or loopholes for months.

> 'It really was very pleasant to go over to what had been the Boche's sixth line on the top of the ridge and look over at land that we had never seen. I stayed awhile as the Notts and Derbys put in an attack against a wood and a farm 500 yards away against a small delaying force which eventually withdrew. It seemed so odd sitting in a dug out that had been occupied by the enemy just a few days before, although many of the dug outs had been burned out as our men had thrown grenades into them after seeing if anyone wanted to surrender.
>
> 'Although the Boche have gone and left large quantities of material, it puts our offensive back many weeks, not least because the artillery cannot get through the morass and chaos of the battlefield. The German retreat has put our lads into a very good mood –it feels like a victory– but we shall knock against them shortly and he will have his trenches and guns all ready that he has installed at his leisure, to say nothing of the yards of wire and the mined areas. So that, in the language of the Gods, we will probably hit a rock!'

The German withdrawal also allowed Reg to help carry out a painful yet deeply emotional and fulfilling duty. When the Battalion moved into billets not far from the Serre battlefield, he went with the Padre one day in early March to visit No Man's Land where the City Battalion had attacked on 1 July. The Padre, Frank Ford, and Reg had become friends while they were out in France, when Reg had often accompanied the singing on a portable organ during the Padre's services in the field. So presumably that was why he had asked Reg to accompany him on his important mission to give a Christian blessing, and a semblance of a funeral service, to the dead who had been lying out in No Man's Land for seven months. Reg wrote later:

> 'Frank Ford was popular in the Battalion, he would go anywhere in the line and help anyone. He would help those who could not write to prepare a letter to send home and he would talk to those who needed some private comfort, especially the wounded and those who knew they were going to die from their injuries.'

Reg must by now have been hardened to the sight of dead bodies, but what he witnessed that day was a particularly desperate experience. These men had been his mates, many of whom he had known since before the days of Redmires, had sailed with them to Egypt and had relaxed with them in estaminets – the bistros where they could get some half decent food, drink and company – behind the lines in France. Nothing so far in the war had prepared him for a sight such as he saw that day, and it was a memory that would sear his soul and he would never forget.

'There they lay in rows just as they had fallen in the battle, but they were no longer recognizable bodies, but skeletons where the white bones were held together by khaki rags and their webbing equipment. Some still had helmets on their skulls, some still had tufts of hair and one shuddered to think how they had got like that in the months since that day in July.

'We walked as far as the German wire and there were bodies all the way up the slope. Then the Padre turned and faced what had been our lines and said an appropriate prayer for the dead and we sang Hymn 437 from the Ancient and Modern Hymn Book that he had given me. The Hymn was "For all the Saints" and for part of the hymn I accompanied the singing on my mouth organ. We also sang Hymn 499 'On the Resurrection Morning' and it was almost unbearably poignant to be standing there among the corpses of our pals. I still have that hymn book and it is a treasured reminder of that morning. The next day it snowed and covered all the bodies.'

Chapter 10

Arras, Gavrelle, Cadorna and Vimy
April – September 1917

During April, the Battalion was part of the First Army reserve and after leaving Merville on 8 April was quartered during the month in three villages well behind the front. For the 12th Battalion this was a quiet month, but it was far from quiet for General Horne's First Army north of Arras. On 9 April, the Canadian Corps of four Divisions, fighting as a unified force for the first time, took the strategic position of Vimy Ridge and its southern flank. This was one of the outstanding offensive successes of the First World War, whilst east and south of Arras the British Army assaulting the Hindenburg Line also made some significant, if less spectacular, gains. However, the Australian 4th Division at Bullecourt could not repeat the success of the Canadians at Vimy and suffered its most disastrous battle of the war, sustaining many casualties and losing many men captured by the Germans.

Meanwhile, Vivian was back in charge of A Company and was again an acting captain with the rank badges and pay to go with the promotion. He wrote to his brother on 18 April:

'I think I owe you a letter, but we are moving from village to village all the time and there are so many things to do when we are on the move. I am tons happier as a company commander than as adjutant and I am thankful to be back. The CO has put me in for a temporary captaincy above the heads of about six other acting captains and lieutenants and if it comes off I will be all serene.

'The company is pretty good now though it was a bit out of hand when I took over again. I think they will do well when the time comes because we train individually as well en masse. As a captain I am entitled to a horse and I am now riding pretty well. I had a fine afternoon two days ago when going to reconnoitre a training area and galloped over field after field. It all gives you the idea of the excitement of hunting.

'The country we are in at present feels very English and reminds one of the Downs, but I expect we are in for something pretty mustard soon. At the moment the Hun is fighting hard for his life and he'll be beaten in the end, though there's no doubt it will be a long job and will take many months.'

The quiet period for the Battalion ended on 1 May, when they moved into a forward position at Roclincourt in support of the 31st Division's assault on 3 May on the German lines from Oppy Wood to south of Gavrelle, north east of Arras. This time, the 94th Brigade was the support Brigade, whilst the 92nd and 93rd Brigades led the assault but were bloodily repulsed by the Germans, with heavy losses in the Hull Pals Battalions of the 92nd Brigade and the Leeds, Bradford and Durham Pals of the 93rd Brigade.

Lieutenant Colonel Riall was based in the 93rd Brigade's HQ at Bois de la Maison Blanc, so that he could be given orders where to send reinforcements from his Battalion to strengthen positions that the Germans might be overrunning. Soon the order came that A and C Companies had to quickly reinforce Hill 80, a prominent feature about half way between Gavrelle and Oppy, because it seemed to be in immediate danger from a German counter-attack. Vivian led A Company and his friend, Captain Robert Leamon, led C Company and they had to cover over a mile as quickly as possible to get to the position before the Germans. It was broad daylight and the only way to get there in time was across open country with all the incipient risks of an artillery barrage on their combined force of three hundred men.

Writing a few days later, Vivian described the events:

'I was detailed to take A Company to defend a flank about five days ago. I got through their guns with just one platoon, then all their guns opened up and cut off the remainder of the Company. I got to the position (Hill 80) without a casualty and we were on this long sloping hill facing Fritz and naturally we got a lot of attention. I was told to hold the flank at all costs even though I had only got forty men there at that time. A few minutes later I saw the rest of my men running to join us chased by shrapnel, but I still thought we were for the long jump. Half an hour later the other Company got through and also some Hotchkiss guns and I went off to my left and found some Vickers gunners and fixed them up. Then we knew we were all right, but it was touch and go for some minutes.'

The prompt action of Vivian and his Company saved Hill 80 and the German attack petered out. But Vivian was not unscathed.

'I was blown over once or twice but finished up rather badly. I was taking an East Lancs officer round who was relieving me, when coming round a traverse we got a whizz bang smack in the bay and it blew me over and the other chap was killed outright. My backside felt very sore when I woke up and when I felt my britches they were wet. I thought I had got a "Blighty" but then found it was a piece of shell lodged in my water bottle and that had saved me. My luck was in because wounds in the buttock are no fun, you lose so much blood. However, my buttock looks as if I have been hit by buckshot but don't worry I'm in the pink.'

The Battalion was back in the line on 9 May, now holding the front line in the Gavrelle sector, an area that included the Windmill spur that many thought was the most dangerous place they had defended in all their time in France. We do not know Reg's exact whereabouts at this time, although he was in the Gavrelle trenches, as always ever present at the Front when the Battalion was in action. It fell to D company to hold the Windmill Spur and Reg, now a fully-fledged Lance-Corporal, was most probably in the thick of it, surviving the German assaults and shells with his usual cheery humour and his refusal to worry about the future too much. The spur was a commanding position and the Germans were as desperate to recapture it as the British were to hold on to it. No one dare move during the day and there were dead bodies and parts of bodies strewn all over the area creating the stench of death everywhere. Also, in the summer heat, drinking water soon ran out and new supplies could not be brought up during the day. In his history of the Battalion, Richard Sparling records that two or three men went mad with extreme thirst.

The Battalion spent twenty days in the sector, almost all of it in the front line but even when they were in a support position near to Bailleul they were sending work parties back to the front at night to rectify damage to the trenches and build new positions for better defence and use in future offensives.

Vivian wrote home, saying:

'The old stately trench warfare has gone. There is now a feverish preparation all along the front for offensives present and future. One lives are in a perpetual state of unrest and when out of the line you're not really out because you return every night to do tasks that cannot be done in the day. We set off about 9.30 pm and go three miles to the front and work for three hours and return about 4am and then sleep if we can. It is tiring work but I've had some ripping times wandering back in the morning just after dawn and enjoying another new day.

The ruins of the windmill at Gavrelle, regarded by many in the 12th Battalion as the worst place they had fought over during their time in France. The Windmill spur changed hands eight times.

'I built two forts in front of our lines within 60 or 70 yards of the Boche and then a communicator to one of them covered by another fort. While we built these forts we were constantly being sniped at and we have driven off some of their patrols. These forts are in front of a position (Windmill Spur) that has changed hands eight times and is jealously regarded by the Boche.

'In the meanwhile I try and dodge Bertha Krupp's iron rations. If you use your intelligence you can time a barrage and then nip in to your next position without casualties. Fritz knows all the positions of our dug outs because these were his trenches, and they shell them unceasingly. One is much happier in shell holes. I am a bit fraggy in the nerve department at the moment but I will struggle to get over it in the next few days.'

One man who did not get over it was the CO, Lt. Col. Riall, who had been carrying the strain of running a battalion and suffering increasingly poor health. He finally felt he could no longer go on when the Battalion was due to go back into the frontline on 18 May and he was evacuated to hospital and Major Douglas Allen, the second in command of the Battalion came from the rear transport lines to assume command. The precaution had been taken to separate the CO and the second in command earlier because of the very real threat that they could both be killed by the same artillery fire whilst in their HQ dugout near the front line. Lt. Col. Riall and Vivian had got on very well and Vivian must have wondered if his promotion to Temporary Captain would now get lost again with the advent of a new CO.

That new CO did not arrive at the Battalion until 1 June, after a month in which the 12th Battalion had suffered the loss of over 150 men, including three subalterns killed and five wounded or gassed. These losses were light compared to other Battalions in the 31st Division, where the total losses for May were 3,211 killed, wounded and prisoners.

Major Frank Hood, the acting OC the 13th Battalion of the York & Lancaster, was well known to the Battalion because he had been in

Lt. Col. Francis John Courtenay Hood, the last CO of the 12th Battalion. He led the Battalion from 1 June 1917 to 28 February 1918 when the Battalion was disbanded. He was well known to the officers and men because he had commanded the Battalion temporarily over the New Year 1916-17.

temporary command from early December to early January when Riall had been away on an extended Christmas leave. Now promoted to acting Lieutenant Colonel, he would remain the CO of the 12th Battalion until it was disbanded in 1918. He had experience of cavalry warfare in South Africa, serving with Paget's Horse (the 19th Bn of the Imperial Yeomanry) before being discharged from the army after the Boer War. He was working as a commercial traveller in 1914 and immediately offered his services and was commissioned as a captain, becoming the adjutant of the 9th Bn The Buffs (the East Kent Regiment) before joining the 14th Bn of the York & Lancaster in 1915 and later becoming their second in command.

The arrival of the new Colonel coincided with a fortnight out of the line at Ecurie, a village north of Arras. Not only did training continue but Brigade thought it would be a good idea to raise morale to organise a Brigade Sports Day and Vivian was dropped on again to be the 'muggins' to organise the whole event.

'I had only 36 hours to run the whole thing from start to finish, but it went off rather well despite that. I managed to get six teams to compete, one each from the four battalions and a couple of extra teams that were made up of Brigade staff, Royal Engineers and the Brigade's other supporting units. It was warm work getting round all the units, who were all over the area, and fixing up the entries, but nothing is impossible in the Army. I get all these kind of jobs but I cannot be spared for leave in England, or a spell at an Army Rest camp and little things like that.'

The event was covered with many column inches in the Sheffield papers, as if the event was down the road at Bramall Lane, proof, if any were needed, that Sheffield still had a soft spot for the 'City' Battalion even though only a minority of the men now came from the city. At the close of the meeting however, the 12th Battalion could only manage third place, unlike their regular success in former events. Proof again of the changing demographic and the stark fact that so many of the star performers in earlier days were now either dead or in long term recovery from their wounds

There was another important job that came Vivian's way in June, after another five relatively uneventful days in the trenches in the middle of the month. He was given the task of planning an attack for the whole Battalion on a critical German position north of Gavrelle. The British called this objective the Cadorna trench, most likely after the Italian Commander in Chief, Marshal Count Luigi Cadorna, an unpopular commander who had a penchant for executing deserters.

The Cadorna attack is usually referred to as a raid, but it was in fact a part of a Divisional assault on a particularly stubborn sector of the German defences. It was one move on the chessboard of British strategy, the main purpose of which was to encourage German uncertainty as to where their main thrust would come in the summer of 1917.

The Battalion trained in model trenches behind the lines near Roclincourt for two days, and then joined up for a simulated attack with the rest of the 31st Division for another couple of days. On 25 June, the Battalion was given a day off to recuperate but by the morning of the 27th, they were back in the line ready for 'going over the top'. For Vivian, but not for Reg, this was the first time he would take part in a set piece assault on the German lines, assaults that had proved so costly in lives at best in the past, at worst unmitigated disasters. There had been a lot of thinking on how best to get over the basic conundrum of overcoming well-fortified enemy trenches defended by disciplined soldiers, who were protected by deep bunkers and supported by machine guns and accurate artillery fire and Vivian tried to incorporate that knowledge into his planning.

Early in 1917, the British Army had introduced some changes to its basic unit, the platoon, after its dire experiences of 1916. It was platoons of forty men each who would be the ones who initially got into the enemy trenches, killed or captured the occupants and then held off a counter-attack. Having found out the hard way that the light machine gun, the Lewis gun, could be a crucial weapon in the attack, and that troops throwing Mills Bombs were very effective in close encounters, the army now ruled that in each platoon of four sections, led by a subaltern, only two sections should be basic riflemen (120 rounds each), with one of these sections containing rifle grenadiers, who would make the assault, whilst one section would now be devoted to supporting and defending the Lewis gunner (20 circular pans of 47 rounds each) and a fourth section were to be bombers (carrying buckets of 15 bombs a time). These changes would allow a platoon to be more flexible and hard hitting and not be stuck helplessly outside unbroken wire unable to fight back, as had happened at Serre almost a year previously.

Zero hour was 7.10pm in the evening, giving enough time to do the job and then be protected by darkness if things went wrong. The order of battle for the 94th Brigade who covered 1000 yards of the front was: the 13th York & Lancaster at the northern end, the 11th East Lancs, the 12th Battalion and the 14th York & Lancaster near the Windmill at Gavrelle

Vivian's A Company was on the right of the City Battalion's assault, with C and D companies alongside to the left. B Company stayed in reserve, moving up into Railway Trench, the British front line, when the three other companies set off behind the British barrage and walked out into No Man's Land. The area the three companies first advanced across is today a massive electricity relay station but then it had all the usual detritus of the battlefield, some of which would provide cover if required. The three companies had to advance 400 yards and then get themselves into a position to run the last few yards and jump into the Cadorna trench before the Germans could recover and come up from their bunkers into the line. To aid their mobility, each soldier carried much less weight than at Serre in 1916, although he still had to carry basic kit, including his rifle and 120 rounds,

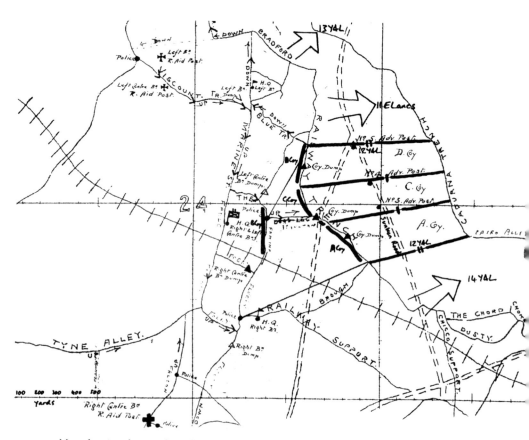

Map showing the attack on the Cadorna Trench at Gavrelle by three companies of the 12th Battalion and the positions of the other three Battalions in the 94th Brigade.

helmet, gas mask, a full water bottle, haversack, a pick, shovel or wire-cutter and three sandbags each, the whole weighing about 35lb altogether.

Once into the trench, the men fought with animal savagery in the confined space. Otherwise civilised men were now behaving with all the desperate energy and cruelty of medieval warriors, because their own lives depended on it. Bayonets were used and taking prisoners in the melee was now a luxury unless they clearly surrendered coming out of a bunker with their hands up. Richard Sparling picked out a few of the men for special praise.

'Vivian led from the front and was the first man into the Cadorna trench and was immediately engaged in hand to hand fighting with the Germans, as was 2nd Lieut. Frank Westby who showed complete disregard for his personal safety and set a fine example to his men.'

Sergeant Reginald Jarvis was reported as leading a section with conspicuous dash and determination and personally engaging in several hand to hand combats with great success, bayoneting all the enemy he fought with. 'His example throughout the day was magnificent,' says Sparling. Others must have agreed because Sergeant Jarvis, a Conisborough man who had been wounded on 1 July, was awarded the Military Medal for his actions that day. Three runners were singled out for praise as well. Private James Briggs, Private Joseph Widdowson and Private Albert Bowyer ran repeatedly through the shelling to deliver messages across very dangerous terrain, including back to Battalion HQ and the Brigade forward signal office, whilst a Lewis gun section commanded by Lance Corporal Clarence Manterfield set up an advanced position beyond the Cadorna trench and harried the retreating Germans. After their gun was knocked out by German fire, they rushed back to the Cadorna trench, picked up another gun and returned to their isolated post and drove off any returning Germans, despite heavy shell fire all around them.

In a letter telling his brother how the attack had gone, Vivian wrote:

'We had a bit of a do the other day, the 28th to be accurate. Suddenly in the middle of a fine peaceful evening the guns along the entire Corps front opened up with one voice and two Brigades jumped out of our trenches practically as one man, and after forming into three waves quickly walked towards the Boche lines. We were on top of his trench before he could get out of his shelters. Where we got in we got nine prisoners straight away and in the confusion I regret to say that I shot their officer myself. I should not have done it, but there were other Germans in the trench who had not surrendered and they might still have caused trouble. It only took us two minutes to capture the trench and immediately we sent any wounded and the prisoners back to our lines. The Boche response was very weak so we suffered only slight casualties, though we had no trench to speak of, because our artillery had nearly flattened it. Then a violent thunderstorm started and it rained like hell but the men quickly dug to get cover as we were staying here and not intending to advance further.

'Our planes were hovering overhead looking for flare signals to show how far we had advanced, I set off a flare to mark my company's position and was delighted to see a line of flares burning either side of me covering 2000 yards indicating that all units of the two brigades had been successful.'

The attack had been a total success but there was no plan to exploit the gain. It was just 'a bite and hold' mission, whereby the British forces did not get over-ambitious but won small victories one at a time and improved their front line positions. However, for survivors of the disaster at Serre, it seemed like a revenge for the Battalion's many dead a year ago and they had suffered so few casualties. In return, the 94th Brigade claimed it had killed 280 Germans and taken over 200 prisoners, with the 12th Battalion's share numbering 28.

We do not have a record of what Reg did specifically during the attack and the consolidation of the next two days. It is certain that he will have been kept very busy, either acting as a runner or laying down telephone lines to the Cadorna trench from a signal relay post in the original front line. One single shell alone severed three telephone lines connecting Battalion HQ to Brigade HQ and it would have been Reg's task to have attended these breaks in the line caused by artillery fire, often in the open under fire.

For Vivian, the job was only half done. He knew that so many newly gained positions were subsequently lost to counter-attacks, because the assaulting troops were temporarily disorganised having captured a trench after a desperate fight. So he had planned what to do as soon as the position was taken with the same thoroughness as he had planned the assault.

'I had made my mind up before hand what I would do next and the men worked magnificently despite the thunderstorm. The Cadorna trench was often just a couple of feet deep after all the shelling and immediately we had secured the trench we got to work digging it deeper again, replacing the revetments, moving the German wire to the other side of the trench and reversing the parapet so it was facing a possible German attack, not our own lines. Now the three sand bags each man carried could be put into use and we filled about 7000 sandbags securing our position. By the time we had finished the Cadorna trench was well nigh impregnable again.

'The next two days the Boche gave us hell with whizz bangs but we eventually came out quite well. I did not lose a single officer and only about ten men were killed in the whole Battalion.

'I took the Staff Colonel from Division round the position the following morning and he wrote to the CO and said he considered that the way we consolidated the position was a model for a textbook on the subject. He added that I had to write up the story of the whole raid and the consolidation and show a plan of how we attacked and how we restored the trench. So that is not bad for my first attack and the Company's reputation is made.'

Indeed it was, and almost immediately Vivian was recommended for the Military Cross for his leadership and courage during the assault, as well as being mentioned in dispatches for the way he had consolidated his position afterwards. Five days after the Battalion was relieved on 1 July, Vivian's promotion to Temporary Captain was announced in the *London Gazette* effective from 21 January 1917. He was no longer an Acting Captain, but despite the word temporary he was now permanently promoted for the duration of the war, and he could enjoy a salary of £320 pa.

He also said in a letter home that he had been recommended for the Belgian *Croix de Guerre* but the paperwork had been too slow at Brigade HQ and the opportunity had been lost, although it is puzzling to understand why he should be eligible for a Belgian award when Gavrelle was at least thirty miles south of the nearest section of the Belgian border. He also told them:

> 'I was fearfully ill both before and during the attack with a temperature and the squitters but just got on with it, but I am practically right now. I also got some lovely loot including a rather nice Boche revolver for myself and one of their rifles that I gave to the CO. I gave the Adjutant a Boche dagger and the Sergeant Major a watch, compass and field glasses. I also kept a receipt I got for seven prisoners. I'll send it to you as a souvenir of the raid.'

In very short time, Vivian was presented with his Military Cross by General Douglas Haig himself on 16 July, a mark perhaps of how the success of the Cadorna attack was viewed in official quarters. Even royalty had forwarded their congratulations to Divisional HQ. The Military Cross was a highly prestigious award introduced for gallantry by officers and warrant officers in December 1914. Its white and purple ribbon was highly prized by officers during the war, although they had to remain modest in public about the award. After the war, the letters MC after your name could open a lot of doors to career advancement and social circles. You had become an unambiguous war hero and you were revered by people as such.

Surprisingly Vivian's award was the only MC won by an officer in the 3½-year history of the 12th Battalion. However, there was another award and that was to RSM Charles Polden, the archetypal Regimental Sergeant Major, who had always been a rock in any crisis. He had been awarded the Battalion's first MC for his cool and decisive action at Puisieux in early March 1917, when the Battalion was chasing German rear-guards who were falling back to the Hindenburg Line and suddenly put up very stiff resistance.

There was a postscript to the story of the award of Vivian's Military Cross and his

Vivian Simpson shortly after the Cadorna raid wearing his captain's three stars and the ribbon of the Military Cross. He was the only officer in the 12th Battalion to be awarded an MC.

subsequent embarrassment. The family back home were so delighted with the award of the MC to Vivian that George gave the story to both Sheffield papers –the *Independent* and the *Daily Telegraph* – and they both printed long fulsome articles about the famous Sheffield sportsman who was now a war hero. Relatives of other officers and men wrote to their family members in the Battalion and the consensus was that the Simpsons had overstepped the mark, as 'blowing your own trumpet' was just not the done thing.

Vivian firmly reproved his brother.

> 'You see, there are three other Companies in the Battalion and there is such a thing as jealousy and one has to be very wary to avoid stepping over the mark. The officers of my Company did not like it either and the whole thing made me damned uncomfortable for days.'

However, they seem to have forgiven Vivian soon enough and he was given a dinner party in the Mess in his honour where they 'flogged the bottle and wet the Military Cross!'

After the Cadorna attack, the Battalion came out of the trenches until 12 July, when they took up new positions north of Gavrelle in front of the Vimy Ridge. Their Corps, VIII Corps, took over from the Canadian Corps that had wrested this key position from the Germans in April. This would be the Battalion's sector as part of VIII Corps until February1918. On the whole, it was a quiet sector and the front lines that Reg, Vivian and the rest of the troops occupied was five miles in front of the ridge, with 1,000 yards of No Man's Land beyond that. At one period during July, Vivian acted as second in command of the Battalion while Lt. Col. Hood was away on leave and he appears to have thoroughly enjoyed the experience. He was clearly now regarded as the senior captain, the go-to man for any difficult or unusual tasks or duties.

There was a considerable amount of patrolling in this period, sometimes in broad daylight using some new camouflaged suits, something that would have been impossible on the Somme or at Gavrelle. However, much of the time, the Battalion was working hard adding to the extensive system of defensive trenches that would make the Vimy area impregnable, even during the German offensive of March-April 1918.

The Battalion was very much reduced in size whilst at Vimy and this was happening throughout the British Army even before the crippling losses sustained in the third battle of Ypres. Haig's new massive Flanders offensive started on 31 July and went on until November, when Passchendaele village was finally captured by the Canadians after so many men of the British and Dominion armies had been killed or wounded in the mud and squalor east of Ypres.

From now on, the Battalion would never number more than 700 men, but at times in the summer of 1917 the 12th Battalion was down to 450 men and there were now only three rifle companies, D Company having being abolished and on occasions there were only two platoons to a company. In one of his letters home to his brother, Vivian wrote:

> 'Our chief amusement is watching Boche artillery potting at our observation balloons just above our heads. Three times he has brought down one of our balloons over the last six days and another time a couple of his planes brought down one in flames. Unless they can get the balloon down quickly, the observer jumps out with his parachute. How paltry Whit Monday parachute descents will seem to the average Tommy now!'

But there were bad moments during the Battalion's time at the Front. At 1.30am on 6 August, the Germans let fly with a tremendous gas attack that only lasted a quarter of an hour but caused sixty men to be gassed, with one officer dying of the effects later. There was another, even bigger, gas attack in early September after Reg had left the Battalion on 25 August to return to the Regimental Depot at Pontefract, prior to starting his training to become an officer. It was the first time he had been back in England since the SS *Nestor* sailed for Egypt in December 1915 and he had been in every action that the Battalion had been engaged in after they arrived in France in March 1916. He would have been given some generous leave and a chance at last to meet up again with Elsie, before she had to leave Sheffield and travel to Truro to start the new term at her teacher training college.

Vivian had also finally got leave on 28 July and was back in Sheffield for a fortnight and the chance to play some golf at Wortley. Now was his opportunity to spend time with May and his son. He wasn't all that complimentary about 'the infant' who he described as 'a fiend incarnate who, having been strafed by his mother, promptly bit her offending hand.

John Simpson, aged one, with his maternal grandfather, John Belcher, in the garden of the Belcher's house in Broomhill, in the summer of 1917.

At the moment at the age of one he looks more like Borstal than Harrow.' Still it must have been a wonderful relief to be out of the line and enjoying life with the family and meeting old friends, especially at the Golf Club, though his enjoyment would have been tempered by the sadness he must have felt at the absence of some of his playing partners from pre-war days, like the Colver brothers both killed in 1915, and Alfred Bond and Brian Heape, both lost recently in May of 1917.

By the middle of August, Vivian was back with the Battalion. It must have been a difficult parting for husband and wife. Vivian and May had been married for over two years but for the last twelve months they had hardly seen each other, except for Vivian's fortuitous tonsillitis that had given him unexpected home leave over the previous Christmas period. May wrote to Vivian every other day when he was in France and, although his letters to her have not survived, we can assume he frequently wrote back to her. Without doubt, May, with a very young child to care for and a brother at the front as well, must have felt particularly vulnerable. Vivian wrote, from France:

'Left Maykins feeling a bit upset though she behaved like a brick. God knows what it costs the women of this and other countries. They never know when we are in danger up in the line or when we are in comparative safety, so there is no relief from worrying for them.'

The Vimy sector however continued to be rather quiet as both the German and British Armies concentrated their men and materiel in the desperate battle further north for control of the Ypres Salient. When out of the line, there was time for sport and Vivian played in a football match between the officers of the 12th and 14th Battalions that the Barnsley men won 1-0. There were more films, especially featuring Charlie Chaplin, and concert parties including a Pierrot troupe called the Nissen Nuts that members of the 12th Battalion put together. They set a fair standard and were much in demand and eventually became the Divisional concert party.

On 5 September they were subjected to a two hour gas attack by the Germans, who fired around 5,000 gas shells but this time the Battalion was more prepared for the attack and casualties were light. One can detect a certain weariness in Vivian's attitude. There were scarcely any officers left from the Redmires days. That summer, captains John Middleton and Eric Moxey joined the RFC and only a few injured officers came back, one of whom was Captain Reginald Moore who re-joined them in May but in September was judged too ill to continue and eventually got a position on the Staff.

Vivian certainly had had enough of living in the countryside, especially in France, and said he longed for life in Sheffield where you could go to the theatre, a cinema, a decent restaurant at one of the top hotels and, of course, play golf at Wortley. Instead his Brigadier had developed an enthusiasm for vigorous patrolling and was even planning a substantial raid in the second half of September that he had selected Vivian to plan and lead.

Vivian wrote home, saying:

'The Brigadier is a devil for stirring things up. I met him in the line the other day and he said to me. 'You've had a pretty quiet time here for a few days and you seem to have tame gentlemen opposite you. I think we shall have to stir him up a bit'. He then proceeded to do just that, causing all sorts of infernal fire to be brought down on our heads.'

It was while Vivian was out with a reconnaissance patrol on 20 September gaining intelligence for the planned raid, that he was hit in the arm by a bullet. It did not seem much at first, but it turned out to be a 'Blighty', and for a start he was sent to hospital in Rouen and later transferred to a recuperation centre in England.

Neither Vivian nor Reg would ever serve in the 12th Battalion again, but they would both be back in action in the Spring of 1918.

The official message from the War Office sent to the family telling them that Vivian had been wounded and was in hospital at Rouen. Vivian had kept George Harold Simpson named as his next of kin, rather than putting May's name forward when they married, possibly to spare May the agony of picking up the fatal telegram at the front door letter box, if that calamity arose.

Chapter 11

An English Interlude
September 1917 – March 1918

Reg finally applied for a commission on 30 May 1917 and he started a process that would see him commissioned as a Temporary Second Lieutenant in February 1918. He was one among 300 members of the 12th Battalion who were commissioned as junior officers during the First World War. Right from the start of the Battalion's life, even before they got to Redmires, men were being encouraged to become officers, because clearly in a Battalion like the 12th York & Lancaster, there was a good level of education and many capable and responsible men.

Reg had been quite happy to stay in the ranks, initially because it would never have occurred to him that a junior clerk in the City Council's Education Department could seriously be considered as an officer. Before 1914, Reg would have regarded officers as above his station, people recruited from the local gentry, even the sons of nobility, along with established professional people who lived in grand houses on the south and west side of Sheffield. Later, when some members of the Battalion left and were commissioned, he still did not want to take the plunge himself, preferring to stay with his friends who he had joined up with, and then served with from Redmires to Vimy Ridge. However, many of the old gang were now dead or seriously wounded and others like his friend, Josias Jago in the signals section, had put in for commissions and had already become officers, more often than not with another regiment.

The process took some time. His application was not approved and signed by Lt. Col. Hood until 19 July, after Reg had been involved in the heavy fighting around Gavrelle and after the Cadorna attack. It was while the Battalion was in the Vimy Ridge sector that he finally got orders to travel to England on 25 August. He first went to the Regimental Depot at Pontefract, presumably for administrative purposes, before going on a well-deserved leave. He must now have felt the most amazing relief that for the next few months he would be certain to stay alive. For the immediate future, he would no longer be in constant danger of death in the front line, or subject to random obliteration from the enemy's artillery that could strike from seemingly anywhere and cause unforeseen, instantaneous death and mayhem even well behind the lines.

How normal England would seem to Reg after the devastation he had lived amongst in Northern France. Even though there were wartime restrictions, life would appear to continue quite normally. When he arrived back for leave at the Midland Station, the Sheffield that awaited him would look much the same as it did when he left. Zeppelin raids had had only a minor effect on the city, there was little obvious bomb damage, industry was booming and the pain of the city felt by so many families in terraced houses or verdant suburbs could not be seen, even if it hung like a malevolent pall across the routines of life and the spirit of the whole community.

How Reg must have enjoyed that first ten day leave, staying with his parents at their new home on Langsett Avenue on the hillside above Hillsborough. How proud they must have been that their son was about to become an officer and how relieved they must have been to have Reg back safe and sound after all they had read and heard about the ghastly conditions and the desperate battles in France, conditions that they could only partially comprehend. They would have friends and acquaintances whose sons had not been so lucky, but for now their son was out of danger and going up in the world.

On familiar ground in Hillsborough and in the countryside up the Rivelin valley, now was the chance for Reg to really relax, meet up with old friends and once again have the pleasure of courting Elsie, before she had to return to Truro for the new term. That first leave would have been very sweet for Reg, a chance to unwind, release tensions and put the gruesome horrors of all he had witnessed behind him for few months. But his leave did not last that long because, although his officer training course did not start till October, the army could not let him do nothing in the meantime. So in September, Reg found himself packed off to Brocton Camp at Cannock Chase, near where he had been with the City Battalion in the summer of 1915. It is doubtful that he found much useful to do there, rather he was just marking time until his officer's course started at Oxford.

Reg had been selected to go to No.4 Officer Training Battalion that was based at New College, Oxford. Here he would undergo four months instruction, leading to a commission after the successful completion of the course. The army had set up these Officer Training Battalions in February 1916 to give a crash course to potential officers when they realised that with the expansion of the army after conscription was introduced and the disproportionate losses of junior officers, they needed to take drastic action to produce a much enlarged officer corps. They could no longer rely on a steady supply of suitable men from the OTCs of public schools and the universities, they would have to look to the ranks of serving soldiers and elevate those who had proved themselves in battle and had the necessary initiative and authority to command platoons. They looked to men like Reg who had come through months of trench warfare and demonstrated their courage, resilience and resourcefulness, men who had been NCOs and proved they had the ability to command at least at section level, although some of the new officer cadets would have been sergeants and often through necessity would have

Reg when at New College, Oxford, wearing his new Officer Cadet uniform with the white banded cap and the No.4 badge.

already been temporarily commanding platoons. As for etiquette and polish, that could be inculcated on the course and rough diamonds turned into 'temporary gentlemen', although in Reg's case everyone who knew him regarded him as a gentleman already by any definition, except one of overt snobbery.

It was soon apparent that Reg's life was about to change. For the journey down to Oxford, after another spell on home leave, he travelled first class for the first time in his life. It was a forerunner of what was to come for the next four months. The army intended that new cadets would fully appreciate that officers were something special, and that from now on, even as cadets, they would be treated like officers, starting with their new uniforms that were the same pattern as the officers' uniforms. They also had the same, better quality, cap, but with a white band that denoted a cadet in training.

By the end of the war there were 28 locations for Officer Training Battalions and they turned out 73,000 officers, whilst Sandhurst only produced 5,131 during the whole war. They were usually housed in grand buildings, often imposing country houses, to encourage the cadets' sense of importance and they were scattered around the country, including one in County Cork for officer cadets heading for Irish regiments. Being offered a place on the course at New College meant that Reg had drawn first prize in the lottery. Right in the heart of the older Oxford colleges, New College lay alongside All Souls' and Hertford Colleges to the west and Queen's College to the south. It had welcomed its first pupils in 1386 after it had been founded by William de Wykeham, the Bishop of Winchester, who also founded the famous school at Winchester a few years later. New College was only new in the sense that it was new in the fourteenth century, when it was built on a graveyard where many victims of the Black Death had been buried, yet from this perhaps inauspicious start, it became one of Oxford's most academically successful and wealthiest colleges.

After all he had seen in the last two years, Reg would not have been easily over-impressed, but even so it must have been an awe-inspiring moment when he first entered the quad of New College and looked around at the castellated buildings that housed the undergraduates' rooms, seeing for the first time the panelled hall where the cadets would dine in style served by the college waiters, the medieval cloisters set around a separate quadrangle and even a section of the old city wall that formed the perimeter of part of the grounds. If the Army was intending to say to new cadets 'you are part of the establishment now and we expect you to live up to certain standards and behaviour', then living in at an ancient Oxford college could not be surpassed in hammering home this message.

No freshman could have been more excited and admiring of his new surroundings than Reg, who took to his new life at Oxford and seems to have

The main gate at New College, Oxford, from inside the quad.

revelled in it to the full. Yet he must always have been well aware of the irony of being a Sheffield lad, who left school at 14, now dining, studying and enjoying rooms in what was then an even more exclusive environment than it is today. He may have also wondered if it was not all a Faustian pact, whereby the cadets were treated with so much respect and importance, but who, in a few months' time, would be back at the front where the chances of being killed as a subaltern were extraordinarily high.

Reg was put into A Company, a group of 150 men from regiments all over Britain and including a number of very tall Australians. Reg got on particularly well with them and discovered that some of them belonged to wealthy families who owned huge farms and others who had been to prestigious schools modelled on English public schools.

'I used to enjoy drilling these tall Aussies. Little me in command of these men, anyone of them could have easily picked me up,' Reg reminisced years later, but their presence at New College was a reminder to Reg and others that this war was the war of the Dominions and the Empire as well, and it is possible Reg had not met Australians before.

As for the training and instruction, Reg found that so much of it was very familiar and he had been regularly doing something similar since he joined up in 1914. They even practiced digging trenches, but the instructors were looking to see if all the cadets had leadership qualities, even when they were drilling Australians who were over six feet tall. The instruction and study they did within the college concentrated on the same topics as Vivian had done when he was at Camberley two summers previously. There were lectures on military law, military organisation, military history, hygiene and a certain amount of political analysis to help produce well-rounded officers, not just efficient combatants.

There was practical instruction in maintaining discipline and Reg still remembered, in later life, two of the questions he was posed by the instructors.

> 'They asked me what would you do if you saw two drunken soldiers arm in arm on Waterloo Station? They may not have liked my answer which was; "There are more Military Police on Waterloo Station than anywhere in the country and I could safely leave the two drunks to them".'

This may have been taking lateral thinking a little too far for the instructors, but Reg produced the accepted answer to another question that they took very seriously.

> 'They asked me what would I do if a soldier passed me without saluting. I told them I would call him back and tell him it was not me he was saluting but the King's uniform.'

There was time to enjoy just being in Oxford and taking the chance to wander round the back lanes between the colleges in what is one of the finest concentration of Medieval, Tudor and Classical buildings in the world. He joined other cadets boating on the Cherwell and playing in the Company football team, and it must all have seemed such a relaxing time after the chaotic, lethal frenzy of the Western Front.

At the end of the course, there were written exams and Reg was confident that he had done well. He never received any confirmation of his marks, but he was told that he had passed and soon he would be commissioned in His Majesty's Land Forces. The date of his commission was given as 30 January 1918 on the commissioning scroll that was given to 'Our Trusty and well beloved James Reginald Glenn' and signed 'By His

Reg in his new Second Lieutenant's uniform with cuff star and three overseas service chevrons.

Majesty's Command'. Shortly afterwards, he received his officer's uniforms from the tailors and felt and looked every inch a proper Second Lieutenant, even if his commission was temporary until the end of hostilities.

Reg was then given the opportunity to choose three regiments in order of preference in which he would like to serve. There was no guarantee that there would be a vacancy in the regiment of your choice, and if you were over ambitious and plumped for a fashionable regiment you might very well be unsuccessful, unless you had connections. Reg made his choices and put the North Staffordshire Regiment as his first choice. He put the KOYLI (the King's Own Yorkshire Light Infantry) next, who were the 'next door' regiment recruiting in the Yorkshire coalfield from Wakefield to Doncaster, but who marched everywhere at 140 paces to the minute and finally he put his own regiment, the York and Lancaster.

His only connection with the North Staffs, apart from spending the summer of 1915 at Cannock Chase, was that a friend he had recently acquired at Oxford had an uncle who was a colonel in the North Staffs and encouraged him to put North Staffs down as one of his options. Reg was not keen to go back to the 12th Battalion. It was not recommended that you returned to the Battalion where you had served in the ranks, but there were other York & Lancaster Battalions where he was not known. Nevertheless, he chose North Staffs and was accepted by them and posted on 21 February to the 3rd (Reserve) Battalion, the North Staffs Depot and Training Battalion, at Wallsend. He spent some time in Northumberland on a Lewis gun course and he also had some generous leave back home in Sheffield, until the end of April when his posting came through. He was ordered to join the 8th Bn North Staffordshire Regiment, one of the Regiment's war time Service Battalions, who were in the 19th Division currently in the Ypres sector.

Vivian also found himself back in England that autumn of 1917. His return was unplanned after he had been discharged from hospital at Rouen following his wounding in the left arm when he was out on patrol on 20 September. He had been lucky up to then, having served fourteen months in France, spending most of the time in the front line or close reserve and seen fellow officers killed literally alongside him. Like Reg, he would be relieved to be out of it all for the foreseeable future. He had copped a 'Blighty one' but it took longer to heal than he originally envisaged and so he was sent back to England to recuperate, spending most of the next two months at home in Sheffield living with his wife and son at May's parents' house on Broomfield Road.

His injury could have been a lot more serious, the bullet could have smashed his arm or elbow and he reflected that it could have seriously compromised his future golfing career, something that he would have found hard to take. Often when in quiet moments in the trenches, he thought of earlier days playing golf at Wortley and told his brother:

> 'I love Wortley so much better than any place I have ever been to. It is so satisfying in every way. I look forward, when mended, to spend a little time there and even more after the war, if the Good Lord is willing.'

It was also a time when he could take stock of his situation and start thinking of the future with May and his son and they had conversations about taking back their new house at Hagg Lane overlooking the road out to the Snake Pass across the Pennines. May thought that in the spring they ought to give the tenants an intimation that they were going to give them notice, and then she could move there in the middle of summer when, hopefully, the war would be over and the family could settle down to a normal peacetime life.

Vivian also increasingly looked forward to the end of the war and a return to his peacetime routines, though he was more realistic about how long it would take to defeat Germany, especially as the overall strategic perspective was changing so rapidly with Lenin's Russia abandoning the War, the US Army beginning its slow build up in France, the defeat at Caporetto and the retreat in Italy, set against the capture of Baghdad, and then Jerusalem, by British Imperial forces in the Middle East.

He was not certain after his time as a soldier that a solicitor's life was for him and confided as much to George:

> 'I often realised in the old days that I was something of an expensive ornament in the office and it used to worry me. I haven't the brain or memory capacity for the Law and my mind can only run on common sense lines. I think it is quite true that I could look after someone else's interests without allowing my own to intrude but I am not sure being a solicitor for the rest of my life is for me.
>
> 'What I need is a good job that I could throw myself into, but they generally go to people with influence and I certainly have none of that, nor do I crave it. Neither do I have any great ambition to pursue a military career. I am all for peace so I shall never make a successful soldier. What success I have had in the Army is because I am usually surrounded by incompetents and I get all the sticky jobs to do and I have done them well enough.'

By the second week of December, Vivian was passed fit for light duties and posted to the 3rd Battalion of the Regiment that was based in Sunderland. The 3rd Battalion was the York & Lancaster's training battalion where new recruits and newly commissioned subalterns were put through their paces and where Vivian was appointed second in command of one of the seven training companies, and the position suited him just fine. He liked and respected the major who was in charge of his company, although he was not so sure about the Commanding Officer who he termed 'a Wild Irishman':

> 'I have been put in charge of 25 new subalterns superintending their training although I do not have very much actual work to do. The officer instructors are very averse to anything savouring of duty as they all expect to be returning to France soon and have nothing to achieve here. We parade in the school yard and the men are billeted in local schools while we have a very nice mess in a large house with a decent billiard room, although my own quarters are devoid of furniture. I shall spend a few shillings brightening it up, starting with a Roorkhee chair, one of those collapsible canvas chairs that officers use in India that will also be useful when I get back to France.'

For the second year running, Vivian hoped to celebrate Christmas in Sheffield and spend the festivities with May and her parents at Rossleigh on Broomfield Road, but it was not to be. He drew the short straw and had to stay at Sunderland with the 3rd Battalion but he did manage to have an enjoyable Christmas all the same.

His friend and C Company commander, Bob Leamon, with whom he had defended Hill 80 at Gavrelle, was home on leave and fortunately he lived in Sunderland and invited Vivian to his family home to enjoy Christmas dinner. Then soon after, at the end of December, he had a new posting and he may not have been able to believe it. Captain Simpson MC was going back to school, as he had been posted to No.1 School of Instruction at Brocton Camp on Cannock Chase, where Reg had been kicking his heels in September. This time, however, Vivian would not be an instructor but instead he was on the course, a course aimed at potential company commanders, or bringing existing ones up to speed with the latest tactics and developments in Western Front warfare. Vivian regarded it as all part of the Army's bloody mindedness that they could not allow recovering wounded officers to do nothing, so they constructed courses like this one to keep them busy.

Vivian arrived in haste just before the appointed 3pm deadline on Saturday 29 December. Having decided not risk the trains, he had taken a taxi all the way from Sheffield to Staffordshire that cost him a cool nine shillings, only to be told that the course did not run at weekends and he could have stayed on leave until midnight on the following day. It was not a start guaranteed to encourage Vivian's appreciation of his new posting, and he was even less enthusiastic when he discovered that for the next eight weeks there was to be a rigorous timetable with every weekday starting at 9am and running through to 6pm with another two hours writing up notes in the evening. He also found the first week or two of the course was just elementary information being passed on by instructors he did not regard as up to much.

On the plus side, they had access to a pleasant Mess, where they were served by charming, competent WAACs, and a sizeable, white painted YMCA hut for officers only that boasted four good billiard tables, comfy chairs and a big open fireplace, 'where you can sit in comfort, read a magazine or a book and forget about the world outside for a while'. He also hit upon the idea of getting May and his son over to Cannock Chase and staying locally at a rented farmhouse. He told her that he could probably be free in the evenings and definitely at weekends and he looked at one or two farmhouses before deciding on one that was well sheltered by a plantation from northern winds and looked fairly clean. It is not certain that May took up the offer. Probably sitting alone with a one-year-old child in the bleak Staffordshire countryside and seeing her husband infrequently did not really appeal. She most probably opted for staying in Sheffield at the family home in Broomhill close to her friends, and letting Vivian come back to join her at Rossleigh most weekends.

As the course progressed, Vivian got more reconciled to being at Brocton, helped by the fact that for once he rather liked all the officers in his hut. He wrote:

'We've had a nice time together. There is no-one in our hut that I dislike which is a great asset when you live close together. There are chaps here from almost every regiment, including one from the Rhodesia Regiment and couple from the Connaught Rangers. I've palled up with a captain in the Argylls, quite a decent chap called Jock Pollock and I am hoping to bring him back to Wortley with me when we get our seven days leave at the end of the course. He is a very useful golfer and I know he will like playing Wortley.

'Quite a lot of chaps here have got the Mons ribbon as they were out in France or Gallipoli in 1915. I do not like the ribbon very much and think they might have risen to greater heights when designing it. There are service chevrons everywhere and I have them too. I am looking more like an advertising hoarding with my chevrons and my wounded stripe as well.'

Eventually, Vivian's competitive nature came through, despite his early boredom with the 'futile' course, and in the final examinations in February he came first in Tactics, third equal in Law and fourth in Topography, and reckoned that he had the best results in his company. Although he felt he had only been given a grudging report, his CO obviously thought enough about Vivian's competence to invite him to stay on for the next course, but this time as an instructor. Some officers, with the equivalent of Vivian's time served at the Front, would have jumped at the chance to have a perfectly acceptable official reason to stay in England, but Vivian now only wanted to get back to France and re-join his Regiment.

In January, he had heard that Major Douglas Allen, the 12th Battalion's second in command, had transferred to the Tank Corps and that left a vacancy that Vivian thought he would have been asked to fill if he had still been In France. He saw himself as the senior captain of the Battalion and he knew that if he had done the second in command job for 15 days, he would have been promoted to acting major, something he was now keen to achieve.

The course ended on 23 February when Vivian got his promised seven days leave, spending it at Wortley where May and the 'infant' joined him. They stayed in the rooms over the clubhouse and after a battle over rations and wines with Mrs. Morgan, the formidable lady who ran the clubhouse, he ate and dined very well, getting rounds in against his brother and all his old pals who were around at the time.

By the second week of March, Vivian was back in France having had the chance to meet up once again with his sisters in London when he again stayed overnight at the Grosvenor Hotel. They had all gone out together for that last evening and dined in New Bond Street, and in the morning his sisters came down to Victoria Station to see him off. Their fear, as at every parting, was naturally a concern that this would be the last time they saw their brother, but Vivian, no doubt, headed off any of their anxieties with his usual breezy, confident manner, and they, no doubt, never spoke openly to him of the dreadful possibility that this time their parting might be final.

Chapter 12

Death at a Crossroad
13 April 1918

Once back in France, Vivian was again sent to the 'Bull Ring' at Etaples to await posting to a front line unit. He already knew that the order to disband the 12th Battalion had been sent on 2 February and the officers and men then serving with the Battalion were being sent to other York & Lancaster Battalions. The 14th Battalion was to be disbanded too and only the 13th Battalion – the First Barnsley Pals– was to continue. This Battalion had first call on the City Battalion men and 300 Other Ranks plus 15 Officers were transferred to the 13th Battalion, including all of Vivian's old company, formerly A Company of the 12th Bn. Roughly the same number of men were transferred to the 7th (S) Battalion of the York & Lancaster, who were part of the 17th (Northern) Division currently near Cambrai, while the Battalion Band was posted en masse to the 2/4th Battalion who were with the 62nd Division at Magnicourt. Vivian was unimpressed with these changes, despite recognising the necessity to reorganise units because of the Army's shortage of men after the desperate battles of 1917 at Arras and Ypres. Rather, he was adamant that as the 12th were the senior Battalion in the Brigade, in terms of when they were founded, it was they who should have survived, not the Barnsley Battalion, who should have been broken up instead.

That had been the principle that had been adopted when the 94th Brigade had been disbanded on 29 January, leaving just the 92nd and the 93rd Brigades in existence. These two brigades were also reduced to three battalions each, with amalgamations taking place of East Yorkshire and West Yorkshire Pals Battalions to produce composite battalions of the requisite strength. The 31st Division was still in existence, but its new Brigade was a rather unusual addition and perhaps seen by the General Staff as affording a strengthening of the Service Battalions, which now had so many new personnel from different parts of England that they might no longer have the same esprit de corps and fighting effectiveness.

The new Brigade was the 4th Guards Brigade with its three Battalions drawn from the Grenadiers, the Coldstreamers and the Irish Guards. Vivian rather approved of this new development. He wrote home saying:

'I am not sure where I will be posted, there are lots of Y&L officers here and I might get sent to a regiment from another part of England. I shall try and get to the 13th Battalion as I am well known there by both officers and the men. Now that we have a Guards Brigade in the Division and the best of the old Sheffield Battalion who have joined the13th Battalion, I think the 31st Division will be as good as ever and as good as most Divisions in the whole Army. My only wish was that I had come out before the City Battalion was disbanded and then I could have been an Acting Major and perhaps been appointed 2i/c in the new 13th Battalion. Instead I was stuck on that futile course at Brocton, however, everything comes to those who can keep their backs to the wall!'

Vivian got his wish and on 16 March he reported for duty with the 13th Battalion who were out of the line at Magnicourt west of Arras in the First Army area. He was given back command of what was in essence his old company, now renamed as C Company the 13th York & Lancaster and met up again with survivors from the previous summer before he was injured. It was like the first day back at school for the new term and there were friendly faces in the officers' mess as well, like Captain John Cowen, who would later win an MC at Vieux Berquin when the British retook the area later in the year. There were also one or two American officers who were attached to the York and Lancasters, including a Captain in the US Marine Corps, who were there to get battlefield experience prior to the US Army arriving in France in strength.

Vivian did not have to wait long to be back in the action, for on 21st March, Ludendorff launched the first of a series of offensives planned for the spring to divide the British Army from the French, then defeat the British in north west France and Flanders and compel them into an armistice, or a 1918 version of Dunkirk. For once on the Western Front, the mathematics of the forces deployed favoured the Germans after they had defeated the Russian Army by December1917 and had recently signed the treaty of Brest-Litovsk with the new Communist government that marked their formal surrender. Divisions could now be switched from the Eastern Front and deployed against the Western Allies and if success was swift, then the Germans could at this late stage rally and win the war, before the US Army arrived in France in sufficient numbers to make a major contribution to the Allied war effort.

The first German offensive called the 'Michael Offensive' was on the Somme and it had immediate success, almost destroying the British Fifth Army. On the first day, the German 2nd Army recaptured almost all the ground that Haig's offensive in the summer and autumn of 1916 had gained at so bloody a price over 140 days. The 31st Division were out of the line at the time but soon received orders to move south to support the Third Army holding back the northern flank of the German offensive south of Arras. The 13th Battalion reached the front line on the morning of 23 March and relieved the 15th Royal Scots who were desperately holding back the German onslaught, spearheaded by massive artillery bombardment and the '*stosstruppen*' tactics of elite shock troops exploiting weaknesses in the British line.

Vivian's C Company took up positions east of the small village of Boyelles, about halfway between Arras and Albert. What followed was some of the most desperate fighting by the Regiment in the whole of the war and C Company were bang in the middle of it. The 13th Battalion was subjected to repeated attacks by massed German infantry backed up by near continuous artillery fire, and although they had to make some retirements to adjust their front, they held their positions, unlike the Fifth Army further south. It was the task of Von Below's 17th Army to smash through them and take Arras and advance to the coast cutting off the British First and Second Armies further north, but they could not do it.

It was the amazing resilience and sheer bloody determination of companies like Vivian's that saved the day and the Allied cause. Arras never fell to the Germans, nor did the Vimy sector where the 12th Battalion had helped prepare such formidable defences in the autumn of 1917. It was all a new experience for Vivian and all the British troops involved to be on the defensive against a major attack. For the last three years it had been the British who had been 'going over the top' to attack static German defences and this had for so long been the reality of the Western Front. So to be on the receiving end of a sustained assault was an unpleasant, if novel, experience. But it was through their efforts and those of many British and Dominion troops like them, that ensured that by 28 March, the German offensive against Arras (known as the Mars Offensive) had failed, and by 4 April, the German offensive also ran out of steam on the Somme as the British rallied, halting the German advance short of Amiens and stabilising the line until August.

For thirty-six hours during the height of the fighting from the morning of 26 March to the evening of the next day, Vivian was commanding the Battalion, after Lieutenant Colonel George Wauchope was injured and until the second in command, Major Robert Goodburn MC, arrived at the front and took over command. Perhaps that is one reason why he wrote;

'Whirling through these eight days have been the most wonderful time of my Army career. Long days of 22 ½ hours labour and fighting and 1 ½ hours sleep, perhaps with food, perhaps not. All the nails in my boots are imprinted forever on the soles of my feet, but I am alive and keep smiling.

'The Battalion has done wonderfully well at everything that has been asked of them, though they have often been without rations, and one time it was for sixty-two hours. It is not easy to keep going through nights and days of nervous tension without anything to comfort the inner man. One can do without sleep, but not without sleep and food and twice I fell down asleep when just walking round our positions. We don't stand down here rather we are always standing to, that is the order of the day here and I would not have missed it for worlds. It's like a Gallipoli evacuation adventure, slipping out of a village with the Boche on our tails and threatening our flanks, but both the officers and men were at the end of their powers eventually even though the spirit of the troops is excellent, providing they get their rations and their beloved rum.'

The 13th Battalion handed over to 11th Bn Border Regiment at the end of the month and went into rear area quarters back at Magnicourt to await developments. They had suffered 400 casualties during their eight days in the line, mainly wounded including eight officers, an overall figure almost comparable to the losses of the 12th Battalion on 1 July. They had been forced to give some ground, retreating for 3 miles (or strategic withdrawal as Vivian preferred to call it) through the village of Moyenneville, but then holding a firm line a couple of miles further west before the village of Ayette. Here, Vivian led the battalion for a couple of days in dogged defence against repeated attacks by the enemy, until the German High Command called off the Mars offensive on 28 March, leaving Arras, and the centre of the entire British front secure for the present.

Ludendorff had always envisaged his *Kaiserschlacht* Spring Offensive as a series of hammer blows against the British, each one aimed at dividing the separate British Armies from each other and from the French further south. His success on the Somme against the Fifth Army appeared at first as an outstanding achievement by the standards of the Western Front in the war, but it drained his forces of manpower and supplies. Especially hard hit were the elite troops, recruited from the best men of every regiment, his shock troopers, always in the forefront of the assaults and therefore sustaining such heavy losses against the retreating British.

Now, on 9 April, Ludendorff launched his last offensive (code named Georgette) against the British in the northern sector of the line. From Passchendale, through Messines to Armentieres and Estaires on the River Lys, the German 6th Army attacked and made some quick early progress, so much so that it appeared that this time they would achieve the breakthrough. On the Lys, in French Flanders, the Germans threw four divisions against the Portuguese Expeditionary Force (nicknamed the 'Pork and Beans' by British troops) and smashed through them leaving a great hole in the Allied line. The Germans attacked what they considered the weakest force facing them, believing that the Portuguese troops were not of the same calibre as the British, Canadians and Australians. The Portuguese soldiers' morale was probably low because they could not understand what the hell they were doing in this war and why their government had sent them to France when their quarrel with Germany had broken out over maritime issues in 1916.

The emergency on the Lys meant that the 13th Battalion's rest period was over and along with the rest of the 31st Division they were sent thirty miles north to plug the gap in the line. The urgency of their deployment was such that they had the rare luxury of being driven all the way in lorries and old London buses, and

The Lys Battle Area showing Vieux Berquin where Vivian was killed and Hazebrouk, the German Army's main objective in the area. The black line indicates where the Front was before 9 April 1918 and the dashed line is the limit of the German penetration.

they arrived in Vieux Berquin as dawn was breaking on the morning of 11 April. Estaires had fallen and their vital task now was to stop the German advance from reaching the main communications hub of Hazebrouck. The task was extremely daunting for the 31st Division, who were given a frontage of 9,500 yards to defend, difficult enough in trenches, but this was in flat open country where German units could suddenly come at you from any direction.

It was on this day that Douglas Haig underlined the seriousness of the situation by issuing his 'Backs to the Wall' proclamation to all British troops under his command. His short address was as famous to soldiers and civilians at that time and in the interwar years following, as Churchill's call in 1940 for 'Blood, Toil, Tears and Sweat' was to later generations, but it did the trick and companies like Vivian's and battalions like the 13th York & Lancaster turned the Field Marshal's words into reality.

As soon as the Battalion arrived at Vieux Berquin, it was marched two miles down the road to Outtersteene, arriving there at 6am. Once there, it immediately began preparing for a counter-attack timed for 7am against German troops who were advancing in a loose formation across open country where the situation was fluid. Vivian was not involved in this action as he was one of the officers who were held back at Vieux Berquin. He was given command of a 'nucleus' company to act as a reserve line of defence if the Germans broke through, and also be ready to support any company in difficulty at a minute's notice.

During the day he would have heard gunfire from the Outtersteene direction and perhaps from further south where the Division's Guards Brigade was involved in a battle, literally to the death, for control of the Estaires to Hazebrouck main road. For the moment, his main problem was the stream of refugees from Outtersteene and probably from as far as Bailleul, even Merville, the attractive little town where he had so enjoyed being quartered in 1916, now reduced to ruins. On 12 April, the Germans counter-attacked the 13th Battalion at Outtersteene and after continuous fighting all day they forced the Battalion slowly back towards Vieux Berquin where Vivian's defensive positions were deployed.

The next day, the situation got worse, with many casualties and in the afternoon a German flanking attack threatened to surround the Battalion, who then withdrew back to Vieux Berquin itself and Vivian's composite company became part of the front line.

What happened next was related in letters to May and the Simpson family by 2nd Lt. John Gill shortly after the 13th Battalion was withdrawn from the line.

'You will have read accounts of the doings of the Division during the last month and will know that most of the fighting has consisted of rearguard actions. The village of Vieux Berquin is just strung out along the main road and that became our front line. Meanwhile Vivian and myself with a platoon of men were separated from the rest of the Company and found ourselves in an isolated position at a crossroads about 300 yards north of the village church. Here we took up positions as evening turned to night, with Vivian at one side of the road and myself, and a couple of sections, about eight yards away on the other side. The enemy seemed to be in the village and we could hear machine gun fire, and despite the dark I could just see Vivian moving amongst the men encouraging them. Then he attempted to cross the road to come to my side but half way across he was shot by a sniper from close range. He fell in the road with his hands pressed to his face and I crawled out to him thinking he had been hit in the head, but when I reached him he just said 'it's my legs'. I managed to get him to our side of the road under cover and tried to dress his wound that was in the groin. I could see it was hopeless from the start and he died about three minutes later without speaking again. Believe me he could have suffered no pain, as there was a smile on his face to the last.

'One of our men so incensed by his captain's death located the two snipers and gave them a pan each from a Lewis gun, firing into them until he was sure they were quite dead. So they did not escape, I'm glad to say.

'We remained in the position for three more hours until such time as a runner brought news of another withdrawal by the Battalion. We therefore had to leave Vivian there at the crossroads, because we had to withdraw by a series of rushes by sections and had great difficulty getting our wounded out. I am sorry we could not recover Vivian's body, but we did cover it as well as we could before leaving.'

The 13th Battalion was relieved on 15 April after more heavy fighting and many more casualties the previous day. They had lost three more officers killed apart from Vivian in the four days they had been in action, with seven wounded. Altogether they had lost 408 men killed, wounded or taken prisoner, a figure that was even higher than the losses for March in the fighting south of Arras. On 15 April, the 13th Battalion could only muster 134 men and 6 officers for duty, but along with the 29th Division of Gallipoli fame, supported by the 1st Australian Division, they had saved Hazebrouck and forced the Germans to call off the Georgette offensive and turn their attention from the British to attacking the French on the Aisne, with the exaggerated hope of a knockout blow against Paris.

Vivian was much mourned by his men. John Gill wrote again to May saying that one comment he heard from one man that had stuck in his mind was; 'I could have gone through Hell with him!' whilst his friend, Bob Leamon, told May that Vivian was the most popular officer in the Battalion. He wrote:

'Simmie's death is felt by many. He had the courage of a lion and always thought about the men first and not of himself. One of the bravest, most efficient and splendid men I have ever met has given up his life for his country in this awful war.'

Chapter 13

The Survivor
April 1918 - February 1919

Three months after being commissioned at the end of January, Reg arrived in Belgium to join the 8th (Service) Bn. The Prince of Wales's North Staffordshire Regiment at Ouderdom, just four miles south west of Ypres. This was a first for Reg, as the Sheffield City Battalion had always served in France, whilst he now joined General Plumer's Second Army that had held the Ypres Salient throughout the war. Plumer was regarded, then and now, as one of the more intelligent and successful generals of the war, who had won the decisive battle of Messines Ridge in June 1917, a battle where two Irish Divisions from different traditions, the 16th Irish and the 36th Ulster, had fought side by side carrying the burden of the fighting. Although Reg did not meet General Plumer at that time, he would some years later when, as Field Marshal Plumer, he served as the Colonel of the York and Lancaster Regiment until his death in 1932.

Reg had picked a good time to arrive at the Battalion as they were out of the line, and for the next fortnight they went back and forth to support positions at Dickebusch, two miles away to the east, but were not involved in any close action although artillery shells could reach their positions. The Battalion, part of the 19th (Western) Division, had had a particularly bad time during April after Ludendorff's 'Georgette' Offensive had started. They were at the northern end of the German assaults that had engulfed Vivian's battalion and cost him his life. They had been forced to abandon Messines and then had fought hard to retain Mont Kemmel, the highest hill in Flanders, until they were relieved by a French Division on 20 April and sent back to rest at Ouderdom.

Reg and the Battalion stayed in Belgium until 17 May when they finally received orders to travel to the Champagne sector of the French line north of Paris. It was seen by everyone in the Division as a just reward for all the hard fighting they had done, because since the failure of the French offensive in April-May 1917 against the Chemin des Dames, the Champagne region had become renowned as a 'health resort' among the Allied armies. The rail journey took 37 hours from Belgium via St Pol, round Paris to Chateau Thierry (soon to become famous in US Army annals) and Epernay, until they finally arrived at Vitry and detrained. The reason for the very long train journey was an incident that occurred during the night when they were all awoken, many of them knocked to the floor, as their train

The Cap Badge of the Prince of Wales's North Staffordshire Regiment.

suffered a rear-end shunt from another troop train driven by a British army driver. They were detained for several hours as some carriages had come off the rails but amazingly, they had suffered no casualties. However, it meant they arrived in Vitry in pitch darkness at 1am on the morning of 19 May.

For nine days, they enjoyed a real opportunity to recuperate as they were billeted at the village of La Chaussee on the banks of the Marne due east of Paris. The old hands in the Battalion considered it the best billets they had ever had and, apart from the obligatory training, they organised football matches, athletic sports and swimming competitions, whilst there was also the possibility for the officers obtaining leave in Paris just down the road. For Reg it was an excellent way to find his feet as a platoon commander and get to know the Battalion, and also something of their recent history.

The 19th Division was one of Kitchener's New Army Divisions and the 8th North Staffs had been with it since 1914 when it was formed. In July 1915, they had arrived in France and were heavily involved in the Somme battles of 1916 and in the third battle of Ypres in 1917. When the strategic reductions in units happened in February 1918 – that saw the 12th Y&L Bn disbanded– the 8th North Staffs escaped this fate but were placed in a reduced three battalion Brigade (the 56th) with the 9th Cheshires and 1/4th King's Shropshire Light Infantry (the KSLI), all regiments from nearby English counties back home. They were looking forward to a prolonged period in a quiet sector of the Front, relieving fresher French Divisions that went north to support the British Army.

Their peaceful life on the banks of the Marne was shattered on 27 May when the Germans launched their new offensive against the Allies, codenamed Blucher-Yorck after two of their most famous Prussian generals. It caught the Allies by surprise and was launched from the Chemin des Dames towards Paris and the British IX Corps found itself facing the apex of the German advance. On the first day, the German Seventh Army made gains of 12 miles and three British Divisions, including the famous 50th (Northumbrian) Division suffered massive casualties and had many hundreds of men taken prisoner.

The 19th Division had been held further south in reserve but was now rushed north to fill gaps in the front and attempt to stem the tide.

Starting at midnight on the night of 28/29 May, Reg and the other personnel of the 8th Bn North Staffs were driven in a long column of lorries to open country west of Rheims to await the German onslaught. They debussed at a farm north of Chambrecy where they arrived at mid-day. By 2.30pm they were ready to move off and take up positions around the village of Sarcy, seventeen miles west of Rheims. By 6pm, new orders came through to move forward a couple of kilometres to the north and take up new positions on a ridge between two villages of Bouleuse and Mery Premecy and await the German Army that was heading their way.

It fell to Reg to lead a small reconnaissance patrol to see if he could gain any intelligence on the advancing Germans. He wrote later:

'I was sent forward to see if I could see the Germans. I only had my revolver and a walking stick but the men seemed to have faith in me. They were just like the men in the old City Battalion and they accepted my authority without question, but we could not have done much if we had run into any German storm troopers. When we got to the top of the ridge, that was in front of the high ground we were defending, we suddenly came under fire from three whizz bangs so I reckoned we had found the enemy and we got back sharpish and told the CO that the Jerries had arrived.'

The Battalion war diary records that, despite Reg's observations, the Battalion had a quiet night, but in the morning of 30 May the German attack began in earnest and the fighting was furious with the North Staffs just holding their own. They were on the right of the 19th Division and next to them were units of the French 45th Division. Later, their troops broke and left the 56th Brigade's flank in the air so that the Brigade had to pivot on the North Staffs and protect their flank as well as their front. Reg recalled years later:

'We had been ordered to stand our ground but one French soldier came running towards me heading for the rear. I pulled out my revolver and threatened to shoot him and he stopped in his tracks. I would never have shot him but he did not know that, and no doubt his officers had tried the same tactic on panicky soldiers and maybe they had shot some of them.'

The situation continued to be grave and the Battalion had to abandon its ridge near Bouleuse at 12.30pm and fall back to a line between Sarcy and Aubilly as they could not maintain a position without support on their right flank. At some point in the afternoon, a shell from a speculative barrage landed close by Reg and his company commander, Captain D.O. Jones, and they were both wounded by shrapnel. Two other subalterns were injured that afternoon, as was the CO, Lt. Col. Dakeyne DSO, but the North Staffs held their position despite coming under heavy artillery fire and maintained a solid line over the next week, when the final German assault was beaten off on 6 June.

Although he did not know it at the time, for Reg the war was over. What he thought was just a minor wound, at best a 'Blighty' one, turned out to be more serious. He had been hit by shrapnel in the left hip and the metal had embedded itself in the bone; he also soon realised that he was injured in the arm just above the wrist as well. Reg described the moment of impact as one of a burning sensation although he was able to hobble back to the regimental dressing station, where they saw his condition was more serious and sent him off in an ambulance. The nearest military hospital was an American one near Epernay and he was initially treated there for a while. Reg stayed in hospital in France for four weeks until he was shipped back from Le Havre to Southampton, before finding himself once again resident at an Oxford college, although this one now catered for wounded and recuperating officers.

As for Blucher-Yorck offensive, it just petered out, although it had seemed so successful at the start. In the centre of the attack, the Germans advanced 40 miles in five days and reached Chateau-Thierry on the Marne. Here, US forces helped to hold the line and later in June to eject the Germans from the town. At one time, the Germans were near enough to shell Paris, but it was an illusory victory. In 1918, after years of attritional warfare, the German Army just had not got the resources to carry through such an ambitious strategic plan, especially as they could not deliver a knockout blow to the Allied armies. By overreaching themselves, they sowed the seeds of their own destruction in the summer and autumn of 1918 when the Allies went onto the offensive.

Reg's active service in the front line with his new regiment had lasted just twenty-four hours, from the moment the Battalion debussed at Sarcy on 29 May to being wounded by shrapnel the following day. The irony would not have been lost on Reg. He had served for sixteen months on the Western Front with the City Battalion and come through unscathed and then, after months of preparation to become an officer with the obvious purpose of going back to France or Belgium to fight the Germans, he had been wounded on an obscure ridge by a shell fired by an unseen hand.

The wound did not seem too much for a start, but it took nine more weeks to heal after Reg had arrived back in England on 30 June. He was sent to the 3rd Southern General Hospital at Oxford where many of the less seriously wounded patients were housed in buildings around the city, including some of the Oxford colleges. Once again Reg had been fortunate, and he was to enjoy his period of care and recuperation living in one of the Colleges again. And not any old College, but Somerville College on the Woodstock Road, the non-denominational ladies' college of Oxford University, founded in 1879 to give women of intellectual ability a first class university education, even if they could not sit the examinations and be awarded a degree. Unlike the overwhelming medieval presence of New College where Reg had been at the beginning of year, the Somerville buildings were in a restrained classical style but with large grass covered quads where recovering officers could play croquet and perhaps find congenial female company among the students. Reg very much enjoyed his time at Somerville and found that handsome, young, wounded officers were rather popular among the Somerville ladies. It was now high summer, unlike Reg's time with the 4th OCB when he had enjoyed Oxford in its sometime bleak and snowy winter splendour, and boating on the Cherwell, afternoon teas on the college lawns or in

Reg guiding a punt at Oxford while recuperating at Somerville College in the summer of 1918.

Christ Church Meadow, while decorously sharing your sunlit days with attractive ladies seemed very acceptable to Reg. France and the war must have seemed far away and Reg said in his letters that he had no wish to make a speedy return to the battlefield.

His wounds in the hip and arm must have been more serious that the formal report records, because he was only discharged from Oxford in the middle of August and was graded as Category B. This meant that he was judged unfit for front line service, so that if he was sent overseas again, he would only be fit to stand service in France on lines of communication, or only be fit for garrison duty if sent to a posting in the tropics. In the event, after a generous period of leave back in Sheffield, much of it spent with Elsie who had just finished her two year course at her Truro college, Reg was posted to the 3rd (Reserve) Battalion of his new regiment up in Wallsend, at the same camp where he had been in the Spring before he went across the Channel and joined the 8th Battalion near Ypres.

With the Allies now prosecuting the war successfully without him, he must have realised that he would most likely sit out the rest of the war in Britain and that he was almost certainly going to survive this most terrible of conflicts. He had been at the centre of events for the best part of two years and he had clearly done his bit. So training others to go and finish off the enemy seemed a fair and equitable outcome to Reg. He said that he was made an acting captain while at Wallsend, commensurate with his duties in charge of a training company, and among the trainees he came across at the camp was a conscripted soldier whom he recognised as his old boss from his early employment in Sheffield. No doubt Reg enjoyed a little mild *schadenfreude* when he found the tables were turned by the fortunes of war, and he may well have got his sergeant to give the man a little extra drill and perhaps some 'jankers' for old times' sake.

It was while Reg was at Wallsend that his friends in the Mess took him over to Gosforth Golf Club and introduced him to the game. Arriving as a novice on the first tee, he discovered that his 'friends' had lent him a bag of left handed clubs, no doubt to the great amusement of all, but he learnt to play the game at Gosforth and later golf became one of his great recreational pleasures, as it had been for Vivian Simpson. Reg, however, got his own back at cards where his regular winnings at bridge helped more than once to pay his mess bills.

Reg stayed at Wallsend until 11 October when he was posted to the 3rd (Reserve) Battalion of the Scottish Rifles, also known as the Cameronians, a Lowland Light infantry Regiment from Lanarkshire. They were based at Invergordon on the Cromarty Firth, and among their varied roles they served as part of the garrison protecting the Invergordon naval base, one of the Royal Navy's main anchorages

The Cap badge of the Cameronians (the Scottish Rifles) the regiment that Reg was attached to at Invergordon at the end of 1918.

on the North Sea and later famous, or infamous, world-wide for the 'mutiny' of sailors in 1931 over deteriorating conditions.

It seems from his service record that Reg did not join the Cameronians but was just attached to them, but he always referred to them as his third regiment. He certainly had a photo or two taken in Cameronians' uniform but he also always wore a kilt in the photos. Yet the Cameronians wore trews in the Douglas tartan and there is a suggestion from the family that he borrowed the kilt from a Highland regiment officer just for the photograph.

Either way, Reg seems to have enjoyed his time in north-east Scotland, especially so when the Armistice was declared on the Western Front and the 'War To End All Wars' was finally over, and he was safe in the knowledge that he would now live and could plan for his future. The Cameronians celebrated the Armistice in style

Reg photographed in a kilt at Invergordon that he most probably borrowed from a Highland regiment officer.

with a big party in the Officers Mess, and no doubt Reg and the other officers called in on other celebrations held by the men and also joined for a while the revelry in the Sergeant's Mess.

It must have been a wonderful, carefree time for Reg. He could enjoy being an officer in peacetime in a regiment with great traditions, but who were no doubt winding down the intensity of their training now that the fighting had stopped and they all knew they were going to live. There must have been darker moments when Reg remembered those from the City Battalion who had not made it. Friends from the days at Redmires, men who had been in the same queue to attest at the Corn Exchange that long-ago day in September 1914, well known and popular officers and senior NCOs like CSM Joe Ellis, killed by a *minenwerfer* bomb before 1 July, or Captain Colley who was certain he was going to get killed that first morning during the assault on Serre. Reg presumably would have also heard of Vivian's death in April from old soldiers when he was on leave in Sheffield, or from the family who would have seen the tributes in the local papers.

Reg had the opportunity to stay longer in the Army and go out to Germany as part of the Army of Occupation of the Rhineland and he gave the proposition some thought. But he was eligible for early release and he decided that he had served long enough and what he really wanted was to get back to his family and Elsie. Get back to his home town and take up his post again in the Council's Education Department and quietly revel in the freedom of survival.

Reg was officially demobbed on 5 February 1919. His letter from the War Office told him bluntly that his pay and allowances would cease on that day. There were no words of thanks for a job well done just sparse instructions of what to do and what not to do. The letter detailed some other regulations:

'You are allowed to wear your uniform for one month only, but you may wear uniform on ceremonial occasions of a military nature. The permission to wear the uniform is for the purpose of enabling you to obtain plain clothes but will not entitle you to concession vouchers when travelling.'

Soon after being demobbed, Reg was back at his job in the Education Department and although much was familiar, even boringly routine, there were other fundamental changes. The younger, junior clerks like Reg had been away at the war, had seen and been through the most extraordinary experiences that could only be imagined by those who had stayed in Sheffield. Reg and some others had been officers commanding platoons, even companies, and now were expected to again accept a lowly status in a hidebound office.

'Inevitably there was a barrier between them and us, between those who had gone to fight and those who hadn't,' Reg commented years later, and it is clear that for Reg, and countless other young men still in their early or middle twenties, the war was the defining experience of their lives, and nothing would ever match its significance or intensity. For some of them the rest of their lives was an anti-climax, but Reg made sure this did not happen to him.

Chapter 14

The Continuum

When the British retook the Vieux Berquin area in the summer of 1918, one of the officers in Vivian's Battalion spent some time in the area around the crossroads where Vivian had lost his life, looking for bodies of 13th Bn men that he might identify and then arrange a proper burial with a marked grave.

He found a body in a water-filled shell crater right by the cross roads where Vivian was shot. Examining the buttons and the rank markings he believed it was very likely that this was Vivian's body, but initially he could find no confirmation. Nor could he recognise the features even though the body was in a fair state of preservation as it had been lying face down in the water for four months. He went to look at one or two other bodies in the area before returning to the officer in the shell hole and started rummaging through his uniform and equipment until he found Vivian's identity disc in a hip pocket.

The officer arranged for the body to be buried close to the cross roads and put up a temporary marker. He returned a few days later with a properly fashioned wooden Celtic cross that one of his men had constructed, inscribed with Vivian's details. He also took some flowers with him that he lay on

The temporary grave marker of Vivian's grave when it had been re-interred at Outtersteene Communal cemetery. When an official stone headstone with the York & Lancaster badge was installed it displayed the wrong age for Vivian. The headstone said he was 33 but in fact he was 35 when he was killed.

the new grave. Later, after the armistice, the Graves Registration Unit exhumed Vivian's body, along with many other British dead dotted around the area where they fell and had them re-interred at a new military extension to the Outtersteene civilian cemetery. This cemetery lies to the east of the village, no more than two kilometres from where Vivian was killed, and his body was re-buried there with the funeral formalities conducted by a military chaplain.

The officers and men who had known Vivian were relieved that his body had been found, when there were so many of their former comrades' bodies that could not be identified, or just did not exist. As the officer involved said, when writing to the family in May 1919, 'It is important that a brave man has not died, to be buried in an unknown grave.'

This must have prompted Margaret, one of Vivian's sisters, who he was close to and who he called Margot, to visit northern France in October 1919. She described her experience in a letter to the family posted in Boulogne before she sailed back to England:

'You will be glad to hear that I have found Vivian's last resting place. It was a great privilege to be allowed to stand there. Though entirely alone on the wind-swept incline it seemed as if one was surrounded by a crowd of witnesses in the low clouds. Next to dear Vivian lies an "Unknown British Soldier", and on the other side a Private of the Lancashire Fusiliers.

'Some time I must tell you about this pilgrimage – the walk from Bailleul to Outtersteene where on either side there was nothing but huge devastation, with only a scattered hut put up here and there and not a blade of grass to be seen. The scene will be forever printed on my mind. God, what a price to pay!

'After visiting the grave I went into a wee chaumiere where I arranged for the mam'selle to put flowers on Vivian's grave that day and keep it supplied with fresh flowers. Her family had lost everything and all they had now was a tiny hut for five people with a scrounged Army stove and newspapers for wall paper, yet they were still carrying on amongst all that utter devastation.'

Vivian's older brother George, to whom he had written regular letters from the front, wrote a series of letters to the War Office chasing up the loose ends created by Vivian's death in April. One such letter in October 1918 asked for clarification of the whereabouts of the back pay and gratuities owing to Vivian's estate that the War Office had calculated as £203, including a gratuity of £196, but had not yet paid over. He also chased up, on May's behalf, the gratuity of £250 to be paid to her as an officer's widow and also financial compensation for all of Vivian's kit that had been lost in the Arras sector when the Germans launched the Georgette offensive. In another letter to the War Office he claimed that Vivian's estate qualified to be free of death duties because his widow was in straitened circumstances with a two year old child, 'and it is quite certain that her father will have to find monies out of his private means for the maintenance of the widow and child in a manner fitted for their station in life'.

All these letters were written on the stationery of their solicitor's firm, where the partners were named as George H. Simpson and Vivian S. Simpson. Vivian's name had been retained with a small black cross in front of his name, a touching gesture to a brother who had given his life for his country and a way of preserving his memory for a little longer. When the probate procedures had been completed, Vivian's gross effects came to £2,052, not an inconsiderable sum, all of which he left to May. Her one good piece of fortune in this whole dreadful business was that she was living in her family home where her father would have been in a position to support her and his grandson, and this would have given her some degree of stability at a time when her world was collapsing around her.

In early August 1918, the situation got even worse for May and the Belcher family, when news came through that her brother, Percy, had died of wounds received at Lens on 20 July. The family in Broomhill would have been barely coping with the news from the War Office that Percy had been injured when they received another telegram that dashed all their hopes that he might survive. Percy Belcher, before the war a manager at the London and City Bank in Sheffield, where he was following in his father's footsteps, had been commissioned early in the war in the Royal Field Artillery and had seen considerable service in France. He had served in the same Division as his brother-in-law, but in the 92nd Brigade, the Brigade made up of four East Yorkshire Regiment Pals Battalions, and he was

The war memorial at Wortley Golf Club, bearing 11 names including Vivian Simpson and Percy Belcher.

commanding the Brigade's C Battery when he was injured, succumbing to his wounds a week later.

For the Belcher family, like millions across Europe and beyond, the tragedy must have been unbearable, but for May the news must have been even more calamitous. Within four months she had lost her husband and her brother – who had been the best man at their wedding three years earlier – when she must have been desperately praying that, as the tide of war had now turned, Percy at least would survive. If that had come to pass, then after the Armistice Percy would have returned home to Sheffield, resumed his post in the bank and no doubt once again enjoyed regular rounds of golf at Wortley Golf Club, where he had been a member for some years before the war. His safe return would have enabled the Belcher side of her family to resurrect some degree of normality, allowing May to bring up her infant child in secure and loving surroundings.

Not only did that not happen, but the death of her father in February 1923 at the age of 69 added to the desolation and uncertainty of her life. John Frederick Belcher's death may have been brought on by grieving for the loss of his only son, in whom he must have invested such hopes for the future of the family as well as the bank. Added to this were his concerns for Percy's young wife Dorothy, who had married his son in 1916 and who now, like his daughter, found herself a war widow. From the happy and successful family they had been before the summer of 1914, living in their mansion in Broomhill, pillars of Sheffield's society, the war had now laid the family very low and they had suffered just about every disaster that could possibly happen to them.

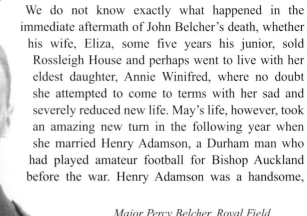

We do not know exactly what happened in the immediate aftermath of John Belcher's death, whether his wife, Eliza, some five years his junior, sold Rossleigh House and perhaps went to live with her eldest daughter, Annie Winifred, where no doubt she attempted to come to terms with her sad and severely reduced new life. May's life, however, took an amazing new turn in the following year when she married Henry Adamson, a Durham man who had played amateur football for Bishop Auckland before the war. Henry Adamson was a handsome,

Major Percy Belcher, Royal Field Artillery, Vivian's brother in law and best man at his wedding in 1915. He died of wounds in August 1918 after being seriously injured at Lens on 20 July.

John Vivian Simpson with Malayan schoolchildren outside the plantation school circa 1928.

taciturn man, usually seen in tweed suits and plus fours, who was currently back on furlough in Britain from his work as the manager of a rubber plantation in Malaya. May and Henry were married in October 1924 and for the next five years they lived in Malaya, taking eight year old John with them, although he would later be entered at a preparatory school at Folkestone, where it is most likely that a Simpson aunt, living in Sussex, kept an eye on him and looked after him during the Christmas and Easter holidays.

John seems to have spent some time in Malaya in the late Twenties, while May and Henry travelled back to England in 1928 when Henry was due for another furlough. But somewhere at the end of the Twenties, the family came back to Britain permanently and settled in East Chinook, Somerset, buying a house called Forday House, a Grade 2 Listed Somerset long house. John, now in his early teens, had by now left his prep school in Kent and was enrolled as a boarder at Sherborne School in Dorset, a school famous throughout the West Country. Built on the site of an old Benedictine monastery, Sherborne could trace its origins to the mid-sixteenth century and even earlier, and was generally recognised as among the top public schools in the country. Presumably the fees would have been paid for by Henry Adamson, or perhaps May had inherited enough money of her own from her father and she was also able to support her son's education at Sherborne, where John remained until he went through the Sixth Form and left in 1934.

John Simpson did not go on to university but led a fairly leisurely existence working for a garage business and looking every inch the carefree young gentleman of the county set. In 1936, he joined the Territorial Army and was commissioned

May Adamson in 1939. Within the family she was always known as 'Doo'. Born Marion May Belcher in 1889, she died in 1958.

into the 5th Bn Somerset Light Infantry. He seemed at last to have found a real calling and with the example of his decorated father to live up to, he became a platoon commander in B Company based in the Drill Hall at Yeovil and threw himself into the training and regimental duties. He went away on several officers' courses one of which was at Sandhurst, another at Catterick and also spent some time at camp in the summer of 1937 with the 2nd Bn Somerset Light Infantry, one of the two regular battalion of the Regiment.

In May 1939, when John was almost 23 years of age, he married Rachel Mackintosh, but their new married life was cut short by the outbreak of war in September. So that winter John found himself in France close by the Belgian frontier, not all that far from where his father was buried at Outtersteene. The 5th Bn Somerset Light Infantry were part of a new BEF and they spent the period of the phoney war preparing defensive positions that would have done the job if the Germans had used the same strategic plan as in 1914 using the same massed infantry tactics. They were straddling the old 1914-18 battlefields and it would have seemed to all of them that the new war, when it eventually got going, would be a re-run of the Great War slogging match along the French/Belgian border. Every man in the BEF was no doubt determined to play their part and match the courage and determination that their fathers had shown just over twenty years previously against the same enemy.

This must have been even more poignant and compelling for men like John Simpson whose father had fought and died defending this same ground in northern France and John must have often reflected on his father's sacrifice during those weeks before the German offensive started in May, and also how his own generation must not let the side down. When the German attack came, the French, who comprised 90 per cent of the Allied armies, and the BEF were outthought and outfought, and in a bewildering few days the German mechanised divisions had forced the BEF to rapidly retreat and abandon its French allies to their fate. Proud Regular and Territorial Divisions and Regiments retreated ignominiously to Dunkirk and evacuated the Northern European mainland for what turned out to be an absence of four long years. It is one of the greatest defeats in British military history that somehow later generations have turned into the 'defiant' Dunkirk spirit and John Simpson was there. Wounded, and no doubt fighting as effective a rear-guard action as he could, just as his father had done at Arras and on the Lys in March and April 1918, Lt. Simpson was one of the many thousands who managed to get away back to England and be ready to fight another day.

In the summer of 1941 John Simpson had recovered sufficiently to be posted to the British Army's main overseas theatre of war. In June, he landed at Suez and took up a post as adjutant at an Infantry Base Depot near Geniefa close by the Great Bitter Lake that formed part of the Suez Canal. Here troops were rested who had been fighting in the Libyan Desert and also where new troops from Britain, India, Australia and New Zealand could get acclimatised and train for desert warfare. Many of the

2nd Lt John Simpson leading his platoon through Crewkerne during the Coronation celebrations in 1937. Note the plus-four style of the officers' trousers.

Commonwealth troops who went through that base would soon take part in the fighting during the British offensives that reached Tobruk and Benghazi in Cyrenaica and later in the autumn of 1942, after a headlong retreat, participate in the victory at El Alamein.

In March 1942 John Simpson got a new and rather unusual, if not exotic, posting, when he was attached to the Sudan Defence Force and given the rank of *El Kaimakam* by the Governor-General of the Sudan. *El Kaimakam* was a title given to British officers attached to the SDF and he undertook similar duties to his work in the Canal Zone, but with Sudanese troops who were engaged in mopping up operations in Ethiopia after the restoration of the Emperor, Haile Selassie, in 1941. His military duties took him all over southern Sudan and over to Asmara in Eritrea, to the Congo border south of Juba and into Ethiopia itself. While in the Sudan he acquired the ownership of a racing camel and also a pet cheetah and when visiting Khartoum, there were more familiar social pleasures, including yachting on the Nile and dining in gracious colonial hotels. He also had time to complete a diary of his life in Egypt and the Sudan, illustrating his entries with brilliantly sketched caricatures of his fellow officers, along with delightful water

John Simpson was a brilliant caricaturist and a water colour painter. This scene shows his Sudanese soldiers on operations crossing a river in Eritrea.

colours of local tribesmen and also soldiers who served in the different regiments of the Sudan Defence Force.

The last year of the war saw him serving in North West Europe and, following the German surrender, he was based for a time in Berlin, where his artist's skills were again called upon to design posters warning of dangers to health in the all but destroyed city. John Simpson was demobbed after the war, but he continued in the Territorial Army, settling down initially with Rachel in Bristol where his two sons, Patrick (in 1946) and Timothy (in 1951) were born. However, after a less than successful opportunity in the export/import business, John Simpson re-joined the Regular Army in 1951 and was gazetted as a major in the RASC based at Maryhill Barracks in Glasgow. Among his more interesting duties in those years was his overall responsibility for all VIP transport to and from Westminster Abbey at the Coronation in 1953.

John Simpson was always happiest in the army. He thought of himself as an army man and when he left in 1954 he was never really successful as a businessman in civilian life. He kept his rank, of course, and always used it so that people always referred to him as 'the Major', but his interests lay also in the arts and he was a member of the Bristol Savages, an arts group of active musicians and artists. He continued with his painting and became a 'Yellow Feather', an award that indicated the quality of his work.

He also threw himself into working with local organisations in the village of Yatton in Somerset where he and Rachel lived out their later years. He served his community as a parish councillor, as president of the local rugby union club and at one time was Chair of the Weston Super Mare Conservative Constituency Association.

One wonders how far his life would have mirrored the life of his father, if Vivian's time had not been cut short in 1918 with only half a life lived. By the end of the war, Vivian might well have been a major and could very likely have used his rank in civilian life. One could well imagine Vivian joining the Territorial Army where he might well have ended up as a full colonel after several years' service, and then play a useful role in the Home Guard in the Second World War. The Simpson family most certainly would have expanded with John having brothers and sisters and who knows where in Britain, or in the wider world, they would have all lived and what careers they would have pursued. Even so, Vivian left a considerable human legacy that includes five great-grandchildren and now ten great-great-grandchildren and in that manner, Vivian Simpson lives on into posterity.

Would Vivian have stayed in Sheffield and continued to be a partner in his family firm, making a comfortable living arranging probates and conveying properties? Would he have been content to spend the rest of his life in his native city and county, living in the house he had bought on Hagg Lane overlooking the Rivelin Valley, or would he have moved down South, or chanced his future out in the Empire as Henry Adamson did? His often-repeated love of Wortley Golf Club would have helped to encourage him to stay in Yorkshire, and one can easily imagine him remaining as a very competitive golfer well into his fifties, whilst in the fullness of time serving a year as captain of the club.

Men of substance who were well established in the professions, especially lawyers, were the backbone of the Conservative party in the city and many of them found their way onto the City Council, a position of high prestige in the inter-war period. For most of that period they were known as the Citizens' Association, partly to reflect Lloyd George's post-war National Coalition of Liberals and Conservatives and partly because they knew what they were against – the rising tide of working class Socialism. What had been a rather cosy gentleman's club at the opulent Victorian Town Hall changed beyond all recognition when the Labour Party gained control of the City Council in 1926 and remained in control until 1999. One somehow feels that Vivian Simpson, a man of firm views and a combative nature, would have thrived, found purpose and relished the fervid, acrimonious world of Sheffield municipal politics. By the mid Thirties he might well have become Lord Mayor, with May as the Lady Mayoress, and as a war hero with the MC who had served in the local regiment, Vivian would have been one of the most respected men in the great Steel City.

Chapter 15

A Smile That Simply Won't Come Off!

Reg Glenn returned to Sheffield in early 1919 and lived happily in the City for the rest of his long life, even though the city he returned to in 1919 could hardly be described as beautiful. Its soot-black buildings bore testament to the rancid outpouring of hundreds of factory chimneys and the hearths of thousands of closely packed terraced houses. Most demobbed Sheffield soldiers returned to the squalid housing in tarnished streets where they had lived before the war and once again took up their jobs in murky steel mills that had made the City's world-wide reputation, where work was so hard and often dangerous.

It was not quite like that for Reg, who after demobilisation returned to what was now the family home on Langsett Avenue where his father and mother had moved in 1915; a house they had named 'Glenholme'. He was to live there until he got married to Elsie in 1925, when they started their married life together in a semi-detached house near Oughtibridge that overlooked the River Don. As a former infantry officer with a good war record holding down a secure position with the City Council and living in the countryside beyond the noise, dirt and clamour of the industrial areas of Sheffield, they were clearly now authentic members of the new emerging middle class. Elsie had qualified as a teacher in 1917 and was teaching at an elementary school in Sheffield and the sweethearts from before the war were now clearly a couple who one day would wed and settle down together and raise a family of their own. In 1919 Elsie was still only twenty, and middle-class decorum required a lady to put off marriage for a few more years until a husband and wife between them could afford to buy a house, have enough money saved up to enable them to furnish it and be able to pay all the household bills.

There was another reason why Elsie and Reg put off marriage for another six years that seems bizarre to people in the twenty-first century. Middle class ladies, whether in the professions or serving behind a bank or exclusive shop counter, were expected to retire from work when they married, and most public bodies insisted on this. Sheffield City Council effectively sacked their women teachers when they got married, although few saw it as starkly as this. Rather it was regarded as obvious that respectable married women of a certain station looked after the family home, raised the children and took up a domestic role within their new close-knit family. If they were wealthy enough, they too would engage a local working class woman to come in once a week to do the cleaning for them, whilst if they had sufficient leisure time they could meet up with friends for coffee or shopping expeditions, even bridge or tennis.

Reg's old job with the Education Department in their impressive Leopold Street offices was, of course, kept open for him on his return from military service, but now the human dynamics of the office had changed. No longer were Reg, and some of his ex-army colleagues, young junior clerks who could be easily bossed around, they were now men of substance and they felt disdainful of the more senior men who had not joined up, many for quite legitimate reasons of age. Nonetheless, there was a certain frisson between the former soldiers and those who had remained civilians, and it made for a difficult working environment for many months as it did in many offices and factories across Britain in the Twenties.

One episode that Reg often mentioned epitomised this new situation. Senior staff halfway through the morning had a break for coffee, served in one of the committee rooms. Junior staff like Reg were expected to work on without a drink, but Reg, fresh from officers' messes of the North Staffs and the Cameronians, led some of his fellow clerks out of the building to Davy's, a city centre cafe down the street and enjoyed a leisurely coffee themselves. Back in the office, they found themselves not unexpectedly on the carpet, but Reg held out for equal treatment for junior staff and the upshot was that a new canteen was provided for clerks where they could enjoy their mid-morning coffee.

Reg felt that there was special resentment among senior staff because he had been commissioned, but things found an equilibrium in time and Reg began to receive promotions in line with his ability and years of service. After the Second World War, Reg became the Senior Clerk in his section, responsible for the upkeep of hundreds of schools and facilities that were the responsibility of the Education Department. In effect, Reg was a third tier officer in modern parlance, under a Director of Education and an Assistant Director of Building Services. The holders of these posts would be graduates with good honours degrees and were probably only working in Sheffield because it was the result of the interview that said yes. The Senior Clerks, like Reg, were men who had lived all or most of their lives in the city and had worked their way up from junior positions over several years, if not decades. They were wise in the ways of local government, of headteachers and building supervisors, and were repositories of huge areas of knowledge of the individual schools and key personalities as well as departmental practice and precedents, across the many city schools.

Reg was a well-respected member of the Education Department team, always courteous and helpful, a man whose advice was often sought and almost always taken. He had dedicated his life to public service in his own city and he played no small part in building up one of the leading and most innovative Local Education Authorities in England, where several of the Directors, such as

Sir William Alexander, were nationally recognised figures in the field of education development. Sheffield was a city where education meant the local authority, with several high performing Grammar Schools and where private education was a minor element in the mosaic of education provision. The Council always made education its No. 1 priority and the Education Department always received the lion's share of the Council's annual budgets. Alone amongst British cities of any size, there was no boys' public school, and only a couple of boys' prep schools alongside the independent Girls High School and two Catholic High Schools, yet there were numerous scholarships to Oxbridge and other universities, as well as a strong link with the local university on Western Bank especially for engineering and medicine.

Although Reg eventually had a senior position with the Education Department, the City Council did not pay him well. After the 1939-45 war he only received a weekly a wage of £7, or just £364 annually, so finances must have been tight. The family budget had been eased by Elsie returning to work as a teacher after the ridiculous rule about married women was abandoned during the war, but she had to make two long bus journeys to High Green School where she had been sent by the Council. Yet when newly married, they still had enough money to enjoy themselves. After their wedding, with all the trimmings at Wadsley Church in May 1925, they honeymooned in the Channel Islands, something that would have seemed an imaginative, if not exotic, location to a young northern couple of limited means. Somewhat more adventurous than a bracing North Sea coastal resort that many Yorkshire newly married couples opted for, if they could afford a honeymoon at all.

What Reg and Elsie had was security. A house of their own and for Reg a job for life, in a turbulent era where Sheffield and the mining districts just to the north were at the centre of the

Reg and Elsie on their wedding day in 1925.

industrial troubles in the Twenties. The area would suffer even greater hardship in the depression of the Thirties, when at one time 60,000 people in Sheffield were unemployed, and Reg will have been thankful he had a position at the Council's Education Department, when so many of his contemporaries with formerly well-paid jobs in industry and commerce were put out of work.

The now popular image of the 'Roaring Twenties' of an 'anything goes' lifestyle, jazz bands, night clubs and Charleston dancing, while quaffing champagne from delicate high heel shoes, was not something that would be recognised by Reg and other solid northern folk, for whom misery was all around them, compounding the pervasive sadness of the very raw memories of their wartime dead. Nevertheless, the newly-married couple would have enjoyed themselves in the freer post-war social world of the Twenties and they could afford an annual holiday, often taken at Whitby or Saltburn on the North Yorkshire coast. Reg played football for the office team and took up golf at the newly established Hillsborough Golf Club that opened in 1920 and was just up the hill round the back of their new house. The game Reg had been introduced to by North Staffs officers in Gosforth had fired his imagination, as it had for Vivian Simpson nearly twenty years earlier, and he played regularly during the inter-war period, sometimes with his sister Ada who was also a useful golfer. Reg also taught photography at night school and gained a reputation, no doubt encouraged by life in the trenches, where you had to turn your hand to every possible practical task, as the man to go to when you needed something mechanical fixing.

He was also the man to whom friends went for solid, wise advice. Always smiling, joking – including a lot of guileless leg pulling – he was a popular chap among his many associates and in time he built up an informal network of friends, old comrades and departmental colleagues. So that within his work and social circles almost everyone seemed to know Reg Glenn and had nothing but a good word for him.

Reg's story up till now would have been much the same had the war never happened. In his twenties he would have started to achieve small steps of promotion at work and that would have encouraged him to stay with his secure Education Department job. He would still, of course, have married Elsie and they would have had children – as they did – and concentrated the focus of their lives on their growing family. He would still have taken up golf and been an ever popular fellow, respected at work and among his wider family and his many friends and acquaintances.

What was different for Reg, and many thousands of others, was the totality of what they had endured during the tumultuous four years of the war. No one could be immune to that overwhelming experience, even if it was for them an ordeal that was so painful or debilitating that they would want to forget it. Reg looked back at the war as a time that defined and established who he was. He had been part of one of the greatest chapters in world history, had faced tremendous hardships, seen appalling carnage but emerged relatively unscathed. If he had black moments of trauma, suffering flashbacks and nightmares that recreated horrific incidents when friends were killed alongside him in violent assaults, or under continual artillery bombardment, he kept it to himself. Reg always presented to the outside world a calm and sunny disposition, but he had a compelling desire to embrace the memory and the camaraderie of his army days and a dutiful obligation to remember those he knew so well who were not as lucky as he was and did not return.

Reg missed the first Reunion Dinner of the 'Twelfth Club', because he was with the Cameronians at Invergordon. It was held in the Grand Hotel off Barker's Pool just before Christmas 1918. A hundred survivors from the City Battalion attended, with automatic membership for any 12th Battalion men who had served before 1 July 1916. When Reg returned to Sheffield after demobilisation, he joined the Twelfth Club and in the inter-war period he went to most of their annual dinners and special parades. The Club was a tangible way he could keep in close touch with former battlefield comrades, men who had not just been in France when he was there, but in Egypt as well and had also suffered the rigours of winter training at Redmires, when the army was innocently new to them and seemed such good fun.

Reg did not hold any position of responsibility in the Twelfth Club at that time. There were so many senior people in attendance, someone who had just been a Lance Corporal signaller when with the Battalion did not rate very highly. Included among the Vice-Presidents were all the living former Commanding Officers as well as the company commanders from the Redmires days, including Majors Clough and Plackett, along with Reg's old D Company commander, the world-travelled Major Hoette, who had been wounded on 1 July 1916 and had not returned to the Battalion after his injury.

In the early days, enthusiasm among Twelfth Club members ran high, Reg among them and the Club organised monthly events usually 'smokers', all male affairs allowing members to chat over old times. Later these became a little less frequent and included whist drives and dances so wives and girlfriends could go along as well. The real enthusiasm of the Twelfth Club however was reserved for designing, creating and then unveiling memorials, a homage to their lost comrades who were always uppermost in their minds. In the early post-war years, memorials to the Fallen were being erected everywhere in Britain, as schools, parishes, villages, companies and even individual streets remembered their dead, usually by a plaque or a simple tall cross, more often than not placed in a very prominent place.

The first of these unveilings that Reg participated in was on 18 December 1919 before the Twelfth Club's Second Reunion Dinner. It was the unveiling of a plaque in the Regimental Chapel at Sheffield Cathedral that was performed by

Colonel Mainwaring, the original regular Commanding Officer of the Battalion who had kept in touch with the Battalion he had helped create, and who provided a clear link to those early days at Redmires and Cannock Chase.

Reg was back at another significant event at the Cathedral in November 1920, when the government finally agreed that war time Service Battalions should have at least one colour to mark their outstanding service during the war. Regular and Territorial battalions had a King's Colour and a Regimental Colour, always regarded as a battalion's proudest possession as it still is for today's soldiers. Although the Service Battalions were only awarded a King's Colour, basically a Union Jack with their Regimental name and Battalion number in a circle in the centre, it still was a due recognition of their contribution and their sacrifice in the war. Captain Norman Tunbridge, one of the original officers of the Battalion, who had served as adjutant during the Serre battle, accepted the Colour on behalf of the 12th Battalion and with due ceremony it was laid up in the Regimental Chapel along with the colours of some other York & Lancaster Service Battalions honoured that day.

On Whit Monday in May 1923, Reg was one of a goodly number of ex-12th Battalion men who went over to France to unveil their own 12th Battalion memorial just outside the village of Serre. Designed by an architectural student at Sheffield University, the memorial was constructed on land donated by the village alongside the main road in a position that had actually always been behind the German lines in the Somme battle. After the unveiling, Reg and the others went back to the actual battlefield half a mile away and stood once again on the British front line running from Mark Copse to John Copse in what must have been one of the most poignant, even heart-breaking moments, in their lives. Here, where so many friends had perished, they scrambled over the still pitted and desecrated landscape that inevitably prompted sad memories, trying to identify familiar landmarks and discovering articles and bits of old equipment from the 1916 battle.

Almost seven weeks, later Reg was parading in mufti at the Midland Station with many other survivors of the 12th Battalion prior to marching through the town to Weston Park for the unveiling of the memorial to all of the York and Lancaster Regiment's dead. 8,814 members of the Regiment are commemorated on the monument, the main features of which are the outstanding life size bronze sculptures of an officer, with revolver drawn, on one side, and a private with rifle slung on the other. Whilst the unveiling at Serre had been a rather private affair, at Weston Park over 20,000 people had gathered, a staggering sight to Reg and his comrades when they eventually marched into the park and took their places alongside a Guard of Honour drawn from men of the two Regular and two Territorial Battalions of the Regiment.

Prominent among the crowd were the wives, children and parents of the dead soldiers as Field Marshal Viscount Plumer, the Colonel of the Regiment,

Reg and a friend slope arms with decomposed rifles they had just picked up on the Serre battlefield.

12th Battalion Survivors at Midland Station on 7 July 1923 prior to retracing their march of 13 May 1915 when they marched past Weston Park on their way to the Midland Station, when leaving Sheffield for the last time.

performed the unveiling of the Memorial after an address in which he talked about the 'spirit of sacrifice – and that the sacrifice of the Regiment's dead must not be in vain'. The following day, a Sunday, there were many more thousands visiting the memorial and to this day, on the Sunday nearest 11 November, former members of the York and Lancaster Regiment parade for a service of remembrance around the memorial that also now honours the 1,222 men of the Regiment who were killed in the Second World War.

Two years later, in 1925, the City's own rather distinctive war memorial was unveiled at a ceremony in Barker's Pool attended by thousands of members of the Sheffield public. The Regular and Territorial Army were represented by smartly turned out honour guards, but pride of place went to 900 ex-servicemen, including Reg, who marched into Barker's Pool in a column of threes, their medals proudly gleaming as they took their place opposite the memorial.

Having been at two Battalion, one Regimental and one Civic unveiling ceremonies, Reg was selected by Sheffield City Council to be in the party representing the city at the unveiling of the great national and imperial memorial at Ypres in July 1927. Built on the site that from mediaeval times had been called the Menin Gate, the new Menin Gate, designed by Sir Reginald Blomfield, created an awe-inspiring entrance to the town and has become one of the most admired, even beloved, war memorials in the world. Reg was among those who were crammed in under its long vaulted roof to attend the opening ceremony, and like all those

The outstanding regimental memorial of the York and Lancaster Regiment in Weston Park close by the University that honours their dead of two World Wars.

who were there that day, and so many among later generations, he stood transfixed by the aura of the spacious sepulchral interior, surrounded, even overwhelmed, on every wall by the thousands of names of dead soldiers of Britain and the Dominions inscribed on high stone panels – soldiers who have no known grave.

For Reg and many thousands of others just remembering the lost friends and comrades was not enough. He often said that he had not fought for King and Country but for his mates in the platoons and companies of the 12th Battalion. Whilst there was little enthusiasm in Britain for the 'German' King George in 1914, Reg did have a deep-set patriotism, that quiet, undemonstrative English love of country that propelled him forward to enlist. However, once serving in the close community of the Regiment, and especially under fire at the Front, he discovered a deeper comradeship. In a newspaper interview he gave later, he said:

> 'I wouldn't have missed the friendship, the travel and the chances to see life outside the humdrum of the office for anything. During the time we were together we were more or less one happy family.'

Reg was to rediscover this spirit of close comradeship when he joined a Sheffield Mess of the Fellowship of the Services in 1933, an organisation that was rapidly attracting members across Britain and whose main purpose was to re-kindle the friendship and sense of brotherhood of those who had faced such terrible perils between 1914 and 1918.

Formed initially in 1927 under the title of the British Service Roll (but changing its name to Fellowship of the Services the following year), it was originally the idea of a former wartime officer who had stayed on in the Regular Army. Captain Cresswell White was one of those middle-class officers who had discovered the working class in the trenches and formed a deep individual attachment to his men, especially his batman who died in his arms and who on two earlier occasions had saved his life. A chance meeting in the Old Kent Road with a former army sergeant and a former naval rating, who were working as watchmen keeping themselves warm around a brazier, inspired him re-create a new organisation to recapture that old wartime spirit of fellowship along with the warmth and banter of ex-servicemen that only they could understand. As the three of them reminisced, they were aware of another need, and that was to help ex-servicemen who had fallen on hard times in the Twenties, lives blighted by the hardships of unemployment as well as war injuries and mental scars in those pre-NHS days.

The aims of Fellowship completely coincided with Reg's yearning for fulfilment of the spirit of the Great War comradeship. The emphasis on devotion to your friends who had been through the same extraordinary experiences and the imperative to help and care for those among your comrades who needed support, all these key principles of the Fellowship very much fitted Reg's philosophy of life and his need for a continued connection with his Army past.

Reg's special blue diamond lapel badge, that indicated that he was past National Chairman of Fellowship of the Services.

He became Companion J.R. Glenn Voucher No. 390 in the No. 3 Sheffield Mess. In 1938, partly because of the popularity of Fellowship, there was a move to open another Sheffield Mess in the Hillsborough area and Reg became the Mess President of No. 10 Sheffield George Burkinshaw Mess and was a crucial figure in the life of that Mess for the rest of his days. Among their activities, one of the most important was to enable members to be able to join companions from other local Fellowship Messes and tour the battlefields of France and Belgium, and from now on Reg visited the Somme, Vimy and Ypres as regularly as he could and continued to do so even into his hundredth year.

The other important part of Reg's life in the Thirties was as the father of two young boys and the family life they all shared at their home on Middlewood Road North. Donald was born in 1929 and Roy two years later in 1931 and both of them were educated at Ecclesfield Grammar School, then a West Riding school with a wide catchment area at the southern end of that ancient county. When Donald left the Ecclesfield Sixth Form in 1947 he went on to study architecture at Hull School of Architecture, and after National Service he obtained a post with Sheffield City Council designing many schools and college buildings. Roy, after leaving Ecclesfield two years later, went to Dudley Training College and trained to be a teacher, eventually landing a post at his old school as the Head of PE in the Lower School at Ecclesfield. For Reg and Elsie who had devoted their lives to education, albeit one in the classroom and one in administration, this was a happy and very worthwhile family continuum, with one son creating the buildings where children could be educated and the other son bringing his skills and knowledge direct to pupils at the school. Reg and Elsie had a total belief in education to change and improve people and to create a better society and a better world, and although Reg had only had two years of secondary education at the Central School from 1905-07, he knew from his personal experience what a game-changer a formal education was. He passionately wanted not just his own sons but all children to appreciate the opportunities that were available to them after secondary education was made available for all after the Second World War and generous grants were on offer for those entering higher education.

Reg on holiday at the Yorkshire Coast with his two sons Roy (left) and Donald.

Also like Reg, Donald and Roy had unforeseen military careers. National Service was re-introduced in January 1949 to counter the new world-wide threats of the start of the Cold War and the possible impending difficulties of the latter days of the British Empire. Donald's period of National Service in the Army was deferred until 1953 so that he could complete his studies, but Roy went into the Army straight from school in 1949 and trained with the Welch Regiment at their depot at Brecon. After training, he was given a choice of where he wished to serve and he chose the Middle East, where Reg himself had been in early 1916. Now posted to the Royal Berkshire Regiment as a Sergeant Instructor, he served in Egypt, the Sudan and Eritrea, where, unknown to him, John Simpson had served in 1941-43. Donald, with his architectural qualification, naturally joined the Royal Engineers and he also was out in the Middle East for most of his time as a National Serviceman based in Tripoli. He remembered getting many letters from his father during his time abroad, finally realising how much Reg must have welcomed those regular letters from home during his time in the trenches, as he himself did forty years later in the heat of North Africa.

Reg was 46 when the Second World War broke out. Too old for military service he continued in his post at the Education Offices and joined the ARP to prepare for the worst that the Luftwaffe could throw against Sheffield. Armageddon from the air was expected from the first day of war but it did not come to Sheffield until December 1940. In the meantime, Reg would have been kept busy supervising the air raid precautions at the schools in the city. The children in the east end, where the steel industry was located, were evacuated to safer small towns and villages, whilst shelters were created as fast as possible for schools in other parts of the city. One of them, under the grounds at King Edward VII School, was started straightaway in September 1939 and took the form of an underground zig-zag passageway using best First World War experience and it is still there in pristine condition to this day. The Council also had plans in place to turn the schools into refuge centres for people who lost their homes in the bombing and Reg would have been involved in the planning which was rolled out for many families after the 1940 Sheffield Blitz. On the first night of the Blitz, Reg was at his ARP post when the call came for volunteers to dig out families from a row of cottages nearby that had been hit by stray bombs. It was like 1916 all over again, with some people pulled out alive whilst others were unfortunately dead when Reg finally got through to them.

Like everyone else in Britain, Reg had feared the day would come when the nation was once again at war. Unfortunately for the next generation, whereas Britain basked in a real sense of victory after 1918, albeit earned at an intolerable price, the German sense of humiliation and injustice after the Armistice and Treaty of Versailles outweighed their fears of the consequences of another devastating conflict. Reg had hoped, like millions of others, that as their life in the Thirties improved, their familiar world would just successfully continue. There were sad moments, of course, along the way. Reg's mother, Elizabeth, had died in January 1931 and had never seen her second grandson, but the following year came a happier event when Reg's sister Edith married the Reverend Samuel Snell, formerly the priest in charge at St. Polycarps at Malin Bridge, with Reg giving the bride away on the day. Though Edith never forgot her first love, Dan Edwards, killed on the first day of the Somme, keeping his photograph and his postcards until the day she died.

Something that Reg never expected was the suicide of his old company commander, Major Albert Hoette in 1935. A popular and effective officer, Albert Hoette had led D Company from its first days at Redmires to the moment when he was badly wounded on 1 July 1916. A keen supporter of the Twelfth Club, like many veterans he had found it difficult to settle down after the war and was something of a 'rolling stone' who flitted from one small hotel to another, never finding a real home anywhere. In a narrow dark passageway in Islington, he took his own life with his old service revolver, his decision possibly caused by increasing poor health. He was only 65 and really another victim of the war.

In the immediate post-war world, Reg was kept busy restoring the school buildings damaged in the bombing, and also meeting the requirement for many more buildings to accommodate the pupils (now staying on till fifteen) in the new secondary modern and technical schools created by the 1944 Education Act. At the age of 65, Reg finally retired from the Education Department in February 1958 having completed 48 years' service with the City Council. In the late Fifties, many men who retired found they had nothing to do and slowly faded away. This never applied to Reg whose approach to retirement was more like today's pensioners. Reg was determined to get out and embrace as many activities as possible and live the fullest, most rewarding and useful life he could, while he could. He was fit and healthy but could never have been certain that he had another thirty-six years to live, although you can bet he said he expected to live to be a hundred.

Now he was free of routine work at the office he became the National Chairman of Fellowship of the Services, able to throw himself into all the Fellowship's activities and his immediate election to the position on retirement shows the high esteem he was held in by his fellow Companions. He would play a part in several other organisations during the second half of the century, but Fellowship of the Services was the organisation that was nearest to his heart and with which he had the longest association. During this time, the Fellowship was booming in membership having received a second lease of life from servicemen who had served in the Second World War, Korea and Malaya or just been in the forces during their National Service. In time, Reg became a Trustee of the Fellowship and eventually Chairman of the Trustees, where he was regarded by all members as the 'Grand Old Man' of the Fellowship. He served as a wonderful ambassador for the organisation where his vitality, sense of humour and friendliness won him respect and devoted friends both inside and outside the organisation.

In the Sheffield area alone, there were over 11,000 Companions of the Fellowship and the organisation was vibrant and flourishing. Not so the Twelfth Club which had gone into decline after 1945. There had been no 12th Battalion of the York and Lancaster Regiment in the Second World War as fewer men in the Army served in the infantry in modern warfare than in 1914. The Regiment still managed to raise ten battalions between 1939-45, six of which fought in Burma, two in Italy and two in North West Europe but there was no Twelfth Battalion to carry on the spirit of the old City Battalion and therefore no new younger members, whilst the surviving ones were beginning to drop out through ill health and early deaths.

In stepped Clem Roberts, a wealthy city businessman who had been wounded on 1 July 1916 at Serre, who, along with Reg, who became the new secretary, resurrected the Twelfth Club in 1961. Through their efforts, and Clem Roberts' financial support, they managed to put on a Battalion re-union at Endcliffe Hall in July with 80 members attending. This event helped to rekindle interest in the City Battalion once again and it was further boosted in the same year by the publication of the novel *Covenant With Death* by John Harris, then a reporter with the *Sheffield Telegraph*, whose fictional narrative followed the story of the City Battalion from its earliest days until the battle at Serre on the first day of the Somme. The book was a best seller nationally, but in Sheffield it brought home the story of the City Battalion to a younger generation and rekindled that special pride in the role their city had played in the First World War.

By 1976, the attendance at the annual dinners was down to 19 members and the decision was taken to disband, thereby having a clear break rather than letting the organisation dwindle down to nothing. The date was also significant, because it was the 'Diamond Jubilee' of the battle of the Somme and the remaining members agreed this was the appropriate time to close this personal chapter of history. The story of the City Battalion was now well known again, and Reg was often interviewed by local papers when significant First World War events, especially the anniversary of the Somme, were featured in the *Sheffield Telegraph* or the *Sheffield Star*. Unfortunately, the 1st Battalion of the York and Lancaster Regiment itself had disbanded in 1968 as the War Office sought to reduce the number of infantry regiments because of changing military imperatives and severely reduced numbers in the services. Most ancient and famous infantry regiments opted to amalgamate. The East and West Yorkshire Regiments, both raised in 1685, became the Prince of Wales's Own Regiment of Yorkshire, but the officers of the York and Lancaster Regiment decided to disband rather than join with another Yorkshire Regiment. So as a regular army regiment it passed into history and for Reg, and all those who had served in its battalions, it was a sad and emotional day, but it made the task of those former members even more important in keeping alive the Regiment's story. Along with the continued existence of the Regimental Association, the presence of the Regimental Chapel in Sheffield Cathedral and the Regimental Museum in Rotherham, they have done a splendid job for the last fifty years in commemorating the old Regiment that played such a momentous part in the nation's twentieth century history.

Reg was interested to note that the only other regiment that agreed to disband rather than amalgamate was the Scottish Rifles (the Cameronians), the regiment that he regarded as his third and last regiment. Perhaps they too had such pride that they too preferred a clean break, committing themselves to history rather than become a reduced presence of their former selves.

The Seventies brought their share of sadness for Reg that might have destroyed someone less resilient. Within a four year period, Reg's wife Elsie died in 1973, then his older sister, Edith, died in Snaith, near Goole in 1976 where her husband's pastoral duties had taken her, then only a year later Reg's younger sister, Ada, died in the Royal Hospital in Sheffield. Ada and Reg had been very close both in years and in friendship when they were growing up in their family home and Ada, who never married, stayed close to Reg who would have felt the loss of his two sisters, in such a short period of time, absolutely devastating. But it was the loss of his beloved wife that must have been the most crushing heartbreak, leaving Reg a widower at the age of eighty needing to fend for himself as well as cope with the deep sadness that must have weighed down on him as he adjusted to his new and tragic situation. Elsie had been his sweetheart in their teenage years, she had corresponded with him and supported him during the long days and months when he was away at the Front and married him as soon as they were able to save enough money to set up in their own home. Now she was gone, and within a short time so had all the close members of that generation of the Glenn family. Yet Reg stayed on alone in the family home on Middlewood Road North, doing his own shopping even into his hundredth year and looking after himself, although he admitted that his family, friends and neighbours who popped in daily were a godsend to him and helped him to cope.

Not only did Reg survive the personal tragedies of the middle Seventies, in the Eighties he branched out even more and became something of a local, even national hero. He linked up with the new Western Front Association, founded in 1980 to resurrect interest in the First World War that they felt was slipping away with the passage of time. Through magazines, conferences, battlefield visits and specific education resources they intended to ensure that the story of 1914-18 was not forgotten by a new generation born years after the Second World War. Reg was the perfect fit for this organisation, a veteran with genuine front line service, humorous, articulate and with the stamina to visit schools, battlefields and conferences and talk in an easy, friendly way about his experiences seventy years earlier. His son Donald said that when he went into schools to talk about the Western Front, it was living history to the children as if a Pharaoh had walked in to tell them about ancient Egypt.

Now a marked man by the media, he found the offers started to come in for interviews, but it was the Channel Four documentary *Lions led by Donkeys* in 1985 that made Reg well-known outside of his native city. One feels that if he had been a few years younger and lived a little longer, he would have become the national face of the last of the surviving 1914-18 soldiers, known by all – a veritable national treasure. That role went to Harry Patch, late of the Duke of Cornwall's Light Infantry, but Reg would have carried off the role every bit as well, as his humour, warm personality and clarity of thought made him a TV natural. In 1986, he was featured in programmes from the Thiepval Memorial when the official celebrations of the 70th anniversary of the Battle of the Somme took place. He told the Duke of Kent, who was representing the Queen, that the reason for his long life was that, 'I eat plenty of cabbage, a lot of sugar and all the fatty meat I can get. I never worry. If I owe you money and I cannot pay then that is your worry, not mine.' And the media lapped it up.

In 1988, Ralph Gibson and Paul Oldfield launched their book *The Sheffield City Battalion*, an excellent and extremely detailed record of the history of the 12th Battalion from the first days in September 1914 to its disbanding in February 1918. They drew heavily on the memories of survivors to add to the authenticity of the text and the book included numerous anecdotes and observations by 12th Battalion men who were still alive. Reg contributed sixteen quotations that were used in the book and some photos, and no doubt his general discussions with the authors helped them to navigate through the crowded narrative of the Battalion's experiences during the three and half years of its existence. The authors' aim was to re-acquaint the people of Sheffield with their own Battalion's history and they succeeded magnificently, with Reg playing a full part at the launch at the Regimental Museum in Rotherham, where he autographed the first 200 books to be sold.

In February 1993 Reg reached his hundredth birthday and his family threw a big party for him at the Hallam Tower Hotel, at that time the smartest hotel in the city. It was also a time for recognition by other organisations of all he had done for

Reg with Ralph Gibson signing copies of Ralph and Paul Oldfield's new book about the City Battalion at the launch in 1988.

them in the years previously. On his actual birthday on Monday, 22 February, the Regimental Colonel of the York and Lancaster Regiment, Lt. Col. John Pattison, laid on a special lunch for Reg attended by senior representatives of the Regiment and the Lord Lieutenant of South Yorkshire. He was collected by car and after a four course meal with wines at Endcliffe Hall, he amused his audience with humorous tales of the trenches, complete with details of how a piece of shrapnel was still lodged in a delicate part of his body.

At the weekend, it was the Western Front Association's time to honour Reg. Lyn Macdonald, the historian, who has written several books about key events of the war in France and Flanders, organised a celebration that included a weekend in London for Reg. They took over the Player's Theatre, at Charing Cross, for a concert that included Reg being invited onto the stage by the cast, only to find that once up there he was left all alone leading the singing of famous songs from that war-time period, all the while wearing a new sweatshirt emblazoned REG GLENN, SUPER STAR, 100 YEARS OLD, a present from his grand-daughter, who was most amused and also very proud of her 'famous' grandad. There were other veterans there who had helped Lyn MacDonald with her books, but it was Reg who the media focussed on with a large coloured photo of him in his special sweatshirt, exuberantly leading the singing from the stage, that appeared in the next day's edition of the Times.

Reg celebrating his 100th Birthday with members of his Fellowship Mess in Hillsborough, while wearing his special T shirt that proclaimed he was 100 years old.

It was a wonderful moment for Reg to have such recognition of his lifetime's remembrance of the sacrifice of his former comrades. So indeed were the 280 birthday cards he received from across the country, including one from the Queen and one from the President of the British Legion. There were only 230 men in Britain at that time who were over one hundred years old and reaching that age marked you out as a remarkably special person just for surviving.

If anyone doubted that Reg was more than just a survivor, they were reminded of his love of life at the birthday celebration in March organised by his own Fellowship Mess in Sheffield. Here he was among his closest mates and friends and Reg's reply to all their congratulations has been preserved on video. It is a remarkable recording with Reg in his most ebullient form, causing his friends among the Companions to erupt in helpless laughter as he cracks joke after joke with perfect timing, while playing his audience like a traditional northern club comic. You have to pinch yourself to remember that this man is 100 years old and as bright, lively and entertaining as a man thirty years his junior.

Still full of vigour, Reg was back in France in November 1993 with the Western Front Association, even though he had the added handicap of a broken arm in plaster. Once again, he could visit the graves of his close friends on the Somme battlefield, including Leslie Morte, at whose grave he always spent a special moment of homage. Reg used to say that he was No 928 in the City Battalion and he always made a point of stopping in front of the graves of No.927 and No.929 who are buried at Serre. He caught a chest infection on that visit, which he may well have guessed was his last, and spent his next birthday in February 1994 in the Royal Hallamshire Hospital. Even then he attracted media attention and the local papers showed him standing by his bed with 'the smile that would not come off' telling everyone that he was being so well looked after by the staff, who had provided champagne and a birthday cake, that he considered his 101st Birthday was his 'best ever'.

He came out of hospital in spring, but complications following an operation finally brought his long life to an end on 24 June 1994. His funeral was at Wadsley Church, where Elsie was buried twenty-one years previously and it was no ordinary affair. The date chosen was 1 July and its significance as the seventy-eighth anniversary of the Serre battle on the Somme was lost on no-one present. A guard of honour was provided by the Royal British Legion whose colour party led Reg's coffin into the church, all filmed for local TV news, before the Vicar of Wadsley led the service that touched all present, including many who had travelled far to honour an old friend and a remarkable man.

Three days later, the Western Front Association held a service for Reg at Serre Road Cemetery No.3 right on the 1916 battlefield. Later his name would be carved on a chair in the Regimental Chapel in Sheffield Cathedral and three years later a number of South Yorkshire Messes of the Fellowship of the Services would give him a singular honour when they unveiled a brass plaque to him in St George's Anglican Church in Ypres, alongside the numerous plaques commemorating every regiment and corps of the British Army.

As the last survivor of the Sheffield City Battalion there were no old comrades to mourn Reg's passing or tell their first-hand story of what it had all been like on that clear summer morning at Serre almost eight decades earlier. But Reg had done more than enough to keep alive the memories of those young volunteers who had died on the battlefield. For him, remembrance was not something you did once a year around Armistice Day, but a duty he would perform every day, as if he was living their life for them. He concluded towards the end of his life:

'Most of my friends are named on those tombstones in those military cemeteries in France, and I could just have easily been one of them. It is nice to have your reunions and your regimental dinners and it's nice to pin on your gongs for Armistice Day parades, but was it worth it? I don't want my grandchildren to have to decide whether or not war is worth it. We do not want any more of that!'

Bibliography

Alflat, John C. *Walter Gladwin Alflat: The War Diary*. Privately published

Bilton, David (2005) *Battleground Europe: Oppy Wood*. Barnsley: Pen & Sword

Cooksey, Jon (1986) *Barnsley Pals*. Barnsley: Wharncliffe Publishing

Cooksey, Jon (2005) *Images of War in Flanders – 1915*. Barnsley: Pen & Sword

Cornwell, John *"King Ted's" The Centenary History of King Edward VII School.*

Crewe, Frank (1921) *The History of the 8th Battalion the North Staffordshire Regiment in the Great War*. Longton: Hughes & Harper.

Gage, Ian & Hoffman, Sydney *High Storrs School a Journey.*

Gibson, Ralph & Oldfield, Paul (1988) *Sheffield City Battalion*. Barnsley: Wharncliffe Publishing

Hutton, S., Curry, G. & Goodman, P. *Sheffield Football Club: 15 years of Football.*

Korfes, Otto (2016) *The German 66th Regiment in the First World War*. Stroud: The History Press

Meakin, Penny (2014) *The Meakin Diaries*. London: Austin Macauley

Rieth, John K. (2017) *Imperial Germany's "Iron Regiment": War Memories of Service with Infantry Regiment 169, 1914–1918*. 2nd Edition. Badgeley Publishing Company

Sparling, Richard (1920) *History of the 12th (Service) Battalion, York & Lancaster Regiment*. Sheffield: J. W. Northend

Ullathorne, Helen (2006) *The Training Trenches at Redmires, Sheffield: The Great War Remembered*. Available from: https://www.sheffield.ac.uk/polopoly_fs/1.703328!/file/Redmires-Report.pdf

Whitehead, Ralph J. (2012) *The Other Side of the Wire*. Volume 2. Solihull: Helion & Co.

Wylly, Colonel H.C. (1930). *The York and Lancaster Regiment 1758–1919 65th Foot: 84th Foot*. Volumes 1 and 2. Frome: Butler & Tanner

Wyrall, Everard (1928) *The East Yorkshire Regiment in the Great War 1914–1918*. London: Harrison & Sons

Newspapers:
Sheffield Daily Telegraph
Sheffield Evening Telegraph
Sheffield Independent

War Diaries:

12 Battalion York and Lancaster Regiment. (TNA: WO 95/4590 & WO 95/2365/1)

8 Battalion North Staffordshire Regiment. (TNA: WO 95/2082/1)

Officers' Service Files:

2/Lieutenant James Reginald GLENN. The Prince of Wales's. (North Staffordshire Regiment) (TNA: WO 374/27586).

Captain Vivian Sumner SIMPSON. The York and Lancaster Regiment. (TNA: WO 339/23222).

Other Sources:

Transcripts of war memories recordings by Reg Glenn (kindly loaned by Col. I.G. Norton).

A Soldier Sportsman Vols 1 and 2. Letters, postcards, news cuttings and photographs of Vivian Sumner Simpson (Rotherham Archives Ref. 578-K/8/2/791).

Index